# THE WILD ONE

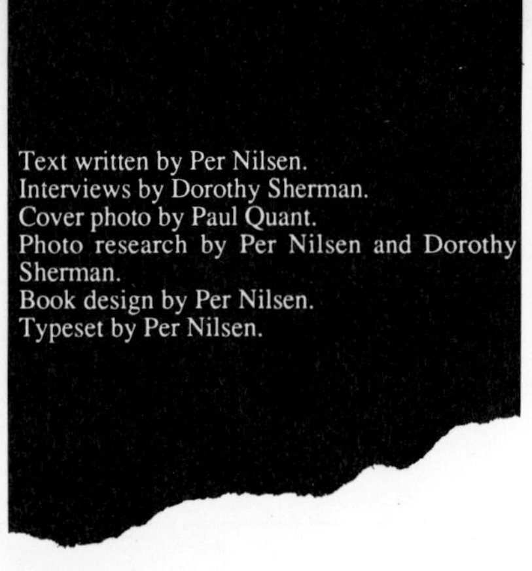




ISBN 0.7119.1643.8
Order No. OP 44551

Exclusive distributors:

Book Sales Limited
8/9 Frith Street, London W1V 5TZ, UK.

Music Sales Corporation
24 East 22nd Street, New York, NY 10010, USA.

Music Sales Ltd
GPO Box 3304, Sydney, NSW 2001, Australia.

To the music trade only:

Music Sales Limited
8/9 Frith Street, London W1V 5TZ, UK.

To a large extent, this book is based on Dorothy Sherman's interviews with friends, colleagues and associates of Iggy Pop/Jim Osterberg. We gratefully acknowledge them all for their time and memories:
An enormous thank you to Ron Asheton and John Sinclair for their endurance. Both waded through several long interviews.
A special thanks to Jimmy Silver for his insights on the early days.
The MainMan days would not have been complete were it not for Tony Zanetta and Leee Black Childers.
Ivan Kral and Rob Duprey filled in the pieces during the endless tour days. Special thanks to Rob for all his last-minute help.
Esther Friedmann. What a saint.
Anne Wehrer. Another saint.
Mrs. Louella Osterberg for her insights. You're a true gem!
Jim Osterberg for his help and support in the project.

We are grateful to Madeline Bocchiaro for all her help. She was crucial in getting this project off the ground and she has been an invaluable aid throughout the making of the book. Kind thanks also to Gilles Scheps, Christoph Thommen, Craig Wilkinson, and John Muir (Babylon Books) for all kinds of assistance.

The following people have contributed interviews, major insights, time, energy, and emotional support to the project and we can't thank you enough: Michael Alago, Frank Bach, Victor Bockris, Harold Corrigan, Jane County, Peter Davies, Michael Davis, Henry Edwards, Chris Ehring, Danny Fields, David Hanna, Mitch Kozuchowski, Wayne Kramer, Sal Lupo, Joe Melnyk, Steve Molton, Stacey Morrison, Elaine O'Neal, "Panther," Neal Peters, Howie Piro, Marcia Resnick, Ron Richardson, Mick Rock, Sheena, Leni Sinclair, Richard Sohl, Johnny Thunders, Karen von Oppen, Michael Wentzel, Lori Whaley, James Williamson, George Witte.

Thanks to Stefan Ahlqvist (Problem), Dana Brutman, Michael Bucur, Elise Chester, Jaime Gonzalo (editor of the Spanish rock magazine Ruta 66, c/Aribau 282-284 7o3a, 08006 Barcelona, Spain), Nic Haygarth, Erkki Kaakkurivaara, Johan Kugelberg, Li Lindström/Polygram, Peter Marttila, Mats Nilsen, Robert Pugh, Paul Quant, the Shermans, and Johnny Volume.

Thanks to the press, record company and industry people: Juliet Johnson (A&M), Jeff Tamarkin (*Goldmine*), Bill Holdship (*Creem*), Richard Hogan and Ben Liemur (*Circus*), Fred Bourgoise (Bug Music), Derik Girdwood (Typex), Bob Talbot (*Detroit Free Press*), Art Collins of Collins and Taylor Management, Alvin Eng of JLM Publicity, and the folks at MTV Networks. Besides material from our own archives, the following people have supplied press cuttings, memorabilia and information: Micke Andersson, Steve Bartels, Josh Emmett, Joe Karoly, John Kleynenberg, David Koepp, Håkan Landsberg, Magnus Lewin, Peter Lind, Dave McBurnie, Jerker Nilsson, Rein Randes, Andrew Rogers, Larry Satterfield, Evan Schwartz, Roeland Suurmond, Pontus von Tell, Monty Wickerham, Tommy Wälimaa. Thanks also to Sytze Annema, Daniel Giboury, Lars-Erik Sjöberg, Julie Stoller, and Jonas Almqvist of Leather Nun fame.

Many thanks to the following: Monica Andersson, Micke Högström, and Kaj Lundbom. Kind thanks also go to Robert Alton, Roy Kirwan, and Amy Muller. They have read and criticized the manuscript.

Excerpts of song lyrics published by kind permission of Bug Music and W.B. Music.

Steven Macanka has photographed Iggy on stage since 1977. A selection of his photos are available from: Mr. Steven Macanka, 182 5th Street, St. James, NY 11780, USA.

Paul Quant's cover photo and a selection of his first-rate Iggy photos are available from: Paul Quant, Storforsplan 1, S-12347 Farsta, Sweden.

Join the French Iggy Pop Fan Club to get acquainted with the life and music of Iggy Pop and the Stooges. Send an IRC for full information to: Iggy Pop Fan Club, 2 Square Trudaine, Paris 75009, France.

Address correspondence to Per Nilsen, Ehrensvärdsgatan 6, 1tr, S-11235 Stockholm, Sweden.

# CONTENTS

# 1 JAMES NEWELL OSTERBERG

**I was born in a trailer camp / Days were cold, nights were damp / Incubator baby, I was half alive / I've been eating lots of shit and jive.**

"Head On" by Iggy Pop and James Williamson, 1973.

Most of the eastern shore of Lake Michigan is tourist country, studded with long stretches of wooded areas alternating with sandy beaches. The towns and villages dotting the coastline are idyllic and tranquil places for those seeking refuge from the hustle and bustle of Michigan's many industrialized centres. Muskegon, one of the larger cities on this coastal cruise, is quite different; it is a pulp-producing area. This is where the story of Iggy Pop begins. He was born James Newell Osterberg Jr. at the Muskegon Osteopathic Hospital on April 21, 1947. His mother, Louella (maiden name Christensen) is of Danish and Norwegian descent. Newell Senior, whose lineage is Irish and English, was adopted by a Swedish family living in the States. Osterberg (or Österberg) is, in fact, a common Swedish name. Louella worked as a controller for Bendix Aerospace, while Newell Senior was a high school teacher.

A year and a half after the birth of James, or Jim as he was and still is called by friends, the Osterberg family moved from Muskegon to Ypsilanti, an industrial town on the outskirts of Ann Arbor. They owned a small mobile home so they simply moved from one trailer park to another, finally setting down in Carpenter Trailer Park near the University of Michigan at Ann Arbor in Ypsilanti. Ann Arbor is a university town, 40 miles west of Detroit, Michigan's industrial and commercial centre. Founded as d'etroit (literally "the straits") by French settlers in 1701, Detroit is also the centre of America's automobile industry and a major seaport. Michigan is one of the seven states making up the Midwest, a primarily agricultural region of the States. The fertile area is also known for its heavy industry, and many of the larger cities (Detroit, Chicago, Cleveland, Toledo, Minneapolis, Milwaukee) have their own particular industries.

Jim was brought up in Carpenter Trailer Park, across from a big shopping centre situated in the middle of a corn field. The trailer park was basically populated by blue collar workers:

*Our family was definitely the only literate occupant of the entire trailer park. The others were mostly heavy truck drivers or low-wage unskilled workers, who were often migratory — guys who would come up from the South when they heard there was some work in Detroit.*

During his childhood and early teens, Jim was badly afflicted with bronchial asthma. He lived a sheltered existence and was under constant supervision. Despite the overprotective upbringing, his mother remembers Jim being a very well-liked and happy child. Quite contrary to many biographers who claim that he was weird and different from the very beginning, Jim's mother maintains that he was just an ordinary kid:

*He was definitely a very normal kid, and he had lots of friends. He would get along well with them even as a very small child. He enjoyed his friendships and got along very, very well.*

Jim was a sharp student and did well academically throughout his school years. Stimulated by his parents, he was an avid reader from a very early age. He always got good grades; he did particularly well in areas related to English, Communications and Mathematics. In many ways, he was a model student, and Louella Osterberg remembers fondly:

*All the mothers I knew would say, "I wish my son was as well-behaved and nice to talk to as your Jim."*

Jim was active in student government, and he was also involved in drama and music at school. He was Vice President of his class in the ninth grade and, according to Louella, was chosen to represent a country in a project called "The model U.N.":

*That was a state thing. I can't remember what country Jim was supposed to be involved with, but they would go away for about three days and they actually had a model United Nations organization. They spoke of the particular issues that were in the real U.N. at the time.*

At the age of 16, Jim switched from the Ypsilanti Public School System to a high school in Ann Arbor, because his father felt he would benefit from the more intellectually competitive environment of the upper-middle class kids there. At Ann Arbor Pioneer High School, Jim went to school with the sons and daughters of lawyers, doctors, professors, and the like. For the first time, Jim was thrown in with kids who had lots of money and lived in large houses. According to journalist Anne Wehrer, who has known Jim/Iggy since the mid-sixties:

*He always felt a little embarrased about the fact that he lived in a trailer. The kids in Ann Arbor did look down on it. They were very snotty about it.*

It was soon apparent that Jim didn't really fit in or feel at home with the often obnoxious and affluent kids at the high school; he didn't share their values or attitudes. Being a poor guy from Ypsilanti and, perhaps more importantly, having lived in a trailer for most of his life, Jim was seen as being somewhat different from the rest:

*These rich kids had sweaters with V-necks made out of materials and things. I'd never seen anything like that*

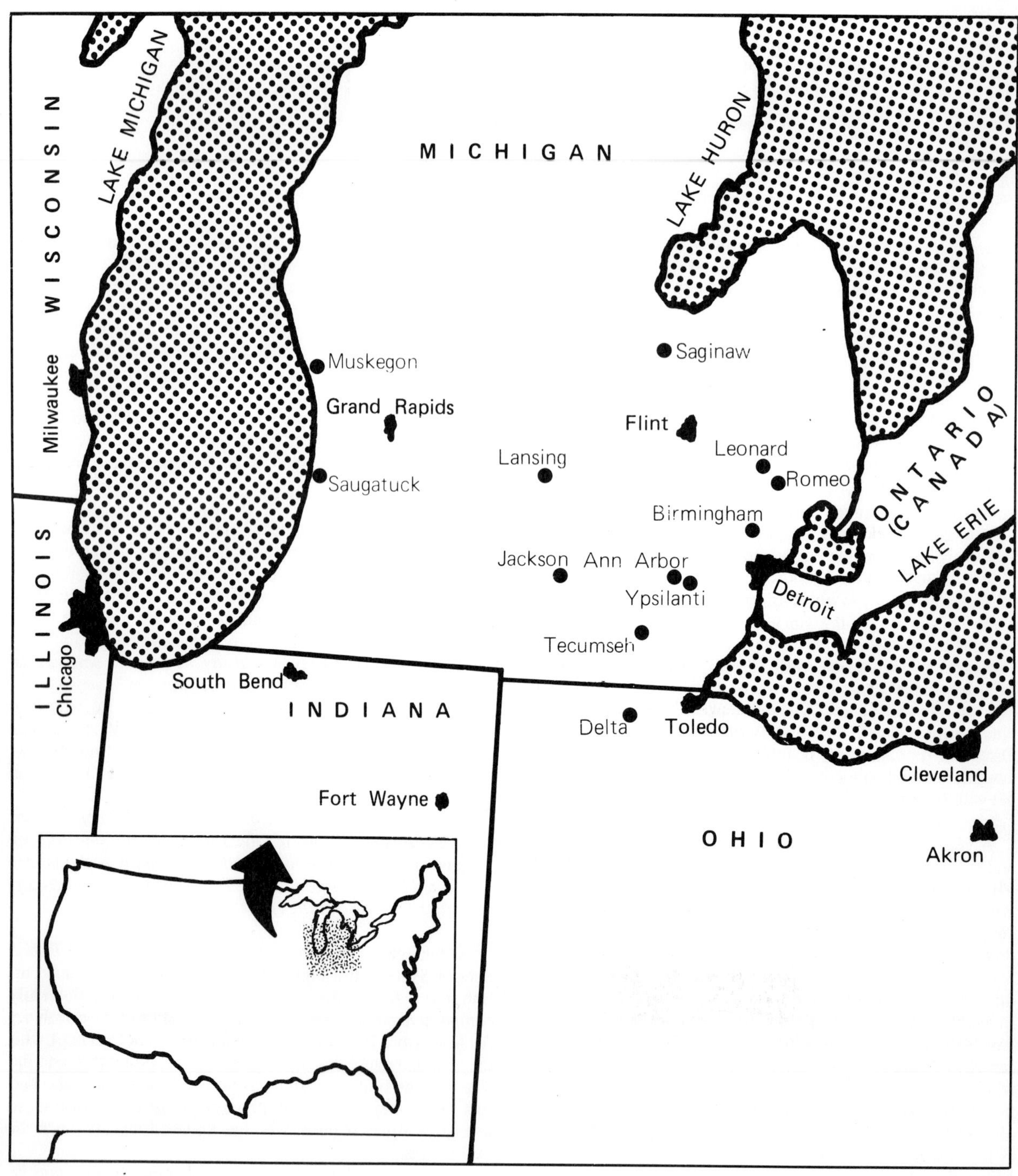

MICHIGAN
WISCONSIN
LAKE MICHIGAN
LAKE HURON
Milwaukee
Muskegon
Grand Rapids
Saugatuck
Saginaw
Flint
Lansing
Leonard
Romeo
Birmingham
Jackson
Ann Arbor
Ypsilanti
Tecumseh
Detroit
ONTARIO (CANADA)
LAKE ERIE
ILLINOIS
Chicago
South Bend
INDIANA
Delta
Toledo
Cleveland
Fort Wayne
OHIO
Akron

*before. ..... I was burdened by the fact that whenever I tried to express myself, I would be laughed at. I was considered weird. A weird kid. I was also very shy, very unhip, very unglib, and never wore the right clothes.*

As with many of his generation, Jim was to come under the influence of rock music in his teens. In fact, his interest in music goes back to the fourth grade when he started playing the drums. To a great extent, music became a way for him to express himself:

*Some people say, "I wanted to show the other kids." It's not that. Everyone has got to find a way sooner or later, everyone does get compelled to try and seek some sort of way to have grace in their life, and that's when I got mine. From music.*

Increasingly, Jim began to find his friends and gratification through rock music.

Jim's very earliest musical impressions were the mechanical sounds he heard while living in the trailer in the industrial environments of Ypsilanti:

*I found myself fascinated by the industrial home that was always around me. Everything from my father's electric shaver to the electric space heater in our metal trailer. And when I was about nine years old, I was taken on a tour of Ford's main assembly plant, in River Rouge, and there I saw my first machine press. A machine press is basically a metal foundation, a giant piece of very heavy metal cut in a form. You put what's to become a fender in the middle, it crashes down, you pull out the form of metal and put another piece in. I loved that sound!*

On being asked in later interviews about his strongest musical influences, he has mentioned names as disparate as the Rolling Stones, Them, John Coltrane, Sun Ra, Archie Shepp, Howlin' Wolf, Carl Perkins, Muddy Waters, Dale Hawkins, Jerry Lee Lewis, Frank Sinatra, the Doors, Velvet Underground, and Bob Dylan.

Much to his parents' chagrin, all his interests gravitated around music and playing the drums:

*My father is a big man, and he said, "You're gonna have to push me out this door if you wanna go off and play the drums with these bums instead of going to school," and I went, "OK dad, here I come, " and at that moment, when the man realized that I was serious — and I was scared — he was very graceful about it.*

According to his mother, Jim won his parents' support from the time he seriously started playing the drums:

*We always encouraged him in anything he did. We have always supported him, and we gave him a lot of financial support. He always knew that he could call us if he needed us in any way.*

10 (+1)
FAVORITE SONGS
OF
IGGY

2120 S. MICHIGAN AVE
Rolling Stones
COUNTRY BOY
John Lee Hooker
MYSTIC EYES
Them
UNDER MY SKIN
Frank Sinatra

A LOVE SUPREME
John Coltrane
SURABAYA JOHNNY
Lotte Lenya
MYSTERY TRAIN
Elvis Presley
UPPER + LOWER EGYPT
Pharoah Sanders
NIGHT AND DAY
Frank Sinatra
MOANIN' IN THE MOON LIGHT
Howling Wolf
MINNIE THE MOOCHER
Cab Calloway

**In 1986, Iggy was asked about his favourite songs.**

# 2 EARLY BANDS

**The reason I started was that I realized that the only thing that was going to make my life worth having, in my mind, had nothing to do with good times or happiness or friendliness or anything. It just had to do with a struggle, a struggle for me — I have to be able to create something myself, which I can then turn around and appreciate, and it can make me feel what I have felt when I heard other people's music that I really like. You know how you feel when you hear music that you really like. When I felt that way years ago, I said that I had to be able to do that myself. That's my whole struggle — to be able to excite myself.**

Iggy Pop to David Walley, *Jazz & Pop*, January 1970.

When he was a mere 15 years old, Jim started the Iguanas after winning a talent show together with school chum Jim McLoughlin. With Jim, picking up the nickname Iggy, on drums and McLoughlin on guitar, they recruited Nick Kolokithas, Don Swickerath, and Sam Swisher. The Iguanas played mostly at fraternity houses and at various resorts in and around Ann Arbor.

After graduating from high school in 1965, Iggy managed to get the Iguanas an engagement during the summer at Harbor Springs, a resort in northern Michigan. They played six days a week, five sets each day, earning Iggy $55 a week. Together with the Iguanas, Iggy recorded a single of which 1,000 copies were pressed and sold at the door at their shows. The record contained a version of Bo Diddley's "Mona" paired with "I Don't Know Why," a Beatles-inspired song written by Kolokithas. During the summer of 1965, they also played some concerts in Chicago, Toledo, and Lansing. Soon, however, it became evident to Iggy that he was the only one in the band who took the music seriously:

*I was the only one in the band who was really into music; the rest of the Iguanas weren't so serious about it. There was a division in the band. They all liked Beatle songs; I liked the Stones, Kinks, and Them.*

Consequently, the group broke up late in the summer of 1965.

Although Iggy dedicated most of his time to music, he also applied for admission to the University of Michigan. Because of his academic achievements and high rank during his high school years, his application was immediately accepted. After the break-up of the Iguanas, Iggy attended the university for one semester with the intention of studying

The Iguanas, 1964. Left to right: Don Swickerath, Sam Swisher, Jim McLoughlin, Iggy, Nick Kolokithas.

anthropology, but he soon lost interest in his classes and got a job working at Discount Records, a record store in Ann Arbor.

Iggy was well-respected as one of the most powerful drummers on the Ann Arbor music scene, and when the Prime Movers, a local blues band, was in need of a new drummer, they contacted him. The Prime Movers were a white blues band, which was quite unusual at the time. Wayne Kramer, who later played guitar with the Detroit group the MC5, remembers Iggy and the Prime Movers:

*If you were black and grew up in Chicago, you knew all about the blues bands, but if you were a white suburban kid from Detroit, blues bands were pretty exotic. The Prime Movers' drummer was this guy Iggy Osterberg. He was really a great drummer: rock steady, no razzle-dazzle, no flash, just pure power rock 'n' roll beat. Their band was popular because they were so different. Everyone else tried choreography and had steps and did instrumentals, and just were like all the other bands of that era. Around 1965/66, when the Beatles broke, everyone had Beatle haircuts and learned to sing in harmony. The idea that Iggy, who was renowned as one of the best drummers on the scene, had joined this blues band was really exciting. The Prime Movers were great!*

The nucleus of the group was the Erlewine brothers, Michael and Daniel; the band also contained Robert Sheff, Jack Dawson, as well as Iggy. According to Iggy:

*The Prime Movers was an effete, bohemian, intellectual blues band of 25 and 26-year-olds. I was 18, which was a big age difference at that time.*

As it so happened, the Prime Movers were also looking for a bass player; Iggy suggested Ron Asheton, a friend from high school. Ron was a year younger than Iggy, and although they had never attended the same classes, they had gotten to know each other in high school. Ron recalls how they met:

*We met through our hair! He had almost a regular hair cut with bangs and I had real long hair, pulled aside and behind my ears. It was like, "Oh, another guy who has got the same hair — I don't feel so bad now." Then we started talking.*

Ron, his younger brother Scott, and their friend Dave Alexander, frequented a cafeteria called The Jug that was popular among students. Ron would see Iggy there, and they struck up a friendship. The Asheton brothers became two of Iggy's closest friends in Ann Arbor. Scott and Ron lived at home with their mother in an area of Ann Arbor they referred to as "the Division," which, in fact, was a typical neighbourhood subdivision. Their father, a Marine Corps pilot, died when Ron was 15 years old.

Ron started playing guitar in a band called the Dirty Shames, which was comprised of his brother Scott on drums, and friends Dave Alexander on bass and Billy Cheatham on guitar, all of whom would later play with the Stooges. The Dirty Shames was strictly a garage band and never played any public gigs. In the spring of 1965, Ron and Dave sold their motorcycles and quit high school to go to England and watch their favourite bands:

*Dave and I went to England to see all of these up and coming bands that we admired so much. We went to the Cavern every night, and for only one pound we got 12 solid hours of incredible music. We saw the Who, the Move, the Yardbirds, Hedgehopper's Anonymous, and we were totally knocked out! I knew that was exactly what I wanted to do.*

The Prime Movers were very accomplished blues musicians and after playing with the band for only a short time, it became obvious to Ron that their musicianship was beyond his competence as a bass player:

*They were very serious. I played with the group for a while. That's when I really learned how to play. I dug the blues, but I wanted to play more straight rock 'n' roll.*

Iggy commented:

*He was really learning to play good. They let him do it for a couple of weeks but he was always too rock and rolly. So, as soon as they had a better chance to get somebody that was really experienced, they gave Ron the boot.*

Iggy later rectified the situation for Ron by getting him a job with a Birmingham (Michigan) rock band, the Chosen Few, in late 1965. Iggy knew the group's singer, Scott Richardson, and since they needed a bass player, Iggy recommended Ron:

*They fancied themselves as the Rolling Stones. James Williamson with his fair Keith Richards look-alike, and Scott Richardson deep into Jagger. I liked Scott because at the time there weren't many people around that wore white shoes and bell bottoms! We hit it off right away and I went to Birmingham. I met James Williamson at the first practice.*

James Williamson, the group's guitarist, only played with Ron a few weeks before he was sent to a kind of reform school in New York by his father. Ron played with the Chosen Few for a year and a half until they broke up in the spring of 1967.

Meanwhile, Iggy continued as a drummer for the Prime Movers. He also played live with many of Detroit's Motown groups:

*I was a pick-up drummer for most of the Motown groups and learned an awful lot about stage presentation. I backed them up: the Velvelettes, the Marvelettes, Shangri-Las, the Contours, the Four Tops, the Crystals, even Bobby Goldsboro, Bobby Sherman. I would play for anybody professional coming through the area to learn.*

Iggy had become infatuated with the blues. After watching the Paul Butterfield Band (one of the greatest white blues bands at the time) play at a club called The Living End in Detroit, Iggy met the group's drummer, Sam Lay. Lay invited Iggy to Chicago to play with the real blues musicians and to learn from black drummers there.

Arriving in Chicago in the autumn of 1966, Iggy lived in the basement of Bob Koestner, who owned the record label Delmark Records, which recorded black blues artists. Iggy became Sam Lay's protégé, and played drums off and on with J.B. Hutto, Johnny Young, and Walter Horton in Chicago's South Side clubs Turner's, Pepper's Lounge, and Silvio's. He worked as a non-union drummer, undercutting other drummers to get gigs.

The more he hung around the Chicago bluesmen, the more contempt Iggy felt for the white guys trying to play the blues:

*When these black men played the music, it almost dripped off their fingers — like honey. It was just oozing out of these guys. It wasn't a studied thing at all.*

After eight months of Chicago and the blues, Iggy had had enough; he had decided that only black musicians could really play the blues:

*When I found that out, I knew I had to come home and make my own music. I used to sit on the bank of the Chicago River with this music in my head. I even used to do little dances with myself. ..... I became convinced that I should go back to Detroit, begin my own group and try to do something as different as possible from anything going on at the time.*

**Iggy in 1967.** (Leni Sinclair)

# 3 BIRTH OF THE STOOGES

**I thought, "My God, I'm free, white and 19. I'm not a 40 or 50-year-old Chicago bluesman. I've got to take what I've learned here and apply it to my own experience. I'm gonna go home to Ann Arbor and find three or four guys who are not impressed with the music scene, who not wanna imitate British bands and not do cover songs." I wanted to make songs about how we were living in the Midwest. What was this life about? Basically, it was no fun and nothing to do. So I wrote about that.**

Iggy Pop in a Dutch TV documentary, December 1986.

Iggy returned from Chicago in the spring of 1967. Back in Ann Arbor, he immediately looked up Ron and Scott:

*As soon as I came back I went to Ron and Scott's house. They were my only real friends in Ann Arbor that I cared for. Then originally, we thought we would have Scott for a singer and me for a drummer and just make a regular band. Then Ron and I decided we wanted a* real *band.*

The Chosen Few, where Ron had played bass, had broken up earlier in the year. Scott Richardson was planning his new group after the Chosen Few, the SRC (Scott Richardson Case), and he wanted Iggy, Ron and Scott to join him. Iggy and Scott would both have played drums and Ron would have played bass:

*I was going to be in the SRC, but I really didn't want to do it. It was going to be double drums, Richardson singing, myself playing bass, somebody on guitar, and Iggy and Scotty on drums. But we really didn't want to do it. We wanted to put our own band together.*

Instead, Iggy and the Asheton brothers decided to form their own group. Iggy, in particular, knew he wanted to express something personal — not necessarily a social or grandiose statement about the world, just something about himself. They settled on calling themselves the Stooges. According to Iggy, the name was a sort of tribute to the Three Stooges, a trio of US TV comedians:

*We loved the one-for-all/all-for-one of the Three Stooges, and the violence in their image. We loved violence as a comedy. Besides sounding right, "stooge" also had different levels of meaning: is calling yourself a "stooge" a self-insult?*

In the beginning, they often called the band the Psychedelic Stooges. In fact, the Psychedelic tag was occasionally used until their first album came out in 1969.

The early-day Stooges were an instrumental trio: Iggy played a Hawaiian guitar and Fender piano, Ron played bass, and Scott played homemade drums. Iggy also sometimes played a vacuum cleaner, a blender, and something he called a "Jim-a-phone." They teamed up with Ron Richardson, who agreed to manage the group and do their bookings. Richardson, commonly called "the Professor," was a schoolteacher, and he worked as a booking agent for groups like the MC5 and Bob Seger:

*I recognized Iggy and the guys as having talent and charisma, or whatever it was. I really liked them and thought they were very good.*

Having spent the best part of 1967 rehearsing and jamming, the Stooges finally made their debut performance on Halloween 1967, at a private party thrown by Richardson. Attending were the friends of the group, among them the MC5, a group from Detroit/Ann Arbor, and their manager John Sinclair. The Stooges' premiere performance was a memorable event, as Sinclair recalls:

*I went with a guy who had rolled up about 50 joints before going there. When he got to the party, he was passing out all these joints. They were inhaling freon at the party. They were taking this whipped cream or some kind of aerosol, and getting the freon out of it and putting it in bags. I just got really blasted. I remember how loud they were. It was incredibly loud in this little house.*

A friend of Sinclair's, Jimmy Silver, was also present at the party:

*It was just the most bizarre music you'd ever heard and I thought it was terrific. Iggy was playing a little modified Hawaiian guitar. It made this incredible sound. It sounded like an airplane was landing in the room.*

The MC5's lead guitarist, Wayne Kramer, also recalls the scene and the reactions at the party:

*Iggy was sitting on the floor and he had a steel guitar with some kind of modal tuning and he was bashing away on it. He had this vacuum cleaner too. He held it in front of the mike and made different noises with it. The whole thing was tremendously abstract and avant garde. People didn't know what to make of it. They didn't know to laugh and they didn't know to take it serious.*

The MC5 had just met John Sinclair; they had wanted this contact because of Sinclair's reputation as Detroit's foremost beatnik poet. Sinclair, a free-form jazz enthusiast and saxophone player, was also a music critic, writing for *Downbeat and Jazz*, as well as the local *Fifth Estate*. A proponent of left-wing political doctrines, Sinclair virtually built an empire founded on the sheer force of his articulate and overwhelming personality. Based in Ann Arbor and called the Rainbow People's Party, Sinclair's communal Rainbow Nation was busy spreading the word of a new world where

The MC5, 1968. Left to right: Fred "Sonic" Smith, Michael Davis, Dennis Thompson, Wayne Kramer, Rob Tyner. (Leni Sinclair)

LSD and marijuana were essential ingredients and where free love was encouraged. After meeting the MC5, he came to the conclusion that rock and roll was a more powerful means of mass communication than any type of traditional propaganda, be it pamphlets or speeches.

Only a few months after the Halloween performance, Richardson decided to quit his job as the Stooges' manager:

*I was managing the Stooges and teaching school at the same time. It was just like being in debt and deeper in debt. There were promises from various promoters, but it was not happening as fast as you should think it should happen. Then we went our separate ways. They were too crazy for me. I liked some of what they were doing but it was getting too crazy for me. They had the energy that they needed to get off in some way. It was hard being around that energy.*

Richardson connected the group with Jimmy Silver, who had attended the Halloween party. Originally from New York, Silver was studying for a Ph.D. at the School of Public Health at the University of Michigan:

*I was supposedly getting my Ph.D. in a field called Clinical Care Organization. However, the drug revolution had struck, and I used to sit around and argue with my professors. I was really getting "out there." My interests were moving in other directions. I wanted to spend all my time hanging out around music.*

Jimmy Silver took over as manager of the Stooges in early 1968.

By February 1968, Dave Alexander had been added as bass player in the group. Ron switched over to guitar, while Iggy decided he would sing:

*Ron said to me one night, "You really need the freedom, don't you Iggy?" And I said, "Yeah, I do." He said, "I think you should sing."*

In subsequent interviews, Iggy has revealed that it was after attending a Doors concert in Ann Arbor that he decided to become a singer:

*It was after I saw Jim Morrison that I decided I'd be a singer, no matter how much I laughed, cried or died.*

In a sense, Jim Morrison had proved to Iggy that you could do virtually anything on the stage and get away with it. Iggy saw a completely loaded Jim Morrison roll around the stage and do gorilla imitations.

With manager Jimmy Silver and his wife, the Stooges moved to a farm house in the countryside outside Ann Arbor. They made up names for their house: "The Old Bear's House," "Loon Hotel," "Stooge Manor." Iggy had his room in the attic, while Ron had a large apartment filled with his Nazi paraphernalia collection of coats, medals, and flags. Iggy described life on the commune in an early interview:

*To tell you the truth we lead a very strange life. It's only recently that anybody has even bothered to consider us part of any community. I sleep a lot. I watch TV a whole lot. I sit in my room a whole lot, and hang around the yard. I don't really have any friends outside the band. I don't really have any fun finding out what's happening in the world. I really don't know what's happening to people outside the band.*

Silver remembers that life centered around TV:

*They were really into TV. They had grown up with TV. They knew everything that was on TV; every late movie and in Detroit they had a really bizarre selection of late night movies in those days.*

Silver became very close to Iggy during this time, and the two of them used to spend hours talking:

*Iggy and I would go out and walk around the back roads. We'd talk for hours out there in the fog. Although I had been to a lot of schools and knew a lot of intellectual people, Iggy was one of the most intelligent human beings I had met.*

During these late night strolls, Silver discovered that Iggy had a very clear picture of what he wanted to do with his music and the Stooges. Sinclair agrees with this view, and feels that the Stooges were designed to be different from the beginning:

*They were never like a normal rock band. They were always pretty far out and that was their premise. It was pretty clear to me that Iggy was trying to do something different.*

Living with the Stooges, Silver soon discovered, was not always easy. They were smoking a lot of dope and occasionally testing out other drugs such as LSD, DMT and glue. Prior to the Stooges, Iggy was very healthy and, according to Ron, he neither smoked nor drank when the group was formed:

*When I first met Iggy he was one of the straightest guys I knew. In fact, he was super-straight! When he first came into the Stooges, he was still that way. I can't really say that we corrupted him, but I believe we brought out a craziness that had been hiding inside him all the time. The rest of us smoked, and we started fooling around with marijuana and such. I think Iggy was a victim of peer group pressure.*

Nevertheless, there were healthy retrievals when Iggy and the boys were served macrobiotic health food by the Silver couple. For Iggy, in particular, with his asthma, it was necessary to have some drug-free intervals. According to Silver:

*Iggy's asthma used to act up in the autumn. It was really bad sometimes. It used to lead him to be incapacitated and he wouldn't be able to breathe too well. Sometimes he would stop smoking cigarettes and dope and eat with us for a couple of days. We'd feed him brown rice and vegetables. It would take maybe a day or two until he would be completely cured.*

The Stooges were less politically oriented than the MC5, but despite this and their relatively secluded life in the countryside, they could not help but be affected by the tumultuous times in 1967-68. As a natural response to race riots (the "Detroit Uprising" in the summer of 1967), "dope raids" and increasing repression by the police and authorities, the Detroit rock scene and American rock music in general were to a large extent politicized. Rock became "progressive" and the lyrics often accused, preached and demanded change. In many ways, rock music created an alternative society in which the youth articulated its freedom from previous generations' preoccupations with work, morals, safety and settling down.

Even though there wasn't yet a mass movement against the US military involvement in the Vietnam War, more and more people were questioning and protesting against Lyndon B. Johnson's, and later Richard Nixon's, foreign policy. In the years 1966-68, all the Stooges members were called to go before the draft board to do their military services in Vietnam. They had seen friends and relatives return from Vietnam in zip-lock bags and they were all determined to stay away from the terror and murder of the war. Ron remembers how meticulously they prepared to avoid getting drafted:

*We all did the homosexual thing — nervous, drug-addicted homosexuals! Each of us went through the whole thing with each other, preparing each other. Iggy was first. We got as high as he did and stayed with him right up to the moment of going. The same for all of us. Then we matched notes. Through the four of us, we learnt all the different aspects of going through it. Later on, through John Sinclair, we advised people who were going before the draft board. We offered our services.*

Iggy has described his draft evasion in great detail:

*The only way to get out was to fag out. They were taking guys with every sort of deformity, so I just forgot to wear any underwear and when I had to take off my pants to get in line, I went and I just beat my meat until it was over a foot long, then I walked out. ..... So I went to the shrink, and he asked me questions like, "What does gay mean? What's a queen?" things like that. By this time I was really into it, and he bought it and took me downstairs to the captain. I was almost in tears, I was so wrapped up in my role — lots of convulsion and tears. ..... It wasn't too much of a problem, really.*

Iggy at the "Loon Hotel," Ann Arbor, 1968. ▷
(Leni Sinclair)

# 4 AT THE GRANDE BALLROOM

**Iggy really started developing his charismatic stage presence at the Grande Ballroom. In those days, he had a lot more of a rhythmic sense of dance than he does now. It was like tribal dancing which to me was very exciting to watch. He was really, really good. It was mystifying and magnetic. He was just stunning.**

Wayne Kramer (the MC5's lead guitarist) to Dorothy Sherman, June 1982.

(Courtesy of David Koepp)

Billed as the Psychedelic Stooges, the Stooges performed for the first time in public on March 3, 1968, only a few weeks after Dave had joined the group. Opening for Blood Sweat & Tears at the Grande Ballroom in Detroit, the Stooges' show was a spectacular and ear-shattering event with various bizarre "instruments." According to Ron, the audience was completely amazed and could hardly believe their eyes or ears:

> *People just didn't know what to think about us. We had our own instruments. For example, we poured water in a blender and put a mike on top of it. We got this really weird bubbling water sound which we put through the P.A. And Iggy danced on a washboard with his golf shoes!*

Jimmy Silver also helped out on stage:

> *They had me play this crazy instrument that they had designed. We took an oil tank that people put outside their houses — not an oil drum — an oil tank that is used to store oil in. We spray painted it white and as the finale to Stooges' act, we dropped a microphone inside this 55 gallon oil barrel and I got to play it with an automobile repair body mallet. It made a noise like it was inside you or you were locked inside the oil drum because it was going through the P.A. system.*

The Stooges performed two songs, if they could be called that: "I'm Sick" and "Asthma Attack," which had its roots in Iggy's chronic breathing problems. Apparently, the audience lapped it up, and the reviewer from the student paper at the University of Michigan devoted almost his entire article to the Stooges. He praised their thrust and intensity and vocalist Iggy Osterberg's originality.

After it opened for regular rock concerts in October 1966, the Grande Ballroom grew to be the single most important venue in Detroit and whole Michigan over the years 1967-70. It became a significant outlet for new and aspiring groups in the area, and in many ways changed the entire music scene, as Silver points out:

> *It was when Russ Gibb started up the Grande Ballroom on a full-time basis that there began to be an opportunity for a*

*kid scene. Previously there was a club scene, but the clubs weren't big enough to have enormous amounts of kids attend them. There were a whole bunch of clubs, in Ann Arbor, Birmingham, Leonard, etc. But it really wasn't until Grande Ballroom opened and the ballroom scene got big that you could have a couple of thousand kids in one place in one night.*

The Grande Ballroom, with a capacity of around 2,000 people seated on the floor, was visited by most of the big names in rock during the 1967-70 period: Led Zeppelin, Cream, Janis Joplin, Frank Zappa, the Who, Jefferson Airplane, Grateful Dead, and the Move all played there. The owner, Russ Gibb, booked the main acts, while local groups were booked by Jeep Holland. Supported by the enthusiastic and patriotic Detroit audiences, the local bands like the MC5, the Stooges, Frost (with guitarist Dick Wagner, who later went on to greater fame with Alice Cooper and Lou Reed), Amboy Dukes (featuring guitarist Ted Nugent), the Up, and the SRC often wiped out the top acts on the bill. Because of this they gained widespread publicity and Russ Gibb was forced to give more space to them.

Largely thanks to the Grande Ballroom, the epitome of raw, powerful high-energy rock 'n' roll flourished in Detroit and Ann Arbor in the late sixties. In a music encyclopedia, Lenny Kaye depicted the music and audiences in Detroit:

*Where Detroit was bland, its rock was vibrant and exciting; where Detroit tried to smooth over interior violence, its rock was consciously and defiantly brutal; where Detroit emphasized middle-class virtues and restraint, its rock promoted running wild in the streets, drugs, any former taboo. What could be turned about was simply subverted. Shying away from technical excellence, the music was raw, performed with intensity and total belief. ..... The Motor City audience sensed this upsurge, breaking ranks to add encouragement at a time when other cities' crowds were beginning to passively sit and nod. In true communal spirit, they felt the bands were of themselves, thrown up from their own number to serve notice of awakening.*

While cars were rolling off the assembly lines at a frantic pace in the Motor City, Berry Gordy and Motown had their own little assembly line of pop hits from their black stars: the Supremes, the Four Tops, the Jackson Five, the Temptations. But to a large extent, it was rock 'n' roll th

**Backstage at the Grande Ballroom, Detroit, September 1968.** (Leni Sinclair)

◁

captured the imagination and interest of the young people in the Detroit area. *Creem*, a Detroit rock magazine established in 1969 (touted as "America's only rock 'n' roll magazine"), wrote at the time:

> *The Detroit/Ann Arbor community is first and foremost a rock and roll culture. Whatever movement we have here grew out of rock and roll. It was rock and roll music which first drew us out of our intellectual covens and suburban shells. It is around the music that the community has grown and it is the music which holds the community together.*

Over the years, *Creem* became a bastion of support for the MC5 and the Stooges.

Besides regular gigs at the Grande Ballroom in Detroit, the Stooges played many teen-clubs (300-500 capacity) all over Michigan: Pop Patrick's in Saginaw, the Fifth Dimension and the Hullabaloo in Ann Arbor, Birmingham/Bloomfield Teen Center, Lansing Hullabaloo, Jackson Hullabaloo, Tecumseh Teen Center, the Loft in Leonard, and venues in Romeo, Dearborn, etc. They also played in clubs owned by Punch Andrews, a Detroit entrepreneur who controlled a string of teen-clubs called Hideouts, including Grosse Pointe Hideout and Leonard Silverbell Hideout.

Despite their highly unusual and experimental stage act, Iggy and the Stooges were usually well received at the Grande Ballroom and teen-clubs. The experimental format with homemade instruments was soon eschewed in favour of a more traditional rock setting where each member stuck to his instrument, while Iggy concentrated on singing and performing. During 1968, the Stooges often shared the billings with the MC5 and the members in the two bands became close personal friends. Michael Davis, the MC5's bass player, closely followed the development of Iggy's stage act in the early days:

> *The Stooges were always different. At first, Iggy had a white face on. It was shocking to see somebody so white — he looked ghost-like. Iggy gyrated around the stage and usually made a crazy fool out of himself to everyone's pleasure. Everybody liked it. Everyone who was at those gigs was shocked in a pleasant way — not in a negative way. They weren't turning people off. They were just weird and different and didn't play songs like everybody else.*

**At the Grande Ballroom, September 1968.** (Leni Sinclair)

# 5 GETTING SIGNED

**The MC5 sent me all this incredible propaganda so I went out to Ann Arbor to see them. While I was there, they said, "If you like us, you'll like our little baby brother band called the Psychedelic Stooges." So I went to see them the night of September 22, 1968. They were performing at the Union Ballroom at the University of Michigan. They were fabulous. Iggy walked off the stage and I intercepted him and introduced myself to him. I found out later that he didn't believe that I was from a record company. I offered them a deal with Elektra at that moment.**

Danny Fields to Dorothy Sherman, April 1982.

On September 22, 1968, the Stooges played a benefit concert for the Children's Community School at the Union Ballroom on the University of Michigan campus in Ann Arbor. Headlining were the MC5 and the Up, another Ann Arbor group, were also on the bill. For all concerned, it was an electric night. Iggy walked about the auditorium assaulting the audience verbally and physically:

*I was playing a free gig, one of my few. It got to the end of our show and I was just letting the amps play and shooed the band off. So I was just wandering around. I had this maternity dress and a white face and I was doing unattractive things, spitting on people, things like that.*

Attending the concert was Danny Fields, publicity director for Elektra Records. He had flown out from New York primarily to see the MC5. Their manager John Sinclair had aroused the interest of two New York journalists, Dennis Frawley and Bob Rudenick:

*I started barraging them with press releases and other types of propaganda material. They used to run a whole story about the MC5 as their column for the week, because they would be too high to meet their deadline. Even before there was any record, we did national publicity ourselves. Part of my strategy in trying to break the MC5 on a national level and get a record contract was to say that there was this whole "scene" out here in Ann Arbor/Detroit.*

Frawley and Rudenick were also disc jockeys at WFMU, a progressive radio station in New Jersey. At the station, Sinclair met Danny Fields, who had a radio show just prior to the two journalists. Sinclair found out that Fields was working for Elektra Records in New York and he cajoled him into going to Ann Arbor to hear the MC5.

Fields was deeply impressed with both bands. Iggy recalls the meeting with him backstage:

*So I wander off the stage and this guy says, "You're a star!" Just like in the movies. I believed he was an office boy, who just wanted to meet me and impress me. He didn't look like what I thought a record company executive should look like. He was dressed like us, in jeans and leather jacket.*

However, Iggy was soon convinced of Fields' serious intent. In a lightning move, Fields offered the MC5 and the Stooges record deals:

*The next morning I called Elektra in New York and told them what I had done, which I really didn't have the authority to do. It wasn't my job, but the deal stuck anyhow.*

Back in New York, Fields was able to persuade Elektra's Chief Executive Officer Jac Holzman and Vice President Bill Harvey to sign both groups despite the fact that they had never even seen or heard them. A few days later, in early October 1968, Holzman, Harvey and Fields, with record contracts in hand, returned to Ann Arbor to see the bands at the Fifth Dimension. Iggy was ill and the performance the Stooges gave was not exactly smooth:

*I was really sick. I had a temperature of 104; there were bruises on my head because I'd had a kind of a fit, and my one ear was gone. Before I went on I was sitting in this blanket, shivering, and then when we appeared I kept falling down. It was really macabre. I was in unbelievable pain and they thought, "This guy is into it." They were so totally freaked that they thought they should sign us!*

Fortunately, Holzman and Harvey were impressed with the show and offered the two groups long-term recording contracts with Elektra. Following the show, they all went to MC5's house in Ann Arbor and signed the contracts.

Originally a folk label, Holzman's Elektra Records started making its first inroads into the rock market by signing Love in 1966. Later the same year, the Doors were signed and, following their huge success with "Light My Fire," the label started looking for further adventurous "underground" acts. Compared to the MC5, who had been doing gigs for over two years, the Stooges' rise was meteoric; only seven months after their debut performance they were signed to a major record company. The Stooges initially received a $5,000 advance, but the sum was later increased an additional $20,000.

Following the signing, the Stooges continued playing around Michigan. Their short 20-25 minute shows contained "I'm Sick" and "Asthma Attack." Later, "Goodbye Bozos" and "The Dance Of Romance" were added. Probably the first rock critic to follow the Stooges was Detroiter Dave Marsh, who later became one of America's best known rock writers. He

The Elektra "signing party," October 1968. Back row, standing (left to right): Jac Holzman, Danny Fields, John Sinclair, Fred Smith, Ron Asheton, Steve "The Hawk" Harnadek (MC5 roadie), Iggy, Dave Alexander, Scott Asheton, Ron Levine (MC5 roadie), Wayne Kramer, John Adams (Stooges roadie), Emil Bacilla (rear)(MC5 photographer/lights), Jimmy Silver and wife Susan, Barbara Holliday (singer and friend), Bill Harvey.

Front (left to right): Sigrid Dobat Smith (MC5 designer/seamstress), Michael Davis, Christine Hovnanian (MC5 designer/seamstress), Dennis Thompson, Rob Tyner, Becky Derminer (MC5 designer/seamstress), Jesse "J.C." Crawford (MC5 announcer).

attended a Stooges concert at the Henry Ford College in Dearborn, outside Detroit, in early 1969:

*As a pot-bellied junior college specimen walked out of the auditorium with his acned mistress, Iggy called out the soul-frying insult, "Goodbye... (long pause) ... you fat mothuh!" sending half the audience to its feet in repulsion, half in response to what they knew had happened — a strong occurence of truth-telling from the platform for liars and sophists. Later Iggy was to hop atop a girl and become slightly too violent, lacerating her or something. Which wouldn't have been so bad if it hadn't been that she was the Dean's daughter!*

In June of 1969, the Stooges went to New York to record their debut album at the Hit Factory, above Times Square. John Cale, previously with the Velvet Underground, was chosen to produce the record. The Stooges' repertoire of songs was quite small. They rehearsed five songs: "Ann" (previously "The Dance Of Romance"), "Little Doll" ("Goodbye Bozos" with lyric changes), "No Fun," "1969," and "I Wanna Be Your Dog." In New York, they played a tape with the songs for Holzman; he liked them but wanted further material to fill out the LP. They assured him that they had hundreds of songs to choose from. Ron continues the story:

*Holzman said, "OK, guys, I'll give you two days to prepare for the recording sessions." We had no more tunes so we brain-stormed back at the hotel. I locked myself up and made the simplest tunes I could, like "Not Right" and "Real Cool Time." I got hold of Iggy and said, "Come in here, check out these tunes." He started writing lyrics and we arranged them. The next day we rehearsed the new stuff. Then it was recording time.*

The album was recorded in the short span of two days. All the songs were first takes. Although the sessions were smooth and swift, Iggy wasn't completely satisfied with Cale's mix of the album. He demanded a re-mix of the tapes and Holzman agreed to do a new mix with Iggy.

While in New York, Danny Fields took the Stooges to the Factory, Andy Warhol's underground/art/film studio. It was among the crowd at the Factory that Iggy met the Velvet Underground vocalist Nico. She followed Iggy back to Ann Arbor and for a while she lived with the band in the farm house:

*She was really lovely, and we were like boyfriend and girlfriend for a while. Whenever we rehearsed, she'd always be right there really enjoying it in a way that you love to see someone enjoying something that you are doing — a very good listener she was.*

Nico didn't exactly discourage Iggy's increasing use of drugs:

*One day she said to me, " Jimmy, you have one big problem: you are not full of the poison! This is not correct. This is not right. How can you perform when you are not full of the poison? Me, I will help you just enough to fill you with the poison, otherwise you have nothing. We do not want to see a person on the stage, no, no, no, we want to see a performance, and the poison is the essence of the performer."*

**Rock festival in Gallup Park, Detroit, May 1969.**
(Leni Sinclair)

**Photo session for the first album, New York, June 1969.**
(Elektra)

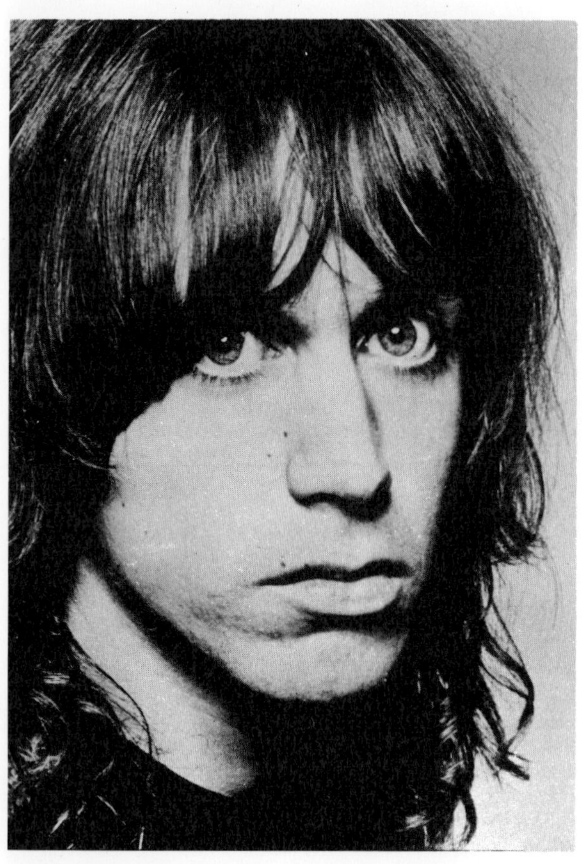

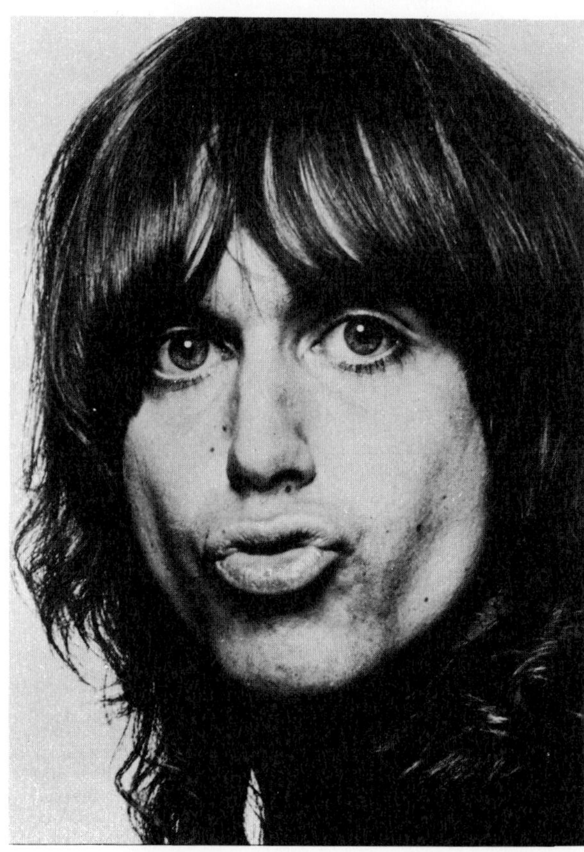

# 6 CROSSING THE PROSCENIUM

**Iggy was so unpredictable — you never knew what he would do. It got to where he would recklessly jump off the stage into a bunch of people on the premise that he would land on them. He'd go out in the audience until he made eye contact with a girl. He would lock eyes with someone, zero in on them, pick them out and go over and throw them over his shoulder or get down on the floor and kiss them. Just do something outrageous out in the middle of the crowd. I'd think, "I wonder if he's going to make it back alive?" Seriously, that's the feeling I got sometimes!**

John Sinclair to Dorothy Sherman, March 1982.

Back in Ann Arbor after the recordings in New York, the Stooges played occasional gigs at the Grande Ballroom and various small clubs. Unlike the MC5, the Stooges didn't play very often — generally only on weekends. Silver explains the approach to live work:

*I had them play as infrequently as possible. There was a point when I could have had gigs for them virtually every night, but they told me not to. They said they didn't want to overexpose themselves. Really, it was because they did the same thing every night. They didn't have a lot of musical breadth to what they could do. They had one show that they did wherever they went. I couldn't book them in the same area night after night. They had to be very widely spread out. It was pop festivals, clubs, ballrooms on weekends mostly.*

John Sinclair's plan for the MC5 was quite the opposite:

*My strategy for the MC5 was to play as often as possible, for as many people as possible. Even if you had to create your own gigs. If people saw it, heard it, they became fans.*

Iggy's stage act was developed at the Grande Ballroom and at the clubs and ballrooms in Michigan. By 1969, he was often leaping off the stage, abusing and attacking people in the audience. Never before had the audience been so vividly confronted with a performer. Wherever they played, Iggy and the Stooges polarized their audience. The response they generated ranged from intimidation and fear to hostility and anger. In *Creem*, Lester Bangs reflected on Iggy's approach to his audience:

*The Stooges are one band that does have the strength to meet any audience on its own terms, no matter what manner of devilish bullshit that audience might think up, Iggy is like a matador baiting the vast dark hydra sitting afront him — he enters the audience to see what's what and even from the stage his eyes reach out searingly, sweeping the joint and singling out startled strangers who're seldom able to stare him down. It's your stage as well as his and if you can take it away from him, why, welcome to it. But the King of the Mountain must maintain the pace and authority, and few can. In this sense, Ig is a true star of the most incredible kind — he has won the stage, and nothing but the force of his own presence entitles him to it.*

Whereas most rock shows are safe and highly predictable, the audience never knew what to expect from Iggy and the Stooges. They were totally unpredictable in the truest sense of the word. David Koepp and Joe Karoly, who saw many of the Stooges' early shows, wrote in an article:

*Would the set last only 10 minutes or well over an hour? Would Iggy keep his clothes on? Would the crowd catch Iggy if he leaped? If they missed, would he pick a fight with some bruiser who could easily flatten him? What girl would he woo tonight? Or vice versa?*

Some reviewers felt that the Stooges were closer to theatre and art than to conventional rock shows. John Sinclair viewed their performances as psychodrama:

*Iggy had gone beyond performance — to the point where it really was some kind of psychodrama. It exceeded conventional theatre. He might do* anything. *That was his act. He didn't know what he was going to do when he got up there on the stage. It was exciting. I'd just watch him and I'd think, "Wow, this guy will stop at nothing. This isn't just a show — he's out of his mind!" Sometimes it was getting too weird. I remember when he started taunting the crowd with broken bottles. He did that as early as 1969. He'd get this audience response. I think he got to where he didn't really have any respect for the audience. So he'd do things to see what would get a response. He was doing something different. He wasn't just another rock star.*

Besides the audience attack numbers, Iggy was a great dancer, even though many of his steps seemed to be James Brown loans. He was also a bona-fide acrobat, easily doing backbends and all kinds of calisthenics. Iggy's act also included self-destructive elements: he often inflicted wounds on his body with drumsticks or the microphone. To many, Iggy and the Stooges' show was highly exciting and it definitely was something new.

By mid-1969, the Stooges had attained celebrity status all over Michigan and their notoriously unpredictable and outrageous reputation preceeded them wherever they went. When they played the Delta Pop Festival, at Delta College in northern Ohio, a contractual stipulation stated that Iggy could not have physical contact with the audience. Not surprisingly,

Iggy went into the crowd:

> *I walked onto the floor and started digging this chick who looked really frightened by our music. We try to play nice songs and establish a sort of a dream meeting between the audience and ourselves. I became carried away, obsessed with this chick and I scooped her from her seat. She screamed and scratched me, so I bit her and dropped her to the floor. I still have scars from her. The school threatened not to pay us, but the people dug it so much that we got paid and asked back.*

At another show, in Romeo, Michigan, Iggy was arrested — to the point of going to jail — after "indecent exposure" on stage. Scott tells the story:

> *Ig was wearing his super-killer low-leather pants and the crotch ripped during the middle of our set. The girls went bananas. They had never seen anyone dressed up in "hobo" clothes before. Ig got a towel to cover the rip, but it fell off. One chick got bummed out and split the joint screaming. It turned out that her old man was a cop, so 25 pigs came back to close the place.*

Gigs in the summer of 1969 included further appearances at the Grande Ballroom and some pop/rock festivals, including the second annual Saugatuck Pop Festival on July 4-5, which featured among others the MC5, Procol Harum, Amboy Dukes, and Bob Seger. The Stooges, along with Alice Cooper, Eric Burdon, MC5, and many others also appeared at the Mt. Clemens Pop Festival in Sportsman's Park outside Detroit in August. At another concert, at the Michigan State Fairgrounds, Iggy's parents for the first time saw their son perform with the Stooges:

> *My father tried to appear cool after the concert, but my mother told me that he had actually climbed a girder in the grandstand to see what I was doing onstage.*

**Ron and Iggy at the Mt. Clemens Pop Festival, August 3, 1969.** (David Koepp collection) ▷

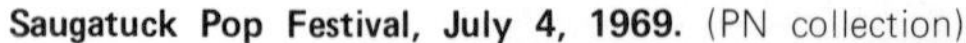

**Saugatuck Pop Festival, July 4, 1969.** (PN collection)

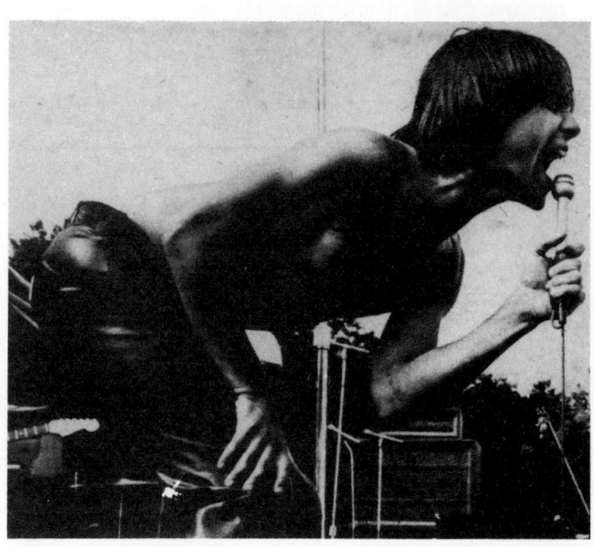

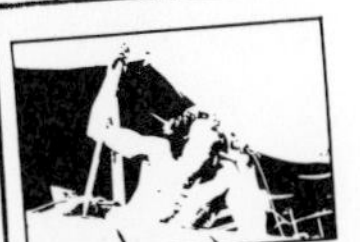

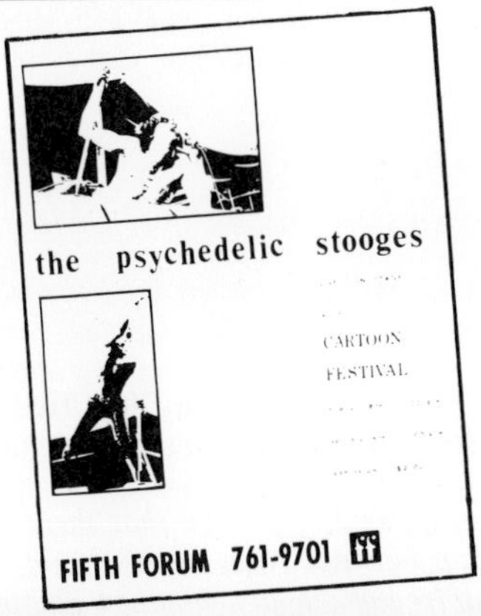
the psychedelic stooges
CARTOON
FESTIVAL
FIFTH FORUM 761-9701

MT. CLEMENS POP FESTIVAL
SUNDAY AUGUST
3
ERIC BURDON
MC5 - JOHN MAYALL
MUDDY WATERS
JOHN LEE HOOKER
ALICE COOPER - CATMOTHER
McCOYS - STOOGES - UP
RUSH - FRUIT OF THE LOOM
RED WHITE & BLUES - SAVAGE GRACE
SPORTSMAN'S PARK
LOCATED ON 28 MILE ROAD - off GRATIOT

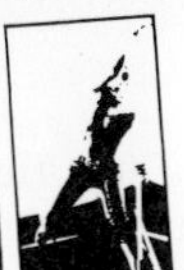

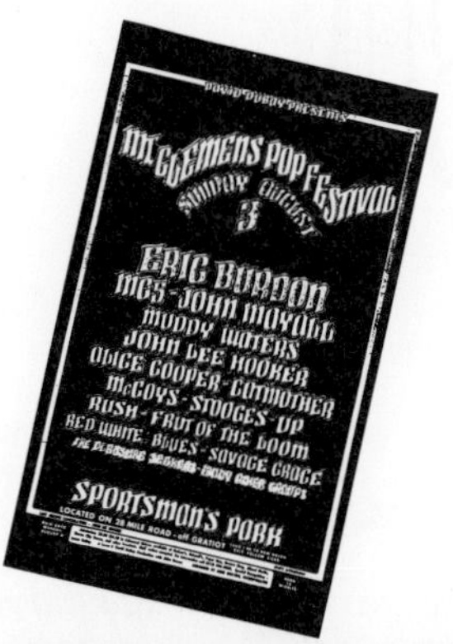

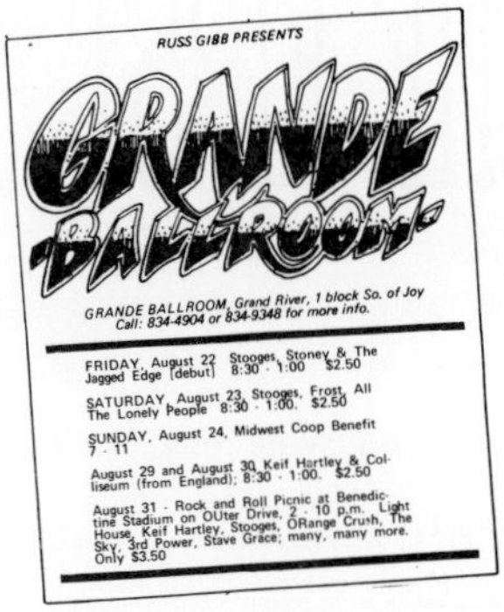
RUSS GIBB PRESENTS
GRANDE BALLROOM
GRANDE BALLROOM, Grand River, 1 block So. of Joy
Call: 834-4904 or 834-9348 for more info.
FRIDAY, August 22 Stooges, Stoney & The Jagged Edge [debut] 8:30 - 1:00 $2.50
SATURDAY, August 23, Stooges, Frost, All The Lonely People 8:30 - 1:00. $2.50
SUNDAY, August 24, Midwest Coop Benefit 7 - 11
August 29 and August 30 Keif Hartley & Colliseum (from England); 8:30 - 1:00. $2.50
August 31 - Rock and Roll Picnic at Benedictine Stadium on OUter Drive, 2 - 10 p.m. Light House, Keif Hartley, Stooges, ORange Crush, The Sky, 3rd Power, Stave Grace; many, many more. Only $3.50

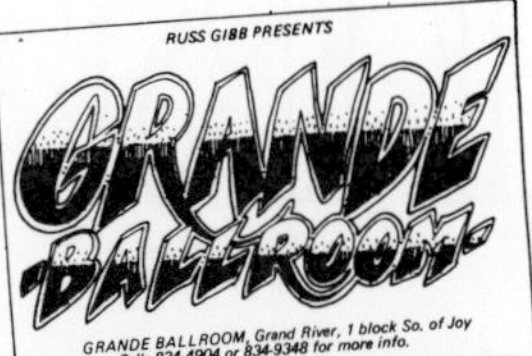

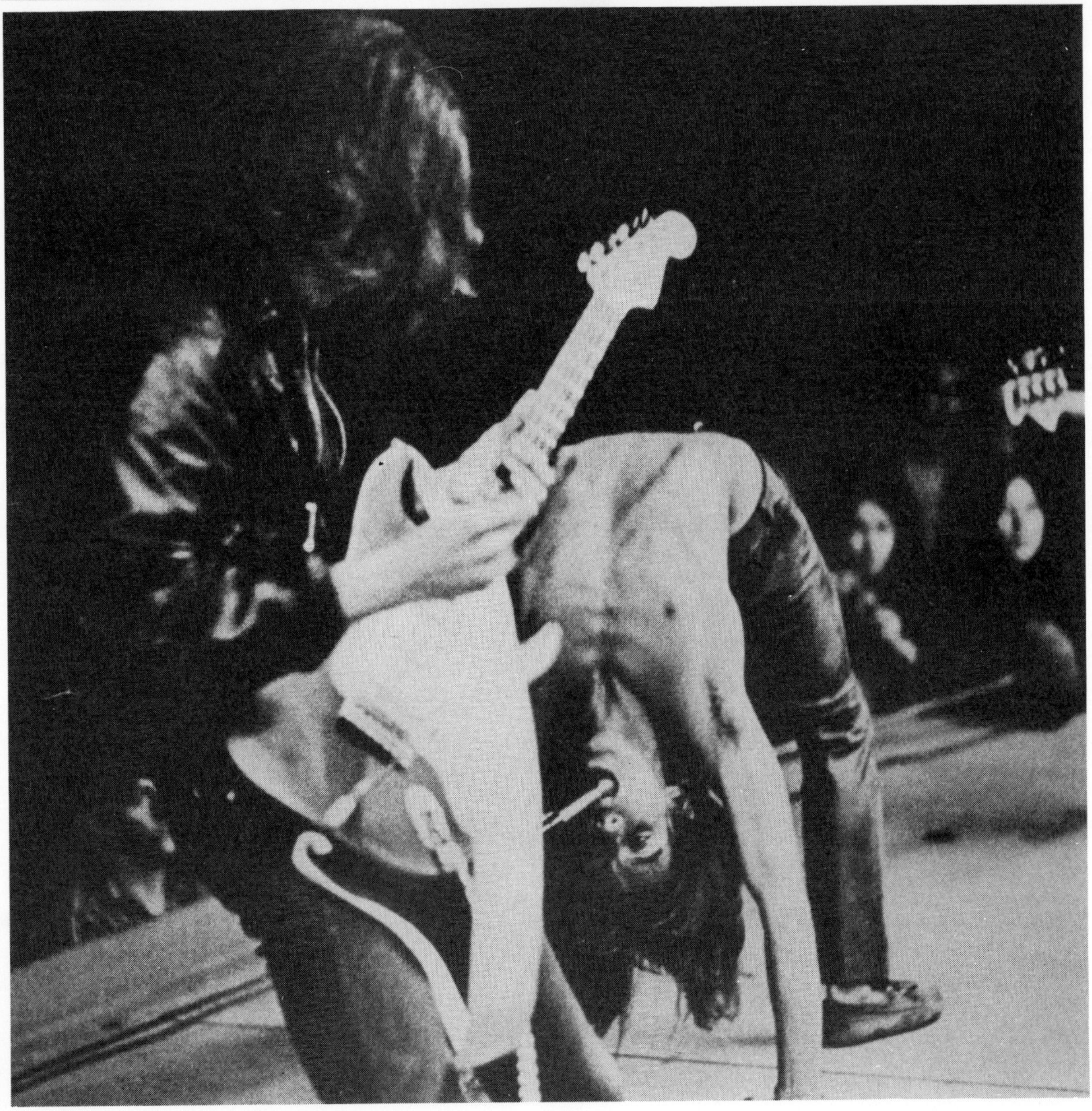

# 7 THE FIRST ALBUM

**I think I helped wipe out the 60's.**

Iggy Pop to Dinah Shore, *Dinah!* TV show, May 1977.

The Stooges' debut album, simply titled *The Stooges*, was released in August 1969, the same week as the giant Woodstock festival took place. The two events could hardly have been more different, though. While Woodstock promoted idealistic "flower power" love and peace, the Stooges' songs spoke of teenage anger, boredom and frustration. The highly realistic subject matters of the Stooges' songs embodied much of the original rock 'n' roll spirit; the lyrics were described as pearls of street-punk wisdom. The reviews were mixed and sometimes contradictory. Some critics complained about simple, minimalist lyrics and repetitive riffs, while others praised Iggy as a visionary. Although the album received very little airplay in the States, it sold fairly well.

*Creem*, the local rock magazine, raved about the album:

> *The dangerous psychedelic Stooges manage to quickly get down to the nitty-gritty of sensual frustration for all of neo-American adolescent malehood. ..... "1969," the lead song on the disc, is the perfect expression of the oldest complaint of rebellious anarcho/crazy youth. Iggy sounds a lot younger than 22 for the horny American youth whose fantasies he summarizes. "I Wanna Be Your Dog" is reminiscent of early Velvet Underground music carrying it into even more bizarre levels. "No Fun" is a crazed song of repressed American boy/girl crazies. "Not Right" features some physically abusive guitar playing by Stooge guitarist Ron Asheton. Throughout the album Asheton reveals himself as an insane master of the power the Stooges channel into their music. This is probably the guitar style of the future.*

The new rock magazine, *Circus* (previously *Hullaballoo*), was also enthusiastic:

> *Nobody ever claimed they were superb musicians, especially they; they just do it as best they know how, not caring much about criticism and caring less about the people not equipped to dig what they're doing. The album is long and rangy, musically average, but emotionally as intense as, well... why don't you supply the analogy?*

Contradicting these views of the album, Chris Hodenfield's review in *Rolling Stone* was highly negative, commencing with:

> *In 1957, it was conclusively proven that there exists a causal relationship between rock and roll and juvenile delinquency. This record is just another document in support of this thesis.*

He called the Stooges:

> *...stoned sloths making boring, repressed music, which I suspect appeals to boring, repressed people.*

*Rock's* Karin Berg wrote:

> *The Stooges' album is certainly not some of the best rock of the year, but it is interesting and provocative in the continuing waterfall of drek relieved by releases of high-quality sameness.*

In England and Europe, the Stooges were an almost unknown commodity in 1969, and few reviews exist from the time of the record's release. In a retrospective article on the Stooges (in 1974), *New Musical Express'* Nick Kent commented on the album:

> *While everyone else was all duped up, dousing themselves in patchouli oil and "getting themselves back to the garden," the Stooges had the collective ear right down on the beat of the street like some thoroughly realistic* Clockwork Orange *manifestation — sans all that ultra-violent nonsense but still toting an attitude of rampant boredom defined perfectly in track titles like "No Fun" and "Real Cool Time."*

*The Stooges* is much more restrained and smoother than the Stooges' live performances. John Cale's production is very "clean," with all the instrumental sections clearly defined. Iggy's vocals are mixed-up high and every word is intelligible. Musically, the album obviously has its shortcomings; it is covered with mistakes and small miscues. In order to make up for technical inability, Ron uses a lot of distortion and wah-wah pedal. The rhythm section, with Dave and Scott, is neither tight nor cohesive. Nevertheless, in spite of technical flaws, the music is brash and powerful, and "1969," "No Fun," and "I Wanna Be Your Dog" are three timeless rock classics. Barney Hoskins wrote about the songs in *New Musical Express* in 1986, 17 years after the release:

> *They remain significant for their conciseness; rarely has such intelligence been invested in something so exquisitely moronic.*

▷

**Elektra promotion photo with Iggy's autograph.** (Elektra)

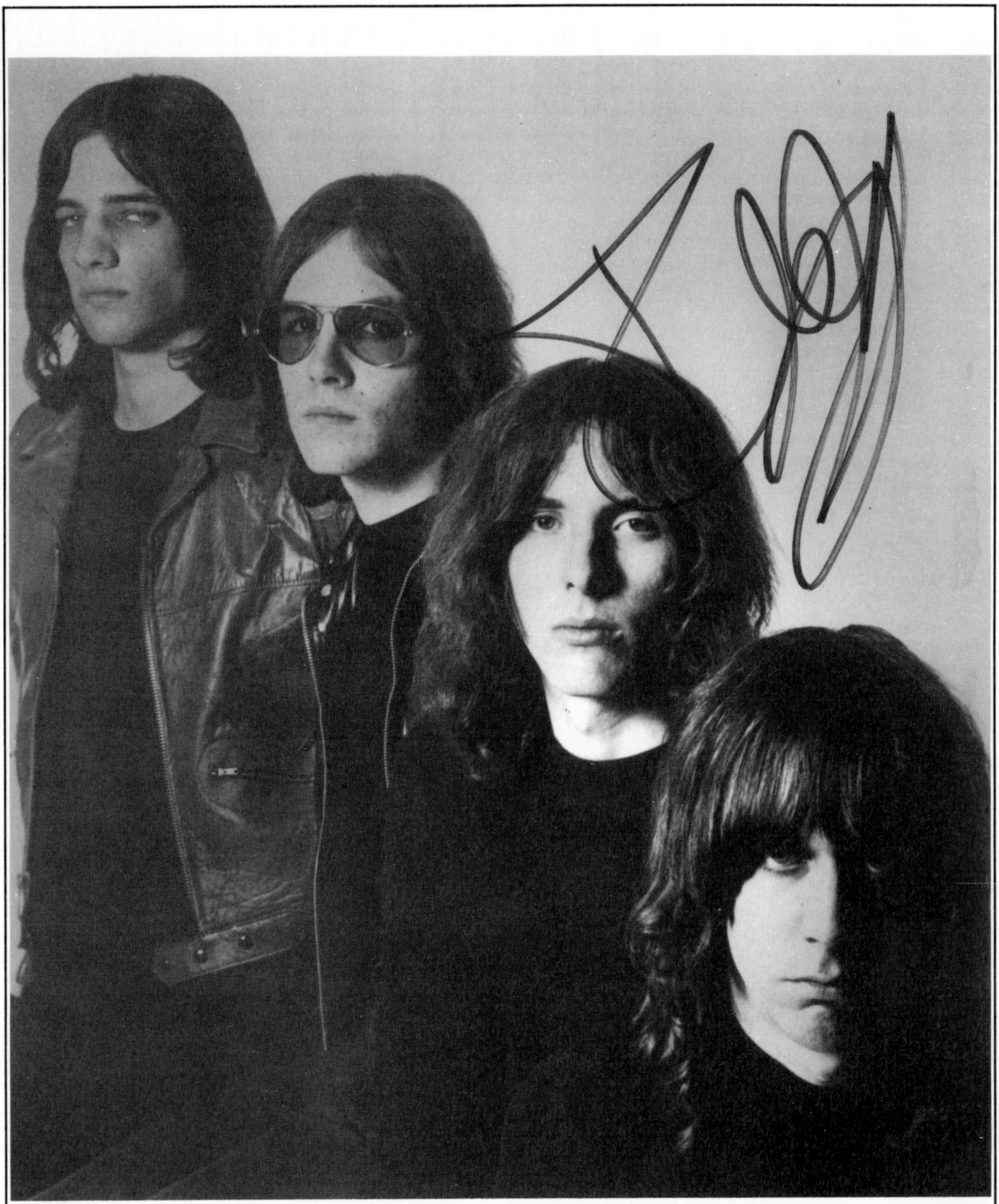

the stooges

scott asheton ron asheton dave alexander iggy stooge

EXCLUSIVELY ON ELEKTRA RECORDS

# 8 ON THE NATIONAL CIRCUIT

**Well, it's 1969 OK / All across the USA / It's another year for me and you / Another year with nothing to do / Last year I was 21 / I didn't have a lot of fun / Now I'm gonna be 22 / I say oh my and a boo hoo.**

"1969" by Iggy Pop and Ron Asheton, 1969.

With the release of *The Stooges* in August of 1969, the Stooges for the first time reached an audience outside of Michigan. Even though it wasn't a huge seller, the record, in combination with the reputation of the band's infamous shows in Michigan, attracted attention from the national music press. To promote the album, the Stooges went on their first national tour. Kicking off in New York, the Stooges together with the MC5 played the New York State Pavilion in Queens, New York on August 29, 1969. It was their first performance in the New York area. *Rock's* Karin Berg was one of the many critics attending the show. Daunted, yet excited, she reported:

> *Iggy is jumping up and down, writhing, hanging onto the stand-up mike, putting it between his legs, rubbing up and down against it...he leans forward, the mike breaks, he's on the floor of the stage, he moans, he yells, "Now I wanna be your dog, now I wanna be your dog, well c'mon!" The fantasies the Ig is conjuring this crowd will not admit to; the Stooges can be a little terrifying — they put on a great show, but the show is not a put-on. The audience is coldly quiet, as if saying, "so show me," and Iggy is showing them!*

As Dave, Ron and Scott left the stage after a short four-song set, Iggy crawled back onstage:

> *Everyone is scrambling to see what he's doing, but no one is saying a word. There is only loud whining feedback. Iggy dawdles over to the drums, plays with them a bit, idly musing, he slowly ambles down to the centre of stage, holding sticks, looks at audience, looks down, pulls it out, pauses, grasps both drumsticks firmly, holding ends out, and slowly cuts long welts into his chest with the tips of the drumsticks. He watches himself and what he is doing to himself, fascinated, fascinating. Then he walks offstage. A few people limply clap.*

Not all critics were impressed, though. Chris Hodenfield wrote a searing report for *Rolling Stone*, and in 1980 he commented on his own review:

> *As the hot summer breeze blew across the stage, and the deranged, forceful music hammered us, Iggy clawed his chest until it bled. He threw himself headlong into the audience. It was spontaneous, not calculated, theatre. Trash*

*showered onto the stage. It inspired me the harshest review I have ever written. What he did to his chest, I did to his act. He was livid about it, and called for my head on a platter.*

The concert was promoted by Howard Stein, and he claims his wife had a miscarriage upon seeing the Stooges; he promised to never present them again.

Immediately after the show, Karin Berg, somewhat hesitatingly, went backstage to interview Iggy:

*I am a little stunned and agog and now I'm supposed to go backstage and I'm dreading it. I have been cowed. In the dressing room, Iggy is putting some cold water on the welts on his chest, the rest of the group is there, things are rather quiet. I walk over to Iggy. ..... "What do you feel when you perform? Do you know what you're doing all the time — what you're going to do?" He smiled, "Does it look as though I'm in control?" "No, it doesn't." "I'm not. I don't take charge. I don't like professionals, they take charge. I don't like to do that. I want to tap energy. I get this feeling, this area of concentration here, the genital area. It starts out that way, I can feel it, I just let it go, and then it moves up my body through here, to the back of my neck, to my head, and it just kind of explodes. That's similar to what happens to people in religious dancing or rituals, the trance-like thing."*

Performing at the Pavilion, Queens, August 29, 1969. (Norm Snyder and Tom Wright)

◁

Following the New York show, the Stooges went to Boston to open for Ten Years After at the Boston Tea Party. The 3,000-strong audience was obviously there only for Ten Years After, and they responded to the Stooges with total silence. Iggy felt something had to be done:

*It was strange to see that many people quiet. I just started the second tune, and beginning with the second tune... I began flinging myself at them! Flinging myself on the floor, drawing blood, cutting myself, taunting, but never direct — taunting them and mimicking them, walking amongst them. Finally, after the third song, there was an outburst of applause.*

In a three-page feature for *Rolling Stone*, Eric Ehrmann interviewed Iggy and the Stooges backstage at the Tea Party, as well as people who had attended the show:

*A few individuals commented on the Stooges after their set: "He has more moves than James Brown, and you can see that he feels every move that he makes. The vibes bounce off the audience, Iggy picks them right back up and, before you know it, the whole place is flipping out with him." "A whole bunch of us drove down just to see Iggy. I had heard about his jumping into the audience and taking off his clothes, but I didn't believe it until I saw it happen. His body animations are hypnotizing, and when he was lying down with the guitars playing by themselves, it looked like he was going to die." "I'm surprised they didn't need a stretcher to carry him off after he collapsed. How long can a guy like that last?"*

In the article, Iggy spoke of the unpredictable nature of the Stooges' concerts:

*The music drives me into a peak freak. I can't feel any pain or realize what goes on around me. I'm just feeling the music and when I dive into a sea of people, it is the feeling of the music, the mood. Nobody ever knows how it's going to end up.*

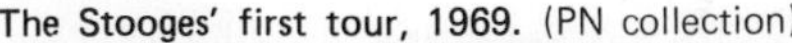

The Stooges' first tour, 1969. (PN collection)

Ehrmann felt Iggy and the Stooges had huge potential to make it big, and he anticipated that they were going to be very interesting to watch in the years to come.

In the summer of 1969, John Sinclair was sentenced to ten years in federal prison for possession of two marijuana cigarettes. The Stooges played several benefit shows for Sinclair in Detroit, where the audiences and performers, including most of the local rock groups, demanded freedom for Sinclair. Former Beatle John Lennon even made an appeal by appearing at a festival to benefit Sinclair. Bowing to public pressure, the authorities released Sinclair in December 1971, after serving 29 months of his ten-year sentence.

The Stooges' tour continued in the autumn/winter, concentrating on the East Coast and Midwest. On Halloween, two years after their debut performance, they returned to Detroit to play the "Black Magic and Rock and Roll" festival at Detroit's 16,500-seater Olympia Stadium, their biggest indoor concert yet. The Stooges' set at this point was only 20-30 minutes long and generally contained no more than four to five tunes. They usually opened with "I Wanna Be Your Dog," followed by "1969." Other numbers they played were also "No Fun" and "Dog Food," a new tune written after the first album.

Earlier in 1969, Iggy got married to Wendy Weisberg, a girl he had first met at the university. Years later, Wendy unexpectedly showed up backstage at a Stooges concert in Delaware, Ohio:

*I saw her before the gig. I was shocked. I remembered her immediately. She was someone you always kept in your mind, maybe to encounter again. ..... She was tomboyish, with a very, very beautiful build — a Jewish girl from Shaker Heights, a wealthy suburb of Cleveland.*

Manager Jimmy Silver married Iggy and Wendy at the farmhouse outside Ann Arbor:

*I was a minister of the Universal Life Church. They asked me to get this ordination so I could marry them. The other Stooges guys called Wendy "the Potato woman." They called her that because she had a lumpy complexion and was sort of suntanned. They lived in the attic in the farm house. She was an absolutely beautiful girl, but it lasted only a few months; they got it annulled. She just couldn't stand Iggy smoking pot and the behaviour of the Stooges guys.*

# 9 LA BLUES

**He tosses himself off the stage, runs into the middle of the audience, leaps onto a table, grabs a burning candlevase and lifts it high above his head. For a moment, it looks as if he'll put it down — dear God, make him put it back down! — but no... Instead, he lowers it over his chest and very slowly spills all its melted wax over his body.**

Review of the Stooges' Whisky A Go-Go concert,
*Entertainment World* , May 1970.

Despite modest sales of *The Stooges*, Elektra remained interested enough in the group to sanction the recording of a second album. Jim Peterman, who had joined Elektra's A&R staff after playing keyboards in the Steve Miller Band, was initially suggested as producer of the album. After reconsidering their strategy, however, Elektra decided they wanted a more commercial producer who could give the band a Top 40 hit. Elektra's president Jac Holzman wanted a producer called John Madera, who had produced hits by Lesley Gore, Danny and the Juniors, as well as Chubby Checker's "Let's Twist Again." Danny Fields, the Stooges' "discoverer," who still worked for Elektra's A&R staff, favoured Eddie Kramer who had engineered records for Jimi Hendrix, Traffic, Led Zeppelin, and the Stones. The Stooges weren't content with any of them though, and as a sort of compromise, Don Gallucci was chosen to produce the album. He had produced the Kingsmen's classic record "Louie Louie" and he played in a group called Don & the Good Times, the house band on an American pop show.

After attending a few Stooges shows, Gallucci told the group that he would capture their live set as faithfully as possible on record; hence, the album would represent a typical live Stooges performance. The Stooges went along with this idea, and in May 1970 they flew out to Los Angeles to record the second album at Elektra's Los Angeles studios where Gallucci worked. It was their first trip to California. They stayed at the famous Tropicana Motel in Hollywood, where Andy Warhol and the whole cast of his production *Heat* were also living. Elektra's studios were only two blocks away on Santa Monica Boulevard.

Shortly before the Californian trip, the Stooges augmented their line-up with saxophonist Steven Mackay, making it a five-piece group. Iggy had heard Steven play in Detroit:

*We'd been rehearsing for the second album when I thought there was something missing. I heard Steven play one*

Recording *Fun House* in Los Angeles, May 1970. Left to right: Dave Alexander, Iggy, Scott and Ron Asheton. (Ed Caraeff/Elektra)

*night and I thought, "Fucking A! This guy has vision and imagination."*

Steven played only a few concerts with the group before following them to California. *Creem's* Dave Marsh felt that the Stooges benefited from the addition of the saxophonist:

*I went to see the band's last gig before they split for the coast to record the second record and Mackay was playing with them on a couple of tunes. The combination ended up as a really stunning and visceral sound.*

The Stooges had been searching for something new and Steven Mackay added an element of jazz to their sound. MC5's manager John Sinclair, himself a sax player, had thoughts about merging high-energy rock with avant garde jazz, to make what he called "heavy jazz." The MC5, essentially a rock 'n' roll band in the tradition of Chuck Berry, rejected this idea, but the Stooges were more open to musical experiments. Ron, in particular, was influenced by Sinclair's ideas:

*Through Sinclair we were indoctrinated into John Coltrane, Archie Shepp, Sun Ra, Pharaoh Sanders. I especially liked Sanders' long suite, "Upper Egypt And Lower Egypt."*

Prior to the recording sessions, the Stooges played two concerts at San Francisco's Fillmore West Auditorium. They topped the bill over San Francisco's Flamin' Groovies and the then relatively unknown Alice Cooper. Jac Holzman flew in from New York to catch the Stooges' show. Ron remembers the meeting with him backstage after their set:

*We went up to our dressing room and there is Holzman with shades and a T-shirt and jeans. He's trying to be cool — getting close to the guys. We were smoking dope and we brought three black kids with us to the dressing room. They were about 11-12 years old, stoned out of their minds on marijuana. The next thing I hear is a girl screaming. We went out and there are these kids — they have knives and they had a girl up against a wall. 11-year-old kids! And here is Holzman. He is so insulted from all this. He had his limousine brought by and he disappeared as quickly as he could!*

Also present in the audience at the Fillmore West were the Cockettes, a gay drag theatre group. They invited Iggy and the Stooges to their house after the concert:

*I [Iggy] remember how penetrating and strange the house felt and how three of them were peering at me — very strange. I had never been exposed to either homosexuality or opiate behaviour.*

The album, *Fun House*, was recorded in a couple of weeks. Although Iggy and the boys were stoned most of the time on grass and cocaine, the sessions went smoothly and they enjoyed working with Gallucci. Ron said:

*He was a fun guy to work with. We'd always try to get him stoned. He wouldn't. He did his job, but even when it was over, he was straight. He was real smooth and it worked really well.*

Elektra had installed a P.A. in the studio to enable Iggy to sing some tunes completely live instead of dubbing the voice over the instrumental tracks:

*I didn't want anybody to fuck with my voice or the sound of my band. To make the music as uncorrectable as possible, I sang through the P.A. We were fortunate that Elektra maintained very high standards of recording quality.*

Despite Iggy's claims that the album was done entirely

without overdubs, it is apparent that Ron overdubbed his guitar parts, playing both lead and rhythm guitar on most tracks:

*Believe it or not, I played the lead parts first and the rhythm guitar second! Just to get the right feeling.*

During their stay in Los Angeles, the Stooges played a weekend gig at the famous Whisky A Go-Go off Sunset Boulevard in Hollywood. Rita Redd, writing for *Gay Power*, reviewed their concert very favourably:

*Iggy wasn't there for the audience's benefit; the audience was there for his benefit and he told them so — when the audience didn't come to Iggy, Iggy went to the audience, knocking plates down, glasses, standing on tables, and telling people to get up and if they didn't get up, he pulled them up and out of their seats, spilling drinks as well as girls' pocketbooks across the floor... And then, when he'd taken complete command of the audience, he turned his back on them. He then proceeded to add insult to injury by proceeding to stand there for 15 minutes while people in the club just stared, their eyes glued to Iggy. They were enthralled by his torso, his silver lamé gloves and his ripped jeans.*

Comparing Iggy to Jim Morrison, Redd concluded:

*The only thing Jim Morrison is into is displaying his cock so he can prove he still has one. When Iggy is on stage, there is never any doubt!*

**Iggy with melted wax at Whisky A Go-Go, Hollywood, May 1970.** (Ed Caraeff)

# 10 SUMMER FESTIVALS

**I turned on the TV and sat down to watch some rock 'n' roll show that I had heard was to be on, and there before my very eyes was a crazed wild man covering himself with peanut butter and screeching out, "She's got a TV eye on me, she's got a TV eye." I couldn't believe it. The fucking Stooges, man! No one had to announce it. I fucking knew who it was, even though I had never heard them before. It was a broadcast of the Cincinnati Pop Festival and the Stooges were there and on my television set! Somehow it seemed only right that I should see the Stooges for the first time in my living room. It was real electric music seen on the technological advancement of the 20th century. The Stooges on the tube was the strangest yet the most logical thing I've ever seen.**

Article in *Back Door Man*, July 1977.

Cincinnati Pop Festival, June 13, 1970. (Elektra) ▷

In the summer of 1970, Iggy and the Stooges attained national prominence in the States when they played a pop festival at Cincinnati's Crosley Field, a baseball field, on June 13. Traffic, Mountain, Grand Funk, and Alice Cooper were also on the bill, but it was Iggy who made the headlines. Pictures of him leaping into the audience, tongue flicking, and being handed around on people's shoulders were distributed to the press throughout the world. The festival was filmed by NBC and was broadcast nationally as *Midsummer Rock*, with very good ratings, in late August 1970. In a review of the TV film, *Rock's* reporter particularly praised the Stooges' appearance:

> *The Stooges are halfway through "TV Eye." Iggy jumps into the crowd, lies down, you can hear one sweet girl's voice ask with soft concern, "Are you all right?" Camera and sound split for a commercial. When we come back to the Stooges, Iggy is back onstage. Lescoulie [the announcer] is saying, "Iggy has been in the audience and back onstage two or three times. The audience seems to be enjoying it and so does he, heh, heh. There he goes again..." And he did indeed. The kids hoisted him up and there are a few great moments for TV film, with lights on Iggy's back, Iggy standing, one leg forward, on the kids' shoulders. Iggy is staring straight ahead, raises his arm. The kids are all laughing with joy because they helped pull that great minute off.*

Even though only two numbers, "TV Eye" and "1970," with the Stooges were broadcast, their spectacular performance was undoubtedly the highlight of the TV film.

During the summer of 1970, the Stooges played several music festivals in America. The pop/rock festival phenomena started with the Monterey Pop Festival in the Summer of Love, 1967. Since then, it has been estimated that over three million people attended music festivals in the years 1968-70 in America. The popularity of open-air gatherings was particularly boosted by the highly successful Woodstock festival in August 1969. It was followed by over 25 festivals during 1970, when the festivals reached peak popularity. In the ensuing years, the festivals were fewer and farther between.

Among the artists appearing at the pop festivals in the summer of 1970 were Ten Years After, Janis Joplin, Traffic, Led Zeppelin, Jethro Tull, Procol Harum, Alice Cooper, as well as many Detroit acts, including the MC5 and the Stooges. There were festivals in Atlanta, Monterey, Winnipeg, Toronto, Forest Hills, and New York's Central Park. One of the largest took place August 7-9 in Jackson, Michigan, in Goose Lake Park. The Stooges appeared on the bill with Alice Cooper, the Faces, and many others. On August 8, the Stooges played to a crowd of almost 100,000 people; it was their biggest audience yet. The audience was separated from the stage by huge perimeter fences, and a trench between the stage and fences was patrolled by policemen on horses. Frightened by Iggy and the Stooges' outrageous reputation, the organizers told Iggy and the band not to incite the kids to bust down any fences. Predictably, that was exactly what Iggy did:

*So I made these little gestures, pointing to the fences. That was all it took: they sort of started tearing the fucker apart. ..... They tried to revolve me off the revolving stage they had. But our equipment guys beat up on them. It was beautiful. You could feel the electricity.*

There were drugs in abundance at the festival, and the promoter was later indicted by a Grand Jury for "aiding and abetting in the sales of narcotic drugs."

With the syndicated photos and film of the Cincinnati Pop Festival, the Stooges were seen by more people than ever before. They started attracting headlines and receiving greater press coverage. The larger audience and increased media attention doubtless meant more pressure for Iggy and the group, and people began to demand greater and greater degrees of on-stage outrage and self-destructiveness. Jimmy Silver feels this development was detrimental:

*I think Iggy began to feel a pressure to do more outrageous things and more and more live up to his billings. He would do things that were physically destructive to him. He chipped his tooth on the microphone one night and he got more into mutilating himself, scratching himself and he would pour hot wax on himself like he did at the Whisky. I think it was partly for effect and partly, I think, he was being somewhat driven to do more and more outrageous things.*

Whereas Iggy's original stage antics had been spontaneous and natural, and only partly pre-conceived, Ron reckons that Iggy now had to live up to the public's image of him:

*He started out doing self-destructive things because that was the way he felt. Then it got to be expected. He'd just try to top himself for the crowd. We would often say, "Give it up Iggy." He's a different person when he gets onstage. It was expected and he tried to top himself every time. I was waiting for him to kill himself.*

**On stage at Detroit's Eastown Theatre, July 1970.**
(Josh Emmett)

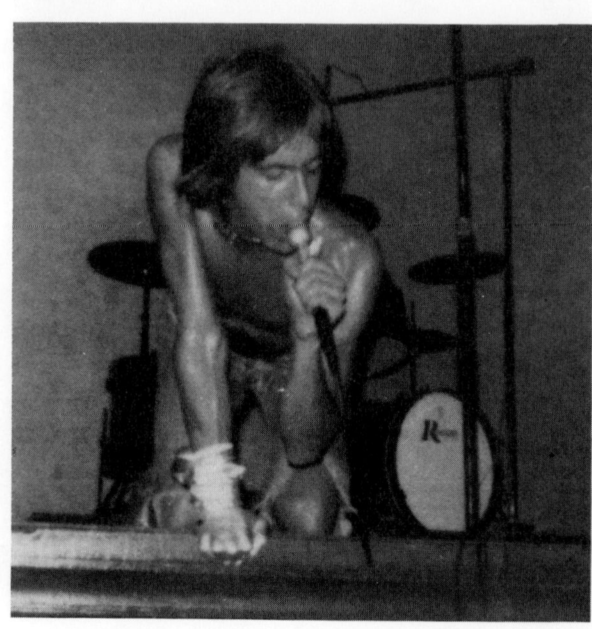

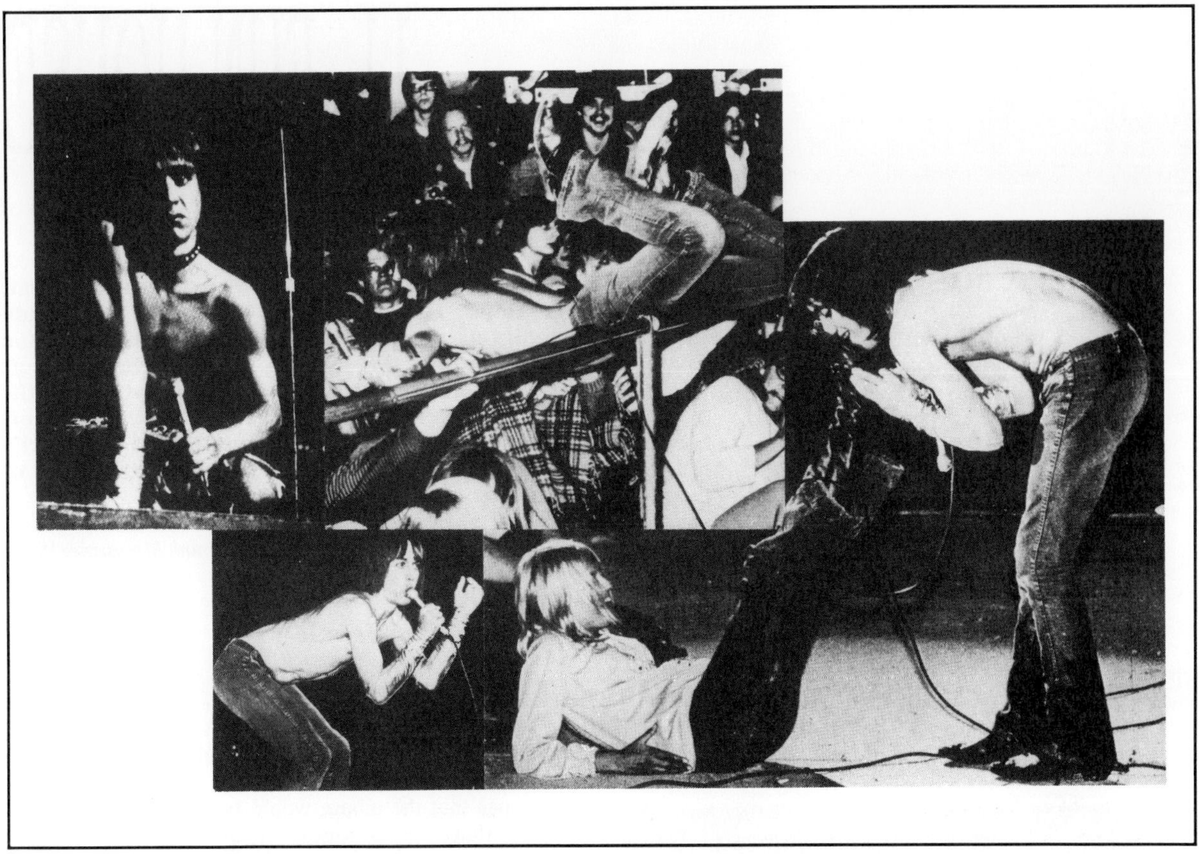

Live in the summer of 1970.
(Mike Barich and Ric Siegel)

# 11 FUN HOUSE

**The war, the riots, the demonstrations and everything else that coed students nationwide were involving themselves in at the time were the other side of the coin to this raging, violent attack of music. These guys were pissed off at the entire world when they recorded this. Pissed off during the years of peace and flowers. Gallucci's production is super-fine, catching every bit of anger the boys translated into music.**

Review of *Fun House*, *Punk Magazine*, 1977.

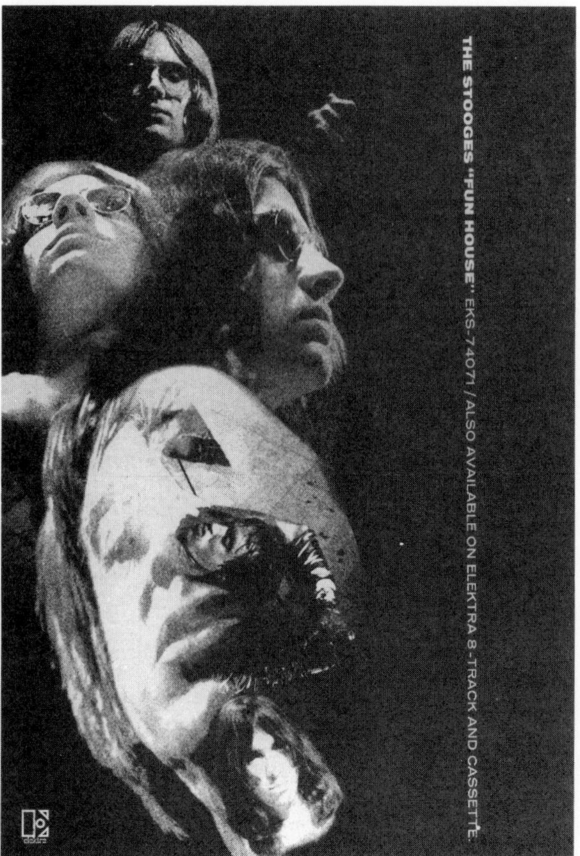


Released in August 1970, *Fun House* was praised by the Stooges' many loyal supporters in the American music press. Regardless of favourable reviews and a lot of coverage, though, it didn't do well commercially. Although Elektra had high hopes that the album would be a good seller, it was evident that the Stooges' music was too brutally uncompromising for mass appeal. Thanks largely to the televised appearance in *Midsummer Rock* and the attention they were gaining, the album sold better than *The Stooges*, almost making the US Top 100. Hot on the heels of the album and TV appearance, Elektra issued "Down On The Street," coupled with "I Feel Alright" ("1970") as a single with a picture sleeve of Iggy standing on the hands of the audience at the Cincinnati Pop Festival.

In *Creem*, Lester Bangs drooled over the album in a hysterical 10,000-word review:

> *It is as loose and raw an album as we've ever had, but every song possesses a built-in sense of intuitive taste which gives them an immediacy and propriety that most heavy groups lack. Everything is flying frenziedly around, but as you begin to pick up the specific lines and often buried riffs from the furious torrent, you also notice that no sore thumbs stick out, no gestures half-realized, or blatantly ill-conceived.* ..... Fun House *is one of those rare albums that never sits still long enough to actually solidify into what it previously seemed. Not always immediately accessible, it might take some getting into, but the time spent is well repaid. Because properly conceived and handled noise is not noise at all, but music whose textures just happen to be a little thicker and more involved than usual, so that you may not hear much but obscurity the first time, but various subsequent playings can open up whole sonic vistas you never dreamed were there.*

Anne Marie Micklo lauded the album in *Rock*:

> *The Stooges can come across on record, too. In "Dirt," for*

*example. Or "Loose." Or anything except "LA Blues," which, while it gives Steven Mackay a chance to do some totally insane things on tenor sax, doesn't make much sense otherwise. This album is a gas! Your own private memorabilia of Stooges trivia is the next best thing to being there: Buy* Fun House *and start yours today.*

An appreciative review in *Circus* concluded:

Fun House *is undoubtedly the cosmic answer to* Let It Bleed *and it should establish the band as to be reckoned with.*

The reviews in England, where the Stooges were largely unknown and only had a small cult following, were lukewarm. *New Musical Express* wasn't impressed:

*The gross Iggy Stooge is said to be a sexy little devil on stage, but not having seen the band perform, and going only on their records, it is hard to see their appeal. Pimply, rubbish rock is how one reviewer has described them in an article. If you can make virtue out of reasonably played rock tunes, sung by a tortured non-voice over repetitive riffs, then* Fun House *is for you.*

Technically, *Fun House* is much more proficient than the debut album and Gallucci's production is excellent, perfectly capturing the Stooges' live sound. As a result of the "live" recording, the album is very raw, making most of Iggy's vocals unintelligible. The material covers a wider range than before, and having worked up the songs live, the Stooges are very tight and together as a musical unit. Steven Mackay's saxophone solos, featured extensively on the album's second side, add a jazz feeling to the simplistic and repetitive riffs. Ron's guitar playing is vastly improved and some of his solos, particularly on "Dirt," are highly effective.

Apart from one tune, "Dog Food," which Gallucci rejected from inclusion on the album, *Fun House* features the Stooges' live set in mid-1970. The songs are even in the exact order of their set at the time: "Down On The Street," "Loose," "TV Eye," "Dirt," "1970" ("I Feel Alright"), "Fun House," "LA Blues." The free-form cacaphony "LA Blues" wasn't really a song per se; as Ron explains, it was the sound the Stooges created when they closed their shows:

*It originally started out as "Energy Freak-Out Freeform." They wanted to incorporate the album as our set from beginning to end, so that was tagged at the end. That was when I'd throw the guitar up or bash anything at the end of the set. There was no real title for it, but we were getting restless in LA, so let's call it "LA Blues," because we were getting sick of being at the Tropicana. Detroit was much more fun.*

Discussing the lyrics of *Fun House*, Iggy revealed to *Creem's* Dave Marsh that he had no intentions of being a songwriter or lyricist:

*I just stand up in front of the mike and the words just start flying. I start picking the ones that sound beautiful. Words that come out that seem to have some truth and some beauty, just anything I like. And after I figure out what the words mean, I start putting them together, so they sound half-coherent, anyway. But when they start out they might make totally no sense. I just scream whatever's on my mind. You can't really write lyrics... because then there's a separation between the lyrics and the music. ..... Frankly, a lot of people aren't far out enough to even understand my lyrics. It's not something that's simple, "Wow this is really obvious." You gotta have a mind. Most people just don't understand where the songs are at all. I'm glad!*

# 12 PERSONNEL CHANGES

**Where are you now my dum dum boys / Are you alive or dead / Have you left me the last of the dum dum daze / Then the sun goes down / And the boys broke down.**

"Dum Dum Boys" by Iggy Pop and David Bowie, 1977.

In the summer and autumn of 1970, the Stooges' line-up underwent a number of changes. Dave Alexander played his last concert with the group at a rock festival in Saginaw, Michigan, in August. He was drinking heavily, and it was almost impossible to rehearse and perform with him. After several gigs where Dave was so loaded that he forgot tunes on stage, Iggy decided to kick him out. Ron remembers the occurence:

> *Iggy didn't dig Dave's attitude, his lack of interest or whatever. He moved out of the band house and was late for practice. At Saginaw, Dave got really drunk and smoked dope, and he sort of freezed on stage and forgot all the tunes. After the gig, Iggy said, "Hey, you're fired. We don't want to play with you anymore."*

Dave died on February 10, 1975, under somewhat mysterious circumstances. Danny Fields was informed that he died from malnutrition, possibly due to anorexia. But Ron claims that the cause of death was an ulcer caused by his excessive drinking. Jimmy Silver talked with Dave a short time before his death:

> *I got a call from Dave. He said, "My folks inherited some money and I've been playing the stock market with it." I was later told that he had made hundreds of thousands of dollars!*

Ron met Dave in 1975:

> *Dave drove me to the airport. "I'll be back in town in about two weeks, I'll see you then." Dave said, "No, this is goodbye." I said, "What do you mean?" "No, this is really goodbye. I won't see you again." "Well, that's ridiculous. I'm going to be back here and you're not going anywhere!" I was back in two weeks and Dave was dead. His mother cremated him immediately.*

Dave was replaced by Zeke Zettner, who worked for the Stooges as a roadie. According to Ron, Zeke wasn't much of a bass player:

> *Zeke had never played before. His attitude was cool, but he couldn't cut it as a bass player. I wanted someone who really could play the bass, but we couldn't find anyone. Zeke was one of the boys so we took him. But he couldn't really play the bass and he learnt slowly.*

**Ron Asheton and the new Stooges members: Steven Mackay (sax), Billy Cheatham (guitar), and Zeke Zettner (bass).** (Leee Black Childers)

Billy Cheatham was also added to the group in August. Ron wanted a second guitarist so he would be able to do more solos on stage. Billy had played guitar with Ron in the Dirty Shames and had worked as a roadie for the Stooges.

In late August 1970, the six-piece line-up, with Billy and Ron on guitars, Zeke on bass, Scott on drums, and Steven playing saxophone, played a four-night stand at Ungano's, a small club in New York City. Prior to the shows, Iggy met a guy who offered them cocaine, which at the time was extremely expensive. Iggy could not afford the drugs, so he went to Bill Harvey, Elektra's Vice President, and actually managed to get him to put up the money:

*I carefully explained that I wouldn't dare to do to my body what my body wasn't accustomed to and that in order to get through the entire gig... "I'm sorry to have to ask you for this, but you're going to have to give me $400 for a one-quarter ounce of cocaine." I was obviously making them flip out. He just couldn't believe his ears. "That's impossible. Who do you think we are? We don't give out... that's impossible!" I'm just leaping around the room. There is no question about this. We've gotta have it... So he did it. ..... I took so much coke through those four nights. If you look at pictures of those gigs, I look like a Biafran or something: skinny isn't the word.*

Iggy at Ungano's, New York, August 1970.
(PN collection)

Tony Glover, writing for *Circus*, was in attendance at Ungano's:

*It's a club called Ungano's in New York, one of the last small rock clubs. The occasion is a press party thrown by Elektra Records in honour of* Fun House, *the new LP by the Stooges. Almost everybody is there. The air is expectant. The Stooges are on the verge of breaking through ("The US Rolling Stones" somebody said). The Stooges are almost an hour late. Nothing happens. Finally, 15 minutes later, the band strides out. As the equipment is readied, Iggy stands shirtless at the mike waiting, eyes self-contained but piercing as he stares around the room. Suddenly the silence is shattered by the loud electronic blast of Stooge-rock. Iggy contracts as though punched in the stomach, his arms flailing. The music pounds on as he dances like an angular snake. He slams the mike against his lips and whoops, then sings in a yelled growl. Iggy bolts into action, stalking out into the audience; people scatter like pigeons in Central Park. Those in the back are standing on their chairs as he goes down on the floor; the audience gathers in a circle around him. "Did he cut himself? Is he bleeding?" Then he's up again dancing through the audience like old Egyptian tomb paintings. The band stand stolidly on stage, pouring out the sounds, all energy focused on Iggy.*

Iggy and the Stooges left the reviewer puzzled:

*What does it all mean? Is it just a hype, an exercise in theatric weirdness? Is it an act, designed to draw attention that the music alone wouldn't? Or is it a "real" stage madness designed to make the audience ask questions about themselves and the nature of what they want from rock groups?*

Danny Fields had brought the whole Andy Warhol crowd to watch Iggy and the Stooges at Ungano's. Attending the show was Leee Black Childers, a young actor who knew many of the Warhol "superstars." He remembers Geri Miller, who had

**At Ungano's.** (Dustin Pittman and Leee Black Childers) ▷

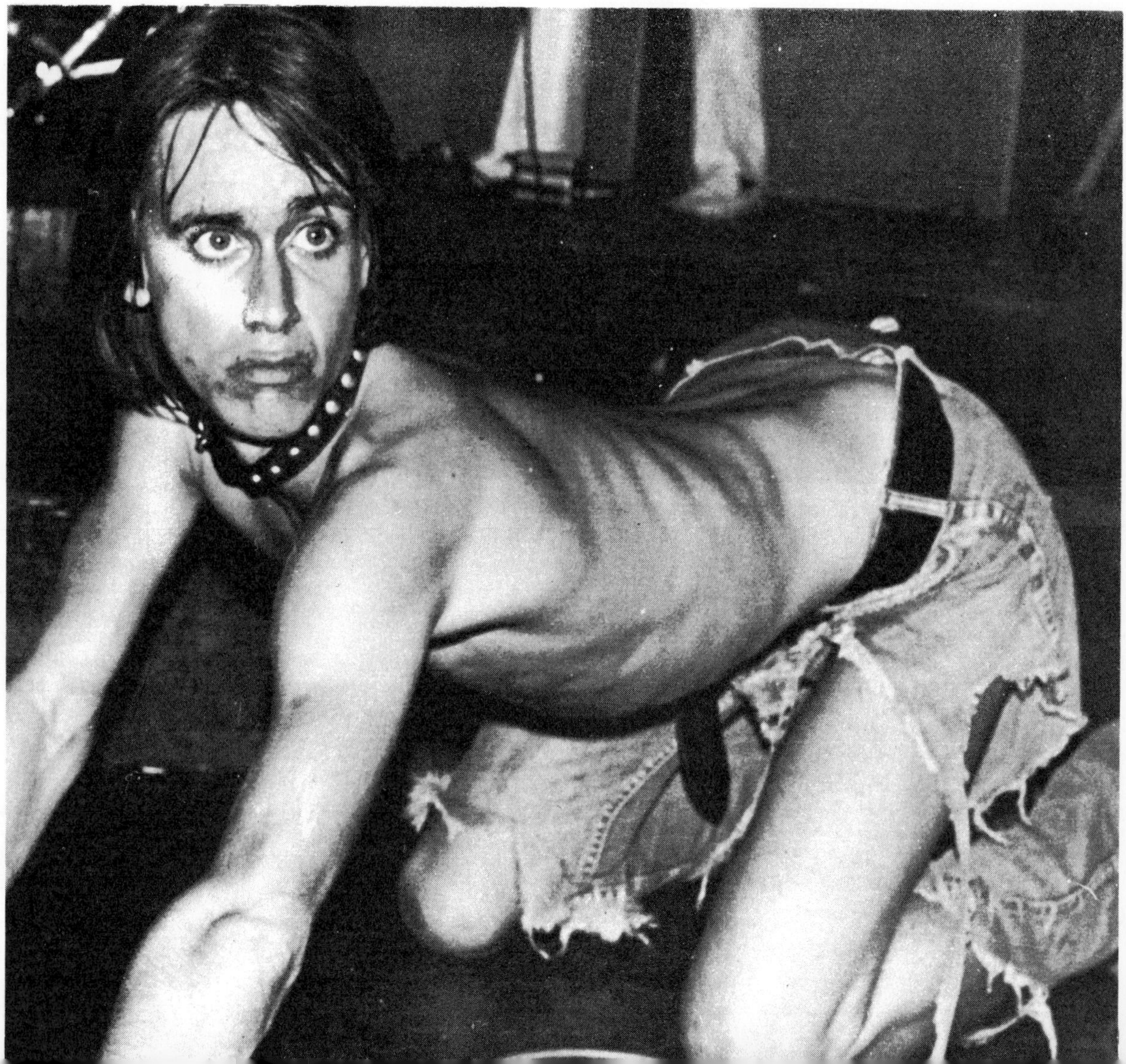

starred in Warhol's *Flesh*, going to the shows to become a groupie:

*She was sitting in the front and during one song, Iggy stalked down to her. She was grinning up at him and he grabbed her by the face. His whole hand covered her face. He dragged her by the face, and when he took his hand off her, she was still grinning. She became a big fan. She had originally gone just to become a groupie.*

After the opening night, Fields took Iggy and the Stooges to Max's Kansas City, a club frequented by artists and various underground "celebrities." Surrounded by Warhol's associates Gerard Malanga, Brigid Polk and Donald Lyons, Iggy was the unquestionable star of Max's backroom. Leee Black Childers and other less "notable" people were only allowed a few words on occasion with Iggy:

*Iggy was very much the focus of the backroom. I remember because I never got to get near to him. Jackie Curtis, Wayne County, Holly Woodlawn, all these people were in the room trying to get near to Iggy. When Iggy walked in the backroom, everyone paid attention. The whole room was centred on where he was, who he was talking to, and who he might leave with. He mostly left with Danny Fields.*

Coinciding with the release of *Fun House* in August 1970, the Stooges went on a national tour. Their set featured mainly *Fun House* tunes: "Down On The Street," "1970," "Dirt," "TV Eye," "Loose," "Fun House," and "Dog Food." As the tour progressed, new tunes were added: "Big Time Bum," "Way Down In Egypt" (or "Egyptian Woman"), "Searching For Head," and "Private Parts." The new songs were more jazz-influenced and less structured than the earlier Stooges material. Iggy later said that at the time, he considered the Stooges a jazz band, rather than a conventional rock group.

By late 1970, James Williamson was back from the reform school in New York and he moved to Ann Arbor. He knew Ron from the time in the Chosen Few, and he started sitting in on rehearsals with the Stooges. He was clearly a better and far more experienced guitar player than Billy Cheatham, so Ron simply asked James to take Billy's place and join the group. Prior to James' arrival, Steven Mackay had left the band and returned to Detroit to form the Mojo Boogie Band. He later played with another Detroit band, Commander Cody and his Lost Planet Airmen.

With the arrival of James in the group, and after Steven had left, the Stooges' sound and musical orientation changed. James was clever at writing simple and highly effective high-energy rock tunes, and he soon started working on new songs with Iggy. The songwriting team of James and Iggy was the beginning of a long friendship between the two. The jazz-oriented style was soon replaced by James' more traditional rock 'n' roll. The new material included "I Got A Right," "I Need You," "Who Do You Love?", and "You're Looking Fine."

In an interview in *ZigZag* in late 1970, Iggy emphatically denied any speculations that the "new" Stooges would become more accessible or softer in order to appeal to a larger audience:

*Mass recognition is not what's important to me, what's important is individual recognition. In other words, it's not how many people recognize you, it's what the people who do recognize you, recognize you for. To me the biggest band is the band that's biggest in the hearts of the people who listen to it. But on the other hand, large numbers of people can... That's attractive too. Fame and notoriety and money and all those things are attractive. But they're not really attractive to me as the musical forest in which I live. I'm not gonna come out of my musical forest for anybody. Because I already know you're fucked if you do!*

# 13 DRUGS AND DISINTEGRATION

**The whole thing was really strange. I had worked for two and a half years on a national scale and had got to the point where we were drawing bigger and bigger audiences for more and more money, but I was performing worse and worse because I was very sick on drugs. This was common knowledge at the time. So I quit. I took the chance that if I stopped playing and tried to straighten myself out, I could start again.**

Iggy Pop to Chris Charlesworth, *Melody Maker*, October 1973.

From the very beginning, the Stooges were involved with drugs, even though their abuse was not much worse than that of the other Detroit bands or even than most progressive rock groups in the late sixties. Iggy and the Stooges were primarily into smoking dope and marijuana, and occasionally dropping acid. Jimmy Silver pinpoints the type of drugs that they used:

*These guys weren't sitting around injecting themselves with heroin. They were doing drugs that I thought were reasonable; things that could be psychologically or intellectually construed as mind-expanding. I'm talking about smoking dope and the psychedelic drugs: acid, DMT, etc. These things were taken in a casual atmosphere and with an amount of care and respect. The idea was that you would emerge from all this as a better person and with a better perspective. Amphetamines were something that people just didn't get involved with. John Sinclair and I used to have long philosophical discussions about what drugs were OK and what weren't.*

However, the drug climate in America changed during 1970; suddenly heroin was spreading rapidly, and its general availability increased abruptly in Detroit and other major cities in the States. Many felt the rising addiction rate paralleled the increasing cultural and political repression of young people. In John Sinclair's opinion, the epidemic of heroin was a result of carefully planned US government strategies, and he wrote in the local *Ann Arbor Sun*:

*Before the Summer of Love, there was hardly any speed around at all, and the kids who were just starting to smoke weed and drop acid had never even heard of it for the most part. The acid was truly dynamite, so the first step was to start cutting the LSD with amphetamine and market it as some kind of powerful new trip: STP! And within a couple of weeks, STP was the hottest thing on the psychedelic market — it debuted in San Francisco and spread back across the country like white lightning. All these were acid or synthetic mescaline mixed with amphetamine, and the speed gradually replaced the acid almost entirely. By 1968, just about every hit of acid on the set was 80 or 90% speed with just a tinge of LSD to make it seem weird and scary enough to pass as a psychedelic. It got so there were thousands of freaks dropping "acid" every day who had never really* had *any genuine LSD, but thought that's what they were getting — they became habituated to amphetamines without even knowing they were taking it. The next step was to slide a few tons of amphetamine crystal onto the scene, and to get people* shooting *it so they could get a* real *flash. Kids who had been dropping a lot of adulterated acid could really dig this new trip — pure speed — because it was like the "acid" they had been taking only without the "scary" side-effects. Once they started running speed, it was just a hot minute until smack crept onto the scene, and it got to be popular first as an antidote for the jangly after-effects of speed runs — you could shoot scag with the same works you used for speed, and it would really cool you out. And besides, everybody thought they could use it without it using them, "Yeah, only fools get addicted, me, I'll just run some of this heroin once in a while and won't get strung out like them nasty junkies." Sure. Only it just didn't seem to work that way.*

Iggy and the boys were soon involved with heroin. It is an extremely addictive drug; tolerance grows fast and junkies find themselves shooting up to kill withdrawal symptoms at a very early stage of usage. Because of its physical addictiveness, heroin is generally considered to be one of the most habit-forming drugs. The use of psychologically addictive drugs like cocaine and marijuana tends to be easier to control. By late 1970, all the members in the Stooges, barring Ron, were addicted to heroin. It was one of the Stooges' roadies, John Adams, who had introduced it to both the MC5 and the Stooges. Jimmy Silver describes their increasing involvement with hard drugs:

*Once they began to get popular and got more money at their disposal and we began travelling more, they had access to other kinds of people. They got into drugs that were beyond where they were at and what I thought was reasonable. They got into heroin and harder drugs. The whole atmosphere of the scene and what was available in it was deteriorating about that time. That was really the end of the 60's and the whole high-minded thing. All the people who believed that drugs were mind-expansive were really going downhill.*

Consuming much of their time and money, the heroin habit completely changed the lifestyles of the Stooges members. The MC5 guys, excluding singer Rob Tyner, were also addicted. Lead guitarist Wayne Kramer explains what happened:

*The choice of drugs shifted. In the 60's it was all marijuana and LSD, an occasional hit of speed. When we got into the 70's, that's when people discovered heroin and coke and every other kind of pill,valiums, etc. There was also a difference in lifestyles; whereas we could always afford some reefer, we had to get out on the streets and hustle to stay high on smack. We all started to get our habits by 1970/71.*

There were several close brushes with death. At one point, Iggy collapsed on the kitchen floor of MC5 bass player Michael Davis, the victim of an apparent heroin overdose. Michael was able to revive him, with the help of a cold shower and mouth-to-mouth resuscitation.

As the Stooges became more involved with heroin and harder drugs, their manager Jimmy Silver lost interest in the band. While they were recording *Fun House* in California he had met some friends who had gone into the natural food business:

*I met some guys that I knew from Boston and I used to hang around with them in the daytime because the band was asleep. They kept telling me that I should come back and go to work with them. ..... We were moving off in different directions and I told the guys that I wanted to go back to California. I wanted to leave the music business and be in natural foods.*

Silver decided to quit the Stooges, and he moved to California. He turned the bank accounts over to Danny Fields, who was asked to take over the managerial duties of the Stooges in the autumn of 1970. Fields had left Elektra and was working for Atlantic Records. Even though the Stooges regarded him as their manager, he says himself of his managerial duties for the group:

*From a professional point of view, I wasn't very much of a manager at all. I was really just a friend in the right place at the right time, but I didn't really do what a manager is supposed to do. I didn't go out there and tell them to shape up and put their affairs in order. I just did patchwork repairs.*

In early 1971, Zeke Zettner left the Stooges. He enlisted in the US Army and went to Vietnam to get heroin cheaper. Zeke died from an overdose of heroin in 1975. His replacement on bass was Jimmy Recca, whom James Williamson knew from Birmingham, Michigan. Jimmy, who also stayed out of the heroin business, became Ron's best friend in the group. Technically, he was a much more proficient bass player than Zeke, and the edition of the Stooges with James and Ron on guitars, Jimmy playing bass and Scott on drums was one of the strongest line-ups of the group.

In June of 1971, the Stooges returned to New York to play the Electric Circus at St. Mark's Place. By now, all the Stooges, excluding Ron and new bassist Jimmy Recca, were physically worn out from their heroin abusage. Prior to the show, Iggy was given some heroin backstage:

*I was in there trying to find a vein and screaming, "Get out! Get out!" to everybody, even my friends — and they were all thinking, "God, he's going to die, blah, blah, blah." Finally, I'm up there on the stage and as soon as I walked on that stage I could feel it. I knew I just had to*

**The Stooges' line-up in the summer of 1971. Left to right: Ron Asheton, Jimmy Recca, James Williamson, Scott Asheton, Iggy.** (PN collection)

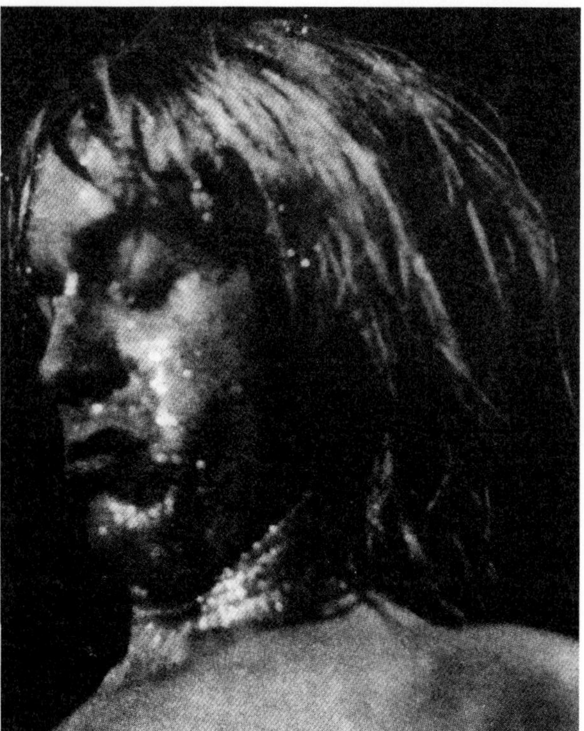

Live at the Electric Circus, New York, June 1971.
(Hank Frank)

*puke. I wasn't going to leave the stage, though, because I felt that would have been considered "deserting one's audience." So I thought, "I'll do a James Brown thing..." A kind of hip side-step move — grab the mike-stand. And then I ended up doing this real elegant jack-back off the mike-stand, then kind of "Que pasa! Que pasa! Hit me! Hit me!" number, and then I heaved off. It was very professional. I don't think I hit anyone in the audience.*

The cast of Andy Warhol's new production *Pork* was rehearsing in New York, and Leee Black Childers was one of the actors who attended the Stooges' show:

*Iggy had gotten an outrageous reputation for self-destruction and being a junkie onstage. Geri Miller was right down in the front again. She had this horrible little voice and she's right down in the front screaming, "Throw up! Throw up! When are you gonna throw up?" And he did! He threw up. Iggy always satisfied his audience.*

The concert ended with Iggy clawing toward the microphone to quote from the *Dracula* movie, "Flies... big juicy flies... and spiders." As he choked and threw up on stage, it was obvious to the audience and critics that Iggy was seized by hard drugs. The whole self-destructive image of Iggy and the Stooges had gone too far; Iggy gave the audience everything they could possibly expect to see short of an onstage suicide.

Although he was no longer affiliated with Elektra, Danny Fields managed to convince Elektra's Vice President Bill Harvey and the *Fun House* producer Don Gallucci to fly out to Ann Arbor to attend a Stooges live session and appraise the commercial possibilities of a third record for Elektra. Fields attended the session, in late June 1971, as the Stooges' manager:

*I was thrilled! They sounded great to me. I was delighted and I remember saying to the Elektra people, "Well?" and they said, "There's nothing there." "How can you say that? It was fabulous." I was thrilled to hear they were making such progress. Bill Harvey said, "There's nothing there. I don't want to pick up the option; it's not worth it."*

Ron remembers the event:

*They couldn't believe it, especially Bill. He was almost afraid, but Gallucci was cool. We took them into the practice room. They were expecting little amps — we had double Marshall stacks! They stood there. It was so hard to play, I was laughing so hard. Bill was in a suit. Gallucci was a little more casual, but still a sporty little Italian. What the hell do they think we are doing? They must think we are the weirdest bunch of guys!*

Elektra decided to drop the Stooges; a third album was not deemed commercially viable. Fields broke their decision to the boys:

*I don't think they were terribly surprised that no one at Elektra believed in their music any longer. They anticipated it, "We expected that. What do they know?" That was the band's attitude. The axe fell.*

In a last attempt to get the group a record contract, Fields started negotiations with RCA. In the end, though, he felt it was not worth taking pains over the group any longer, and he quit the job of manager soon thereafter. It was impossible to handle the band; three of the members were junkies and their business was in a shambles. According to Ron, they owed Elektra $80,000 and had to sign away their future record royalties to pay off the debt.

After a show at Detroit's Eastown Theatre, Iggy finally decided to quit the Stooges. He was completely run down by his drug abuse and he needed some time off to cure his addiction. He has spoken of his decision:

*I never planned to stop. I felt forced into it because I was in a position where larger and larger audiences were paying more and more money to see us and because at the same time I hit a point where I had a lot of professional problems. I was unhappy. I felt badly myself. We'd just show up somewhere and there would be all these people, and I really wanted to do good for them and I didn't. I had too much at stake personally to go out and do a crummy show. ..... The disintegration of the Stooges at that point was also, at least in my mind, a reflection of the germinal growth of what I wanted to do with James. Because we knew we could do something better.*

# 14 ENTER BOWIE AND DEFRIES

**I was sitting around Danny Fields' one night watching *Mr. Smith Goes To Washington*, and I was deep into it when Danny calls from Max's. Says, "You remember this guy David Bowie?" A year ago he'd listed me as his favourite singer or something. So Danny says, "Grab a cab down to Max's, he wants to meet you." So I said OK, but I couldn't tear myself away from the movie, cause Jimmy Stewart was so sincere. Fields kept calling me, saying, "Listen, man, do yourself a favour." Finally, I made it down there. Bowie and Defries saw I was hungry so they invited me to breakfast. I came up and ate about six breakfasts the next day and started hanging out with them.**

Iggy Pop to Lester Bangs, *Creem*, April 1974.

Without Iggy, the Stooges played one further show, in July of 1971, which they were contracted to before Iggy left. It was a concert at Punch Andrew's club in Ann Arbor. They went on and Ron explained to the audience that Iggy had quit the Stooges:

*They were disappointed, but ironically the thing turned into an amateur night! There was a kid about 15 years old in the audience who was really into Iggy, and imitated him perfectly, even down to hitting me in the knee with the mike stand. So this kid filled in for Iggy the entire show.*

The break-up of the Stooges was formally announced on July 9, 1971. Following the split, Iggy, James and Scott started methadone programs to quit heroin. The methadone cures, where methadone is substituted for heroin taken in reduced quantities, were eventually successful.

In August 1971, Iggy received an offer from Steve Paul, the manager of Edgar and Johnny Winter, to come down to Florida to start a band with Rick Derringer and some musicians from White Trash:

*I knew it was going to be bad, I went down, though, and took my golf clubs with me. ..... "You'll be allowed to write the words. Everything else is strictly..." I felt like a puppet even listening to shit like that, so I wasn't buying any of it.*

Iggy also turned down an offer from an Elektra producer to sing what he called "David Cassidy-type" songs.

Almost completely broke, Iggy hitchhiked from Miami to New York to see if there was anything that he could get involved with. In late August, discontent yet irrepressible, he came to New York City, staying with friends Danny Fields and Gerard Malanga. There were no concrete offers or work for Iggy, and by September 1971, he was disillusioned and ready to give up completely on the music business.

Once again, it was Danny Fields who was responsible for making possible the next stage in Iggy's career. As it happened, Fields had gone out to dinner with Dennis Katz, head of A&R at RCA Records, and Lisa and Richard Robinson, Tony Zanetta, Lou Reed, Mick Ronson, David Bowie and his manager Tony Defries. Bowie and Defries were in town to sign a record contract with RCA. Tony Zanetta, who knew Lou Reed and the others, had met Bowie in London the previous month, when he was playing in the Andy Warhol production *Pork*.

Zanetta played the part of Andy Warhol in *Pork*, which also featured Geri Miller, Leee Black Childers, Wayne County, Kathy Dorritie (Cherry Vanilla), Via Valentina, and Jamie de Carlo Andrews. The play, directed by Tony Ingrassia, opened on August 2 in London to wide media attention. David Bowie, who was playing a series of gigs at Hampstead's Country Club, saw the play and became friendly with some of the actors. Zanetta remembers how the friendship was established:

*I met David in London while we were doing* Pork. *We met a few times and then we became friendly in my last week in London. He did a couple of small gigs while we were there. We went to them, to a place called Country Club. Then David and Angie came to see us in* Pork *a couple of times. We also went to their house in Beckenham.*

At the RCA dinner party at Max's Kansas City, David Bowie told Fields that he wanted to meet Iggy. Fields immediately called up Iggy, who was staying in Fields' loft, watching a late night movie. Finally Iggy switched off the TV and headed downtown:

*So finally after about a hundred calls, I made it down there, just as they were about to close. It was ridiculous, here's all these people with money and everything, all waiting for this little scumbag that's got nothing. I finally stroll in, and there's Bowie and Tony Defries and a couple of the company freaks. David and I got along, and his manager and I got along too.*

David Bowie remembers meeting Iggy:

*I was at an RCA party at Max's Kansas City in New York and was introduced to Lou Reed. He immediately started telling me some story about a guy who injected smack through his forehead — that's typical Lou. Anyway, up comes this funny ragged, ragged little guy with a broken tooth and Lou says, "Don't talk to him, he's a junkie" — that was Iggy. You can't help loving him, he's so vulnerable.*

David Bowie had apparently admired Iggy and Lou Reed a long time. He was very impressed with the Stooges' Elektra albums and he had seen their famous Cincinnati Pop Festival appearance. In fact, Bowie had said as early as April of 1971 that his forthcoming Ziggy Stardust stage act would become more theatrical and outrageous than Iggy and the Stooges had ever been.

When he became Bowie's manager in 1970, Tony Defries was working for the Gem Group in England, a company he ran with an accountant friend, Laurence Myers. However, he already had elaborate plans for a new management/production company of his own, which would manage Bowie as well as other artists of his choice. Although the company, MainMan, wasn't formally founded until 1972, Defries started planning by inviting some of the *Pork* actors to work for him.

On September 8, the day after the Max's meeting, Iggy met with Defries and Bowie at the Warwick Hotel for breakfast. On Bowie's recommendation, Iggy signed a management contract with Defries. Zanetta recalls what happened:

*Defries and Bowie liked Iggy immediately. Tony Defries really like helping people out. He knew David and Angie [Bowie] were into Iggy. Iggy came up to the hotel and he started spending a lot of time with David. They made plans right then and there that they would bring Iggy to England. Tony would manage him. Iggy was on methadone at the time and was cleaning up his drug act.*

The plans for Iggy evolved over the next few days: as soon as Iggy was through with his methadone program, Defries would get him a record contract, after which Iggy would go to England to record an album. Defries wanted the album to be recorded in England for several reasons. Iggy's reputation in the States couldn't be worse. Everyone in the music business knew of his drug abuse and he was branded an eternal loser.

Upon his return to Ann Arbor, Iggy told James Williamson about the bright new prospects, and they made vague plans to start a new group together. Iggy was closer to James than to any of the other Stooges members; they had worked closely together as a songwriting team and been through their heroin trips together. Iggy considered James to be a better and more experienced guitar player than Ron. In effect, Ron wasn't asked to join the new group:

*Iggy had more of a rapport with James. They got tight through drugs, they were junkies together. And James was a better songwriter and a more accomplished guitarist.*

Ron was upset when he heard of Iggy's and James' plans to carry on without himself or Scott, but he was even more exasperated when he was told that they intended to call themselves the Stooges:

*I felt the name Stooges was really Iggy, Scott and myself. We started the group and I was really furious when I heard they were going to use that name for their new band.*

So, while Iggy and James planned their new group and upcoming trip to England, Ron and Scott were out of work in Ann Arbor, living with their mother.

In December 1971, Defries returned to New York. He sent for Iggy from Ann Arbor and arranged for him to stay at the plush Warwick Hotel. Tony Zanetta was employed to look after Iggy and take him shopping:

*He was totally off drugs at that point. I went up to the Warwick every day; I was kind of babysitting. Tony Defries gave me the money to take Iggy out shopping. We went to some shops on Madison Avenue. Tony gave us $400-500 and we spent the whole $400 in the first half hour on two pairs of pants! The way Defries acted, we thought he had millions and millions of dollars. We spent the $400-500; that was a lot of money to both of us. We didn't know each other so well, so were both pretending that it wasn't.*

Together with Defries, Iggy visited RCA and Columbia. A deal was struck with CBS/Columbia and Iggy signed a lucrative two-record contract:

*I sang "The Shadow Of Your Smile" for Clive Davis and just did a little softshoe. And totally, just whatever he asked. He asked me if I'd do this or that or the other thing, I'd say no. "Will you do Simon and Garfunkel?" "No, I won't." "Will you be more melodic?" "No, I won't... but I can sing, ya wanna hear it?" And I just sang that, and he said, "OK, enough, enough!" And just picked up the phone and said, "Yeah, call the legal department." And that was it.*

# 15 LONDON BOYS

**We all went over to England, lived in a lovely place in London, and rehearsed and rehearsed and rehearsed. Every morning the Stooges would troop dutifully to this filthy basement to practice. After about two months they said, "Iggy, what are we practicing for?" It was like *The Bridge On The River Kwai.* I felt like Alec Guiness. Why are we building this bridge? To blow it up! Defries didn't want us to gig because Bowie was hot then. If I had been on the road I would have been hot too. I bitched to Tony Defries, "We're a band, let us play!"**

Iggy Pop to Scott Isler, *Trouser Press*, January 1983.

Finally, in March 1972, Iggy and James, both completely off heroin, went to England to recruit a new band and start recording the album for CBS/Columbia. They were put into the first-class Royal Gardens Hotel in London. After a month at the hotel, Defries decided it was too expensive and instead rented them a small house in St. John's Wood, London. Throughout April and May, Iggy and James auditioned several musicans for their band, in search of a bass player and drummer:

*The more we got to know England, the more we felt there wasn't anybody there we wanted to play with. Because Iggy and I knew what we wanted, but we were just really disappointed with the whole thing.*

Eventually they decided to call up Ron and Scott in Ann Arbor, asking them to come over and play. Scott was excited by the idea of going to England and to play drums again, but Ron was wary:

*Iggy calls me up and goes, "We can't find any guys that are good enough on bass and drums." At first I thought, "Well, fuck, thanks a lot man! You're calling me out of desperation after you have tried out every limey that was available in England."*

Although Ron previously had played the bass in the Chosen Few, he was much more interested in playing the guitar:

*I felt it was a blow since I considered myself a guitarist. Iggy was saying things like, "Eventually you'll switch over to guitar, we'll get another bass player." I wasn't thrilled, but I wanted to go to England to do something. Just do something.*

Immediately after arriving in London on June 6, Ron and Scott started rehearsing with Iggy and James. MainMan had secured them almost unlimited studio time at CBS' new

**Iggy in London, March 1972.** (Melody Maker)

## Are Those Iggy Stooge-Judee Sill Rumors True?

Our favorite all-American boy, James Osterberg aka Iggy Stooge aka Iggy Pop aka Pop, is beginning to make his presence known in England, the base of operations for his comeback thrust. His hair is longer now, we're told, and he's given to wearing old hats and leopard-skin jackets. The following are excerpts from his English press coverage.

*On his problems: "I got a real man-size habit, and then I didn't want to be onstage anymore 'cause I knew I couldn't do my best under those circumstances. It got to the point where I'd get on stage and then puke. The people didn't care. Their attitude would be, 'I've seen him do so many far out things, now let's see him kill himself'."

*On Marc Bolan: "Kinda chipmunky."

*On his drumming experiences with the Iguanas: "Where I came from I was a legend."

*On himself: "I've always been lucky, I've wanted everything in the world. I've wanted it all. I'm as dishonest as the next guy, ya see. I'm greedy, crooked and vain, and I like to profile. Everybody has a shadow and I like to project a big one."

And it appears that the rumors about him penning a tune for gentle songstress Judee Sill have a basis in truth. Apparently she was on a British television program he happened to be watching, complaining about how she didn't like rock and roll bands because they were all so "young, loud and snotty". He wrote a song which will immortalize that wisdom, and it will hopefully be available on the next Stooges album, due in late fall from Columbia. It is not yet known whether Mr. Osterberg has approached Ms. Sill to sing counterpoint on the song he wrote for her, but it might certainly be good therapy.

studios in London. They worked five to six days a week in the studio, writing new tunes, rehearsing and recording. Defries wanted Bowie to produce the album, but Iggy objected strongly to this suggestion, wanting to do it by himself:

> *We didn't want David to be in the studio every night. We didn't want to contend with him, trying to gain artistic control while we were actually recording.*

It was decided that Iggy would produce the album himself, while Bowie would be responsible for mixing the tapes. There were several reasons for letting Bowie mix the album, according to Iggy:

> *David is talented and could probably have improved the tapes, but also it would have been a good selling point to have his name on the album. I didn't want Bowie to produce the album and I got my way.*

During June and July, Iggy and the Stooges were working hard in the studio. Several new tunes were recorded: "Nigger Man," "I'm Sick Of You," "Tight Pants," "Scene Of The Crime," "Gimme Some Skin," "Fresh Rag" (a re-working of a Joe Tex number), "Penetration," "Search And Destroy." They also recorded some material they had played live in 1971, among them "I Got A Right" and "I Need Somebody."

With David Bowie's breakthrough album *The Rise And Fall Of Ziggy Stardust And The Spiders From Mars* out in early June 1972, and an American tour planned for the autumn, Defries decided to fly a number of select American journalists to see Bowie's acclaimed Ziggy Stardust set at Aylesbury Friars on July 15. After Bowie's show, there were buses outside the building carrying the journalists to London to watch Iggy and the Stooges' comeback concert at King Sound, a new venue utilizing the old King's Cross Cinema. Lou Reed had made his solo debut to a packed house the previous day. The King's Cross Cinema show was the only concert Iggy and the Stooges played during their stay in England; it was to be their only show outside America.

The British music press and audience had only read and heard about the Stooges' infamous concerts in the States; the Stooges were still very much of a cult band in England. Dressed only in silver lamé trousers and sporting silver hair, Iggy was as wild as ever, and lived up to his outrageous reputation. Nick Kent reported for *New Musical Express*:

> *Iggy started off demonstrating his own demented version of the boogaloo, progressing to some particularly impressive acrobatics and then into his audience assault numbers. Once he grabbed a chick and stared blankly into her face, almost beating up some poor wretch who dared to laugh at him. ..... The total effect was more frightening than all the Alice Coopers and* Clockwork Oranges *put together, simply because these guys weren't joking.*

One of the invited journalists was Glenn O'Brien, writing for *Interview*. In his review, he questioned whether the English audience was really prepared for Iggy's manic on-stage behaviour:

> *Iggy was walking in a circle ten feet in radius from the microphone... the ultimate rock and roll body clad only in silver lamé pants, bagging enough in back to show black bikini briefs, and black boots. The upper torso is greased and silvered. The hair, chin length, is silver. They eyes are made up black, the lipstick is black, and the nails. Iggy stares like an amnesiac Hamlet into the audience. He*

In the recording studio, London, June 1972.
(Photo © Mick Rock)

*glares, circles, but doesn't speak. Minutes pass. The audience begins to titter at the touch of his theatrically outraged stare. Iggy begins to insult the audience. He tells it that it doesn't inspire him. He sits down on the stage. After a minute he rolls over on his belly like a centrefold girl and continues to wonder at the mediocrity of half a theatre full of London hippies. ..... Iggy does several things London has never seen. He swings his microphone around his head in a big circle just like Roger Daltrey, but when Iggy wants it back, he lets it wrap around his neck. Iggy likes to visit with the audience. He likes to sing a song to a particular girl in the audience. He likes to grab her by the hair and shake her head like a handful of dice when he sings to her. ..... Iggy was gone. The battery of amplifiers screamed a dull but deafening scream which drowned out the calls for encore, the applause, conversation. Absolutely stunned kids of London went home.*

The Stooges' 40-minute set at King's Cross Cinema consisted of tunes they had rehearsed and recorded in London during June and July: "Gimme Some Skin," "I Got A Right," "I'm Sick Of You," "Scene Of The Crime," and others. During a break in the show, when his microphone broke down, Iggy sang an impromptu version of Frank Sinatra's "The Shadow Of Your Smile." It was completely new repertoire to the audience since nothing from the Elektra albums was played.

The following day, MainMan arranged a press meeting at the extravagant Dorchester Hotel in London with Iggy, Bowie and the Spiders, and Lou Reed, who was recording *Transformer* and performing in England. Bowie, interviewed by Charles Shaar Murray in *New Musical Express*, talked about theatricality in rock music:

*There will only be the odd few bands who have the knowledge to master their theatre. Iggy has natural theatre. It's very interesting because it doesn't conform to any standards or rules or structures of theatre. It's his own and it's just a Detroit theatre that he's brought with him. It's straight from the street.*

Iggy and the Stooges continued writing and recording new songs throughout the summer. When Defries finally heard the tunes, he hated them and found the only acceptable tracks to be an early version of "Search And Destroy" and the riff to "Tight Pants" (which became "Shake Appeal" after some lyric changes). He ordered them back into the studio to record more material. In comparison to the material that finally ended up on the album, *Raw Power*, many of these pre-*Raw Power* tunes seem to be just half-developed songs, consisting of ultra-fast riffs with an odd solo thrown in. Stand-out tunes of the early material are "Search And Destroy," "I Got A Right," and "I'm Sick Of You," with its slow mesmerising, jangling riff suddenly exploding into a stuttering riff before returning to the opening phrase.

The *Raw Power* sessions were a prolific period of songwriting for James and Iggy. Although Ron had some tunes and ideas he wanted to include on the album, all the songs were penned by Iggy and James:

*My brother and I put a lot of input into it. James would structure tunes and we would help arrange. We never got*

SAT. JULY 15TH.

FROM U.S.A. 1ST LONDON APPEARANCE OF

EX IGGY AND THE STOOGES

FLAMIN' GROOVIES

F.F.& Z.

★FILMS, HAPPENINGS, AND CRAZY SUPRIZE ATTRACTIONS★

Advance tickets available at Cinema £1

**Performing at King's Cross Cinema, London, July 15, 1972.** (Photo © Mick Rock)

**King's Cross Cinema.** (New Musical Express)

*any credit. It was this Jagger/Richards trip. James fought tooth and nail that all tunes were written by Iggy Pop/James Williamson.*

Antagonism welled up between Ron and James. Ron claims that James was arrogant the entire period in London; he considered himself Iggy's right-hand man, and he treated Ron and Scott more or less like studio musicians, ordering them around at his every whim. In spite of their differences, Ron and James worked effectively together and Ron still has a high regard for James' songwriting.

In comparison to the heroin period in 1970-71, everyone in the group was pretty healthy during the London sojourn. No one was involved with any hard drugs. Defries and MainMan were adamant that their artists should be clean. According to Tony Zanetta, the company was very anti-drugs:

*MainMan was never drug-oriented. No one was into drugs. Later on, people got involved with drugs, cocaine, etc. It was never the hip thing to do at MainMan. We drank too much. We were all so chic, sitting around in restaurants drinking white wine and brandy. Leee [Black Childers] and I used to fill up bathtubs with ice and we'd order for bottles of white wine, keep them on ice, so that we'd have wine after we'd gotten back from gigs or whatever. David [Bowie] didn't do any drugs. He didn't smoke pot; he hardly drank a glass of wine at the time. Iggy didn't do any drugs either.*

Nevertheless, Ron and Scott spent half of their weekly MainMan salary on hash:

*We lifted off our salaries to buy us half an ounce of hash every week. My brother and I chipped in some of each of our money every Monday to have this guy come to our house and bring the hash. We were just smoking hash — no one was into harder drugs.*

Upon completion of the album in September, everybody in the band wanted to go back to the States. Defries and most of the MainMan staff went with Bowie to the States for Bowie's first large-scale American tour, leaving Iggy and the guys by themselves in London. According to Leee Black Childers, they felt left out, and reacted against being neglected by demolishing parts of the rented house:

*They wrecked the house and disrupted the neighbourhood totally until they were thrown out. That's why they ended up being brought back from England. They could find no place for them and they were afraid that Iggy was going to be deported any minute.*

# 16 MAINMAN HASSLES

**We lived in this huge, beautiful mansion in the Hollywood Hills. We rehearsed every night; wrote new tunes and kept the band in shape. We thought Defries was trying to get us gigs so we kept on rehearsing. But nothing happened. We said, "Come on Tony, let's get going, we wanna play!" But at that point — we didn't realize it then — Defries concentrated everything on breaking Bowie in the States. He couldn't care less about us. He did real shit by us!**

Ron Asheton to Dorothy Sherman, March 1982.

In the summer of 1972, the MainMan organization was officially founded. With Tony Defries as Chief Executive Officer, Tony Zanetta was appointed President of the American department with Leee Black Childers as Vice President and Cherry Vanilla as Director of Publicity. The English office, including Corinne Schwab, who later became Bowie's personal assistant and close friend, and Don Hunter, soon faded into the background of the American department with all its colourful people. The MainMan artists, including David Bowie, Iggy, Mott the Hoople, and Annette Peacock, were paid a weekly salary. Originally, Iggy was the only member of the Stooges signed to MainMan, but Ron, Scott and James each received a weekly $150 as sidemen. This was, in fact, more than Bowie's musicians received, as Ron soon discovered:

*I'm talking with Woody and Trevor [Bowie's drummer and bass player] and we started talking about money. Trevor goes, "What are you getting every week?" I told him that I got $150. He flipped out! They're on top of the charts. "I only get $75 a week," said Trevor. I dug a little bit and I found out that Mick Ronson [Bowie's guitarist] was getting something like $2,000 a week! Trevor and Woody got $75 a week and Bowie got a cut of the action. That's what Defries tried to set up with the Stooges: Iggy would take a percentage of the action, and the rest of the guys would get a salary. They wanted to make James' bigger, but Iggy, knowing my brother and myself, knew we wouldn't go for it, so we got the same amount every week.*

Presumably, Iggy received more, but how much is not known. During the stay in London, MainMan also paid for the rental of music equipment and studio time, as well as the house rent. The Stooges also had a car with a chauffeur at their disposal for which MainMan paid.

For a long time, Bowie had been the darling of the music press in both America and England; he was regarded as a highly talented singer and songwriter. However, it wasn't until he started touring in 1972 that he emerged as a big star. During the British tours, Bowie had gradually built up a larger audience, and by the summer of 1972, he was front-page news in the British rock press. Iggy expected that he and the Stooges would be handled in a similar manner: playing small gigs and slowly building up a following:

*I was told then that I was too big to start little gigs, that I was too well-known! I fought this, but it didn't matter. I was told this by a man I looked up to [Defries] and who helped me out, so I went along with it.*

It was MainMan's policy that their artists should act as if they were huge stars, regardless of their actual commercial status. Besides this reason for the absence of tours in England for the Stooges, Defries also wanted to avoid the competition between the stage acts of Iggy's group and Bowie. Undoubtedly, it was frustrating for Iggy and the Stooges to be confined to the recording studio when they saw how much publicity Bowie was getting for his "outrageous" show.

In mid-October 1972, Iggy finally flew out to Los Angeles with the completed *Raw Power* tapes to join Bowie's entourage who were staying at the Beverly Hills Hotel. All the musicians in Bowie's band, the roadies, bodyguards, MainMan people and various friends lived at the hotel for 10 days while Bowie played shows at Santa Monica Civic Auditorium and San Francisco Winterland Auditorium. Tony Zanetta recalls the scene:

*We all had bungalows. There were 30 of us! Everyone was at the Beverly Hills Hotel. Iggy was really healthy. He was eating only vegetables; he was a vegetarian. No drugs. He was in a really good state of mind and he wanted to stay in California and bring his band over there.*

The rest of the Stooges returned to the States a few weeks after Iggy, and came to Los Angeles in early November.

While Bowie's American tour continued in November and December, Iggy and the Stooges stayed in Los Angeles at the Beverly Hills Hotel, running up huge bills. Leee Black Childers was sent out to find them a house in the Los Angeles area:

*I found them several houses, but Iggy wouldn't settle on any of them. By his choice, he was going out in Beverly Hills Hotel limousines to look at the houses. It all went on the hotel bill. He found a house on his own. It was an incredible, beautiful, magic house! Right on top of the Hollywood Hills. From one window you could see all of Burbank and from another you could see all of LA. It had a huge, huge swimming pool and absolute privacy. It was a gorgeous place. We rented the house for $900 a month.*

As his first assignment for MainMan, Childers was sent to live with the Stooges in the Hollywood Hills mansion on the fashionable Mulholland Drive. He would take care of rehearsals and deal with everything that had to do with Iggy. Most days of the week, Iggy and the guys went down to the nearby S.A.R. Studios to rehearse and work on new tunes. There was still no live work as Defries didn't want the band to tour. Zanetta explains the absence of concerts:

*Tony Defries wanted the band to be in demand. He had theories about that kind of stuff. He wanted to create a demand for the band and he didn't want Iggy to do small clubs, or as an opening act or any small gigs. He wanted everything to be right, but none of us at MainMan had the time to make that happen.*

Meanwhile, Bowie's second American tour opened at New York's prestigious Radio City Music Hall (February 14, 1973), and the MainMan staff was preoccupied with Bowie's career.

As the months passed and there were no concerts to play, Iggy and the guys grew impatient and complained to Childers about the situation:

*They weren't working and Iggy was feeling second banana to Bowie. He was feeling left out and he was most insecure and upset. I guess I wasn't very good at receiving all the complaints. We were all so in awe of Tony Defries. He was like a god. I just didn't want to disturb him. Iggy's complaints disappeared into me. Very few of them were communicated to Defries in New York.*

Eventually, Childers managed to persuade Defries to schedule a concert for the Stooges in Detroit for late March 1973.

David Bowie arrived in Los Angeles in early March 1973 for the last two concerts of his American tour (Long Beach Arena and Hollywood Palladium). He had some time off before the Japanese leg of the tour in April, so, with Iggy, he went into Hollywood's Western Sound Studios to mix the *Raw Power* tapes. James also attended the studio:

*The tracks were really complicated because this was our first shot at production. But even though he understood what this meant, he was saying, "Well, listen, this is the track that goes here," just trying to rearrange all kinds of shit.*

Although Iggy in recent years has said that he thinks Bowie's mixing was the best under the circumstances, he openly confronted Bowie at the time:

*Half the time the good parts were mixed out by that fucking carrot-top... sabotaged! I think he tried to bury parts so you would hear them faintly, rather than doing a straight mix.*

A tape of the Stooges' original mix of the album was actually played on WABX, a Detroit radio station, and it does sound better than the final mix; the instruments are mixed much clearer. The final mix by Bowie and Iggy has very little drums and bass, and very "close" vocals with high mixed-up guitars. Without doubt, the person most disappointed in the mix of the album was Ron:

*We did a rough mix when we recorded the album and it was much, much better. I was so bummed out when I heard Bowie's and Iggy's cocaine "artsy-fartsy" mix. It was mostly Bowie. He just fucked that album up! Really fucked it. I know what the album could have been.*

After waiting over four months in Hollywood, the Stooges eventually got to play their first US show on March 29; it

Iggy and the Stooges at the Hollywood Hills mansion, early 1973. Left to right: James Williamson, Iggy, Scott and Ron Asheton. (Leee Black Childers) ▷

was their first concert since the King's Cross Cinema gig almost a year prior. It was a highly successful "Welcome Back To Detroit" concert at the prestigious Henry and Edsel Ford Auditorium, a location normally used by the Detroit Symphony Orchestra. Prior to the show, Iggy appeared on a Detroit radio station. Childers vividly remembers what happened:

*He took all his clothes off and was jerking off on the radio! "I've got all my clothes off now. I'm playing with my balls..." Later he locked himself in the radio station's elevator with Cherry Vanilla and tried to rape her! Tony Defries was beside himself with anger. Iggy was totally out of control this whole time in Detroit. But when he got on stage, he did a brilliant show.*

Glenn O'Brien's review in *Interview* was full of praise for the Stooges' return to the stage:

*Iggy is still the same. He projects danger like no other rock performer. He walks a line between entertainment and attack, bringing the violent roots of rock out in the open. He's still the best dancer in rock, out-stepping what James Brown and Mick Jagger were at their peaks and out-outraging prime-time Jim Morrison. ..... The highlight of the show is when he enters the audience. It's the theatre of cruelty come alive. Iggy jumps off the stage. He grabs a girl in the first row and kisses her hard. He holds her and grinds into her while he sings. When he's finished he pushes her down to the floor. Then he goes chasing after a boy. The boy doesn't want any of what Iggy might be offering, but he gets grabbed anyway by the silver-haired black-lipsticked singer. But Iggy doesn't kiss this time, he shakes. Some kids run, afraid that they're next. Others watch in awe. Nobody's going to rush the stage. The stage has rushed the audience. ..... What we saw in Detroit was one of the greatest rock and roll shows ever.*

Iggy and the Stooges left the stage after a short 35-40-minute set, which contained mostly *Raw Power* material, including "Search And Destroy," "Raw Power," "Gimme Danger," "Penetration," "Shake Appeal," and "Death Trip." By orders of Defries, they didn't return for an encore. In true MainMan fashion, there were lavish parties after the show, first at the Ford Auditorium and then later at the Hilton Hotel in Detroit. Ron recalls the backstage party at Ford Auditorium:

*Defries had laid out this gigantic spread of food and alcohol. But we weren't allowed to be seen when we had played. We said, "Alright, just some drinks." They said, "Out in the limousine. You guys aren't going to be seen. This is for the peons." We were grabbing things off the table, into the limousine and back to the hotel.*

After the Detroit concert, Defries got into an argument with James:

*He figured he'd put me out of the way, and that way he could control Iggy. Drugs were involved, even though it was only a minimal kind of thing.*

Defries presumably considered James and the Asheton brothers to be replaceable sidemen to Iggy. According to Ron, Defries had reacted against James' arrogance and "I'm a star" attitude. Considering MainMan's puritanical position on drugs, it is also likely that he objected to James' drug habits, although James was no worse than Iggy or Scott. Matters came to a head when Defries issued an ultimatum that James would have to leave the group, otherwise, not only would they be booted out of MainMan, but he would see to it that the group could never perform on stage again.

As a result, James agreed to leave the Stooges and they were all sent back to the Hollywood Hills mansion. They started working with a Los Angeles session guitarist called Sky Warnklein, who used the stage name Tornado Turner. Defries approved of another show, and in April they played a concert in Chicago with Warnklein on guitar. However, it was evident that it wasn't working well without James; the songs were all written by him and his guitar playing was essential for the group.

According to Zanetta, Iggy became uncontrollable back in Los Angeles:

*He was all down the tubes again. It was drugs as far as I could tell. He began calling all the time. He was looking for attention and there wasn't anybody to give him that. He felt left out. Everybody at MainMan was really too busy to deal with that kind of behaviour. There were robberies, there were abortions, there was this and there was that. It was a new problem every day. No one had the energy to deal with Iggy any longer.*

Childers, living with the group, testifies that the situation was getting out of control:

*They had a lot of unauthorized parties. A lot of broken glass in the pool. A lot of fights with me. They brought in a bunch of junkie groupies and they were shooting up around the pool! All I ever said to Iggy was, "Be discreet, just be discreet." Therefore, the one thing he couldn't do was to be discreet. It's the old "I must break the rules" syndrome. He did!*

But, somehow, Childers feels Iggy's reaction was justified:

*Iggy should have been out of control! He should have burnt the house down and run screaming down Sunset Strip. It's understandable. He was driven so crazy because he was totally ignored until he went completely bananas.*

Word of Iggy's behaviour reached Defries while he was in Japan on tour with Bowie. He decided to terminate Iggy's management contract and release them from the MainMan contract:

*Tony just called me [Childers] and said, "Get them out of the house!" Lo and behold, they all did. No fuss. They didn't destroy things. They didn't pour cement down the toilet or sugar in the gas tank. They just packed up and left.*

Bowie, having been the main force behind Iggy's entry into the MainMan stable of artists, felt very apprehensive about dropping the group. Zanetta recalls the discussions in Japan:

*There were arguments, "Here is this problem and that problem and none of us have the time and you [David] don't have the time, and we just feel..." David was very frustrated. There was a helplessness about it, but he realized that he wasn't going to go in there and sort it out by himself. It would be best for Iggy to go his own way.*

The "Welcome Back To Detroit" concert at Ford Auditorium, March 29, 1973. (Leee Black Childers)

# 17 RAW POWER

**Only a truly diabolical mind could have made the best album of the 70's, and Iggy apparently has it because he's summed everything up and it took him only eight songs to do it. And he didn't have to write any songs about being/not being/wishing he was cosmic, or a star or some bullshit.**

Review of *Raw Power*, Dave Marsh, *Creem*, March 1973.



The long delayed *Raw Power* album was finally released in May, nearly a year after it was recorded. The reception everywhere was overwhelming; it was immediately hailed as a masterpiece and a brilliant hard rock album. The general consensus in the music press was that the musicianship was superior to and technically much better than anything on the previous albums. Somewhat surprisingly, many reviewers also praised Bowie's mix of the album. Although far from being a huge seller, the album reached the US Top 100 and sold very well in Detroit, Los Angeles, and New York, the Stooges' strongest footholds.

The American reviews were excellent. Lenny Kaye lauded the album in his *Rolling Stone* review:

*With* Raw Power, *the Stooges return with a vengeance, exhibiting all the ferocity that characterized them at their livid best. ..... There are no compromises, no attempts to soothe or play games in the hopes of expanding into a fabled wider audience. ..... For the first time, the Stooges have used the recording studio as more than a recapturing of their live show, and with David Bowie helping out in the mix, there is an ongoing swirl of sound that virtually drags you into the speakers, guitars rising and falling, drums edging forward and then toppling back into the morass.*

In *Creem*, Dave Marsh raved about the album, calling it the best LP of the 70's:

*Iggy kicks it loose from the beginning. The guitar charge is just like the old MC5 guitar work, tremendous bursts of apocalyptic interstellar energy, limited only by contemporary technology, harnessed to a strong, if unsteady backbeat. Bassist Ron Asheton pulls down the sound, melding it into something almost earthly, just like a great jazz bass player does, while the rest of the band accelerates beyond anything that's been recorded, or played live or even dreamed of, in years, so hard and so fast that if Iggy wasn't the singer you'd wonder whose record it was.*

A bit more composed was Robert Felden, writing for *Circus* :

*The album is as much of an emotional and audio holocaust as its title indicates. Electric guitars play ferociously and jump back and forth from speaker to speaker. Eerie chorus effects insinuate themselves into some songs.*

In *Stereo Review*, Lester Bangs called the album:

*...a staggering dose of bonescraping rock frenzy straight from the heart of adolescent darkness... fascinating and authentic, the apotheosis of every parental nightmare. The by now banal words "heavy metal" were created for this group.*

The British reviews were likewise enthusiastic. Roy Carr commended the album in *New Musical Express* :

Raw Power *celebrates Armageddon in the form of pathological gutter-level rock 'n' roll. In one searing blast it strips away the layers of veneer and commercial compromise that has — apart from a few rare occasions — defused the whole essence of rock. Much of the success of this set is due to David Bowie's expertise as master of sound. Without distorting the motives or tempering the personality of the Jean Genie, Bowie has contributed to an album which exemplifies the latest spirit of teen discontent.*

Without doubt, *Raw Power* does contain some of the Stooges' most powerful music and Iggy's most effective and haunting vocals. James' guitar playing far surpasses everything on the Elektra albums; some of his riffs and chord sequences are highly original and inventive. His power chords and technically crude guitar, closer in character to early Kinks (Dave Davies) than anything else, became a blueprint for most punk guitarists later in the 70's. Iggy's vocals, alternately screaming and crooning in a voice close to Jim Morrison's are stronger than ever. His voice is double or even triple-tracked on some tunes to great effect. Ron and Scott proved to be an excellent rhythm section, albeit slightly covered up in the poor mix which emphasizes guitar and vocal tracks.

The lyrics of *Raw Power* were more complex and thoughtful than on the Elektra albums:

*My first album had titles like "No Fun" and "Real Cool Time." The songs were almost monosyllabic. People who didn't know me had an impression of some guy just above the moron level. But now all that has changed. These songs are related to my own life.*

Iggy explained the inspiration for some of the songs:

*When I wrote "Gimme Danger" I was just sick of girls. I was really alone at the time I wrote it, and the song was the kind of excitement I wanted. ..... ("Search And Destroy" :) I used to walk around London with this leopard jacket with a big cheetah on the back, and all the old men in London would drive their cars and they'd stop and try to cruise me. All I liked to do was walk around the streets and, you know, "heart full of napalm." I thought "Heart Full Of Soul" [by the Yardbirds] was always a good song and I thought, "What's my heart full of?" I decided it was basically full of napalm.*

A tortured love affair with a girl named Johanna in London motivated Iggy to write "Your Pretty Face Is Going To Hell." She got her thrills from climbing into bed beside Iggy, driving him wild and then running off just before the crucial moment. Iggy later wrote another song about their relationship, "Johanna." He also elucidated the somewhat dubious lyrics of "Penetration" and "Death Trip":

*Part of "Penetration" is about mainlining, but most of it's about the act of penetration as I do it. Penetrating people, events, breaking through doors. Books and people especially. ..... ("Death Trip" :) I just felt that way. I felt very weird. I felt that you can't win. But when I say on that song, "I'll strip you," I don't mean physically, I mean expose.*

The Stooges themselves were pleased that the album was finally out. But, besides the poor mix, they were disappointed in the cover, depicting a rather camp looking, full frontal and half nude Iggy, and MainMan's decision to credit the album to *Iggy and* the Stooges (the Elektra albums had been by *the Stooges*). Said Iggy:

*When I saw that "Iggy" on there like that [looking like a take-off on 50's monster films poster lettering] I flipped right out. I could have screamed! The cover was just the shits. Elektra's were better.*

# 18 OPEN UP AND BLEED

**I was sort of doing to my own body what Pete Townshend used to do to a guitar. First I was using my fingernails on my chest like a windmill, and it made little cuts. It seemed to get the audience excited and the sight of blood got me a little excited too. One night at Max's Kansas City, I fell on the base of a margarita glass. That was accidental. And a lot of blood gushed out of my chest. I carried on doing the show. It wasn't really a serious injury. I do have scars from it, but they have healed now to the point where you'd have to be very observant to spot them.**

Iggy Pop to Bill Forman, *BAM*, November 1986.

Having severed the ties with MainMan for good, the Stooges didn't get their weekly salaries any more, so the only way to survive was to go out on the road and play gigs. To this end, they contacted Jeff Wald, Helen Reddy's husband and manager, who had a small management firm in Los Angeles. He promised to arrange a tour on a very loose "handshake" agreement with Iggy and the group. Iggy also hired Danny Sugerman, once a Jim Morrison confidant, to be his publicist.

After the break with MainMan, James returned to the Stooges again. As rehearsals for the upcoming tour commenced, they decided to thicken their sound by instrumental augmentation. The idea of a second guitarist was dismissed by James; he was simply too egotistical to play with another guitar player. The natural choice, then, was a pianist. After auditioning a couple of guys, they found Scott Thurston, whom James had seen play in a bar in Los Angeles.

On July 30, 1973, Iggy and the Stooges opened a four-night stand at Max's Kansas City in New York City. The audience was full of celebrities and people who knew the band: Lou Reed, Alice Cooper, the New York Dolls, Todd Rundgren, Danny Fields, Tony Zanetta and Leee Black Childers (both remaining good friends after the split with MainMan), as well as various Warhol associates. It was their first concert in New York since the fatal Electric Circus gig in 1971. Lenny Kaye, writing for *Rock Scene*, reported:

> *Iggy Pop was still walking toward the stage when guitarist James Williamson scissored the proceedings with a poker face of stuttering guitar riffs, the opening random violence of "Raw Power." The sound was loud, ripe and full, though Iggy's microphone was barely audible. ..... But overall, it wasn't a good night. The Stooges had yet to feel out their environment, to learn how to move under lights whose positions were set at the beginning of each show, how to talk to an audience who wasn't hostile, not stricken by sudden panic, but one which was ready for anything the band might care to deliver.*

The set included four post-*Raw Power* songs written during rehearsals in Los Angeles: "Head On," "Open Up And Bleed," "Cock In My Pocket," and "Heavy Liquid" (an adaption of the 60's song "New Orleans" with partly new lyrics by Iggy). The partly autobiographical "Head On" and "Open Up And Bleed" were not yet fully developed; Iggy tried out different word combinations in the course of the four shows. "Head On" features a driving bass line by Ron, more or less lifted from a segment of the Doors' "LA Woman." "Cock In My Pocket" is a powerful hard rocking number, in the style of "I Got A Right":

> *It's like an Eddie Cochran thing and nobody sits down and writes a song called "I Got My Cock In My Pocket." But that was basically what I carried around to keep myself alive, so I just stood up at the mike and there it was.*

"Open Up And Bleed" is a slow and haunting tune, featuring some excellent harmonica by Scott Thurston. The song was used as the closing number; it usually finished with Ron and James leaving their instruments on the amplifiers on full volume, creating a deafening feedback.

The following day, the Stooges played their second show. After "I Need Somebody," halfway through the set, Iggy sank to his knees and swiped at the litter and broken glass on the small stage. Lenny Kaye wrote:

> *"My granny dances better than you do!" some cat-caller from the audience advised, but when Iggy rose to his feet, all sound was suddenly hushed. "Will somebody please pick up this glass," and they're not, no one is even making an attempt, and he starts hitting himself across the chest. He picked his hand to his chest, smeared at the crimson, wiped his stained fingers on Scott's denim shirt. "The next song of the evening is entitled..." He finished the set that way, two deep gashes bubbling over their seams.*

Henry Edwards wrote in *After Dark* about the incident:

> *Mid-set during his second evening's show at Max's, Pop stood centrestage, blood pouring from a number of gaping wounds on his face and body. Insiders reported that Iggy, distressed about his attachment to a local beauty named Bebe [Buell], announced, "My heart is broken" and went to work with some pieces of broken glass.*

After the show, Iggy was taken to a hospital for emergency treatment. Under doctor's warning, the remaining two concerts were postponed four nights until Iggy's stitches would have time to set. Later the same week, Iggy and the guys watched Mott the Hoople and the New York Dolls at Felt Forum in

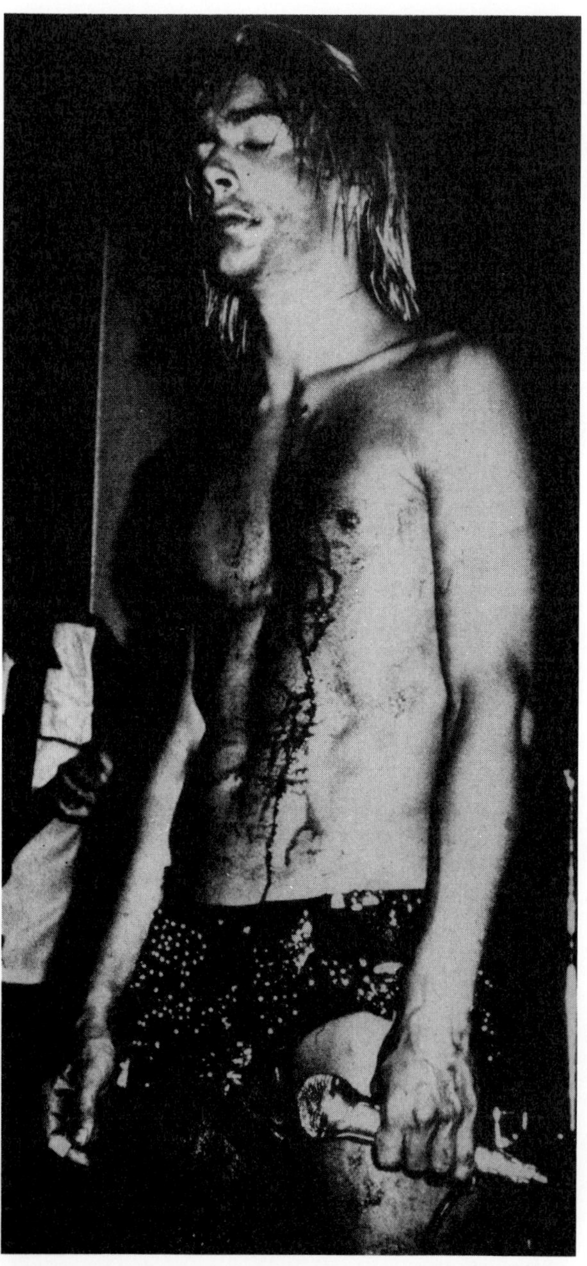

**Iggy on stage at Max's Kansas City, New York, July 31, 1973.** (Billy Maynard)

Madison Square Garden. Once again, Iggy had to undergo treatment after colliding with a door, and he spent the Dolls' set in the Garden's emergency room.

A few days later, on August 6, Iggy, still stitched up and bandaged but irrepressible as ever, was back at Max's again. In Lenny Kaye's opinion, the fourth and last show (August 7) was their best performance:

> *"You can't slander the Stooges," Iggy said after a round of band introductions, followed by a cooling bath of beer borrowed from an adjacent table. It was then that the newly-written encore "Open Up And Bleed" abruptly assumed its final shape. The words had been changing all week, but suddenly mumbled passages became clear, the lyrics in flick-of-the-wrist focus, the music delivered with nary a falter or misstep. "I've been burned..." he sang at one point, "I've been pushed aside, sometimes I've even fixed and died..." Then, "It ain't gonna be that way no more..." with an emphasis on the last word.*

After the last show, Iggy was interviewed by Henry Edwards for *After Dark*. On being asked what he thought of David Bowie, Alice Cooper and other artists borrowing from his act, Iggy couldn't conceal his bitterness:

> *Personally, I think David's a fine fellow. There are so many who stole a lot of shit from me, but the way David did I minded! Look at the photographs of me taken in 1970 and then look at the way David Bowie looks. Check out my lyrics and see how David Bowie has re-written them. Alice Cooper is a hell of a man, he really is. We were working out in California and he saw us working and he said, "Ummmm!" Then he turned up in Detroit a few months later to see us work again and pick up a few more points!*

Following the Max's stand, the Stooges began their first proper concert tour in over two years. Jeff Wald, in association with ATI Booking Agency, had lined up a string of dates throughout August and September. The tour kicked off in Vancouver, Canada, followed by shows at the Phoenix Celebrity Theatre and the American Theatre in St. Louis. Other dates in August included Washington D.C. and Philadelphia, where the Stooges' fan club had been established.

During the Stooges' two-year absence from the rock scene, the world of pop/rock music had changed a great deal. After years of drab super-groups like Emerson Lake & Palmer, Jethro Tull, Ten Years After, Led Zeppelin, Deep Purple — often technically and instrumentally brilliant, but boring to watch — the years 1971-73 saw the rise of a loosely defined genre of glam or glitter rock. In many ways, it was a revival of pop stars, and it introduced new fashions and a new approach to performances (theatre and showmanship) and records (more singles-oriented). Suddenly, everyone camped up in glitter, satin, lamé, and make-up. The new stars included Elton John, Sweet, T.Rex/Marc Bolan, Alice Cooper, Roxy Music, and David Bowie. Iggy and the Stooges also showed a high degree of glam influence, wearing make-up, satin and lamé, and James dressed up in a *Star Trek* costume and platform boots.

# rock scene goes to an OPENING

*Max's Kansas City was full of mayhem & madness the week that Iggy & the Stooges returned to New York. Simply everyone showed up in the standing room only, . . . . Iggy injured himself, and a good time was had by all.*

*Three Stooges–left to right, beloved bassist Ron Asheton, glam guitarist Jones Williamson and the inimitable Ig itself. (Photo by Danny Fields)*

*Columbia Record's Steve Harris is knocked out by the crowds who have come to see Iggy. Iggy's smiling. (Photo by Danny Fields)*

*Ron Asheton watches as Jackie Curtis poses over Iggy & Lou Reed. (Photo by Danny Fields)*

**Max's Kansas City.** (PN collection)

Alice Cooper, who often shared the billings with the Stooges in 1969-71, had made it big and achieved international stardom in 1973. To a certain extent, both Alice Cooper's act, with gallows, guillotines, snakes, etc, and the performances of new groups like the New York Dolls, Black Sabbath, and Kiss, exploited and built upon Iggy's performances with the Stooges. At last, many critics seemed to believe, the time was ripe for Iggy and the Stooges to break through. Glenn O'Brien expressed such expectations in *Interview* :

*Given the fact that Iggy was perhaps the most defiantly ahead of his time performer in 1969-70, and given the fact that many acts have come around doing poor imitations of Iggy's inimitable routines, it should be star time for somebody who was the real star all along!*

Returning to Los Angeles in September, the Stooges went into the Doors' Workshop studio with Todd Rundgren to record some tracks for a possible single but nothing came of it. Said Iggy of working in the Doors' studio:

*Working where Jim Morrison worked is like being in heaven. Jim Morrison was my idol — if he were alive today, I'd die for him.*

During the stay in Los Angeles, the Stooges played a five-night stand with two sets each night at the Whisky A Go-Go in Hollywood. They were very well received; they played to full houses and people had to be turned away each night. Mike Saunders, writing for *Phonograph Record* , attended the shows:

*It must be demanding having to live up to your legend, but Iggy did enough every night to keep his rep intact. Whether falling into the crowded dance floor, pouring pitchers of water on himself, doing his famous dive across the stage into the mike stand, or dry humping into the thin air, it was the Ig all the way.*

Saunders finished his review objectively, pointing out what he felt were the strengths and weaknesses of Iggy and the band:

*Most glaringly, they had only a few songs worked up, with the result that both sets every night were almost identical. Iggy's vocals, strangely enough, were the other weak part of the show. The P.A. was constantly screwed up, with his voice often inaudible as a result. And when it was working, Iggy simply didn't pay enough attention to his singing. His stage act is equally important, sure, but for someone who is as great a vocal stylist as Iggy is in the Dylan/Lou Reed monotone tradition, he should get down and get with it. He wasn't even doing dog barks any more! But that's pretty irrelevant. What's more important here is that the Stooges have come back from the dead to become one of the most powerful groups in the world today. They still have their prime asset: stark energy. Williamson's addition has made them a potential super-group, and Ron Asheton has proven to be an equal dynamo on bass, playing it almost as if it were rhythm guitar.*

Some of the Whisky shows were possibly the best concerts the Stooges had given. In a retrospective article on the Stooges, the *Back Door Man* magazine felt they were among the best rock concerts ever played:

*The Stooges' Whisky performances were the best live rock and roll I have ever witnessed, and I seriously doubt that anything will ever come close to their intensity level. They are the criteria by which I judge any other band live. No one even approaches the energy level.*

**Gigging at Whisky A Go-Go, Hollywood, September 1973.**
(PN collection)

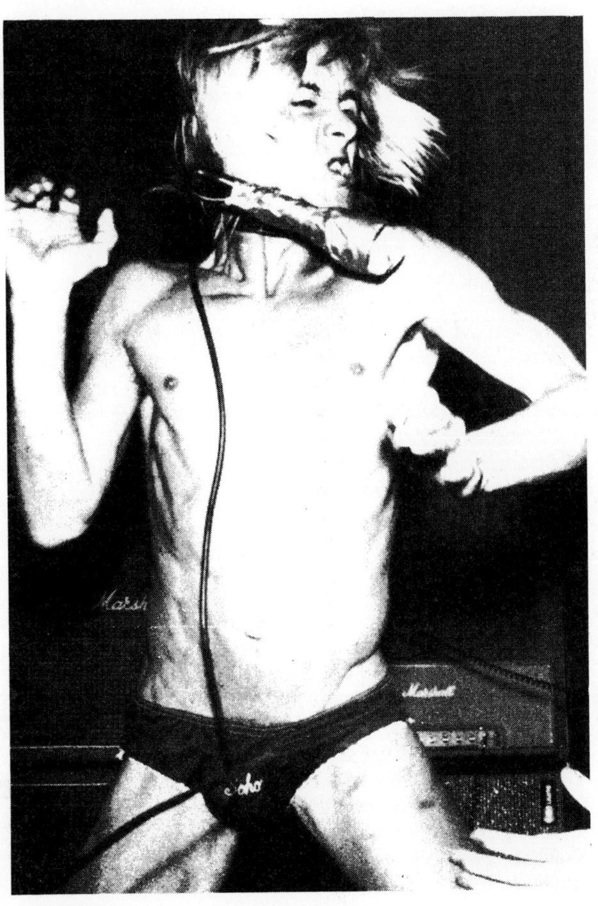

# 19 ON THE ROAD

**After the *Raw Power* album, I just went out and toured until I dropped. As soon as I was dismissed by my management firm, I knew I was playing a losing game. But I thought what I was doing was so good. I was so proud of it that I was determined to let people see it. So I tried to organize things myself. I went after any bookings I could get. It was crazy: five nights at the Whisky, four at Max's, then five in Atlanta, two in Vancouver. There was no pattern to it. I'd just do the shows and then stumble back to LA with a couple hundred bucks and just flop for a week until I could go out again. Whatever I didn't spend on the motels, I'd spend on drugs.**

Iggy Pop to Robert Hilburn, *Los Angeles Times*, March 1977.

In late September 1973, the Stooges were back on the road. In October, they played a show in Memphis with the New York Dolls. Trouble was expected and the concert hall was full of policemen. The chairman of the Memphis Board of Review was in attendance to ascertain if the Dolls were a group of female impersonators, which was illegal in Memphis, or if either act contained obscenity. Miraculously, the Stooges' set went smoothly without interruptions, but the Dolls' show was closed down after an hour and David Johansen, the singer, was taken to a local jail for disorderly conduct after kissing an ardent admirer who rushed the stage.

Concerts in November included Baltimore's Latin Casino and a week-long stint at Poor Richard's, a club in Atlanta. Chris Ehring, who was the Stooges' road manager during the tours in 1973-74, regards the Atlanta shows as the best the group ever played. At one of the shows, Elton John unexpectedly showed up on stage dressed in a gorilla suit. Ehring remembers the episode:

*I went back to the dressing room when someone tried to physically stop me. I said, "This is our dressing room!" Someone from the club said, "Elton John is in there." "Big fucking deal! What's he doing here?" I go in and there's Elton John getting into a gorilla outfit. "He's going to go up on stage and sing with Iggy." I just laughed. "Fine, maybe I should warn the boys?" "Oh, no, he wants it to be a surprise. He wants to come out on stage during 'Search And Destroy.'" He was supposed to scare Iggy! Scare Iggy in this gorilla suit? "You don't seem to understand what these guys are about. They are from Detroit. They're not going to let you up on their stage!" Moments later, out of the dressing room comes Elton dressed as a gorilla, and he goes up on stage. The band all look at him. "Who is this?" James looks at me and shrugs his shoulders. Iggy looks over and walks away. The gorilla starts chasing him, pushing him away. It's really bad.*

Unbeknownst to Ehring, Iggy was apparently genuinely scared:

*A doctor had to shoot me full of methedrine just so I could talk. I was seeing triple and had to hold on to the microphone stand to support myself. Suddenly this gorilla walks out from backstage and holds me up in the air while I'm still singing. I was out of my mind with fear. I thought it was a real gorilla.*

Following the Atlanta stint, the Stooges went to Washington D.C. for a concert with Mott the Hoople at the J.F. Kennedy Center for the Performing Arts. It was a prestigious concert since rock groups weren't usually allowed to play there. According to James Williamson:

*We stayed at the Watergate Hotel, and Iggy and Ron had some chicks down from New York to stay, see the show and stuff. These chicks came in with this goddamn crystal THC. Crystal THC, you don't fuck around with: a little bit goes a* long way. *Iggy probably thought it was cocaine, so he sticks his nose down there and does about six lines; he was so out of his mind that he was seeing green Martians, couldn't walk, couldn't do anything. We had to go on stage in like half an hour and it was really serious: he was so bad he should have gone to hospital but we had a gig to do. We needed him!*

As expected, the concert was a total disaster. Ehring resumes the tale:

*He walked up to the edge of the stage and fell off. Just stumbled off and wiggled his way into the audience. People were throwing him around, pushing him from side to side. He turns around and his whole chest is dripping red. I said, "Someone has slashed him with a knife!" I got one of the equipment men from Mott the Hoople and we ran down and dragged Iggy back onstage, only to find out that it was a jelly sandwich smeared all over him.*

By this time, Iggy literally couldn't stand up or sing, and the show was closed down after three numbers.

As December approached, the Stooges went down South for gigs in Jacksonville, Daytona, Nashville, and Knoxville. In late December, they played some concerts in the New York area. On New Year's Eve 1973, they played the Academy of Music in New York (billed as just Iggy Pop). Also on the bill were Teenage Lust and the headlining Blue Öyster Cult. The newly-formed Kiss were added to the bill at last minute. Journalist Anne Wehrer, a friend of Iggy's from Ann Arbor, attended the Academy of Music show on the advice of Andy Warhol, who told her that Iggy might commit suicide on stage:

*Iggy sang with demonic energy, in his hot pink pants and high top black boots. But his body control was off: backbends collapsed, and he missed the ramp, falling into the audience. He pleaded to be touched. He asked to be destroyed but with no intention of destroying himself. Backstage he was flat out on the red concrete floor, rolling in spilled beer, dead cigarettes and broken dreams.*

Wehrer and Iggy met on New Year's Day for a talk and a photo session. They discussed writing a book about Iggy's life, which eventually became *I Need More*, published in 1982.

The Academy of Music concert was recorded by Columbia for a possible live album, but Iggy's performance was simply too bad. Clive Davis, who had signed Iggy to the label, had left Columbia, and when the Stooges' contract came under review in early 1974, it was terminated.

During the winter 1973-74, the Stooges were constantly on the road, criss-crossing the States. To get money and survive they had to play more frequently than ever before. Gradually, the pressure of the non-stop touring began to take its toll. Although everyone in the band was much healthier than in the heroin days of 1970-71, they were not exactly drug-free. Iggy had developed a downer habit and, unable to afford the more expensive drugs, he was drinking a lot. He later referred to the tour as his "Vodka tour."

Money was usually scarce, and the life on the road was a bare existence for Iggy and the guys. Ehring describes some of the problems they encountered:

*It was a disorganized tour. We didn't have any money at all. We'd just go out and play shows. No one wanted to touch a band that was somewhat unreliable in their attendance — not in their ability to draw people, but their ability to put on a show! When we showed up at a place to play we had to scrounge around to get our equipment. We had to really hustle here and there. We had to pull a lot of moves just to get ourselves staying in a hotel, to eat, to get rental cars, etc. It was very tough for a band of five guys to support themselves playing that kind of music on their own. It was a nickel and dime operation.*

Nevertheless, Iggy and the Stooges were drawing good crowds all over the States, playing mostly first-billed at 1,500 to 4,000 capacity theatres and concert halls. The press reviews were generally positive and, despite a few lapses such as the incidents at Max's and J.F. Kennedy Center, Iggy cut down on his on-stage excesses, and concentrated on doing a professional high-energy rock 'n' roll show. In an interview with *Melody Maker's* Chris Charlesworth, Iggy talked about the response to the concerts:

*The reaction has been encouraging. I've spent a few nights sleeping in cars, and there have been a few problems, but all in all I'm much happier than when I was a recluse. I'm playing and that's the important thing. I think I've surprised the audiences who come to expect some kind of clown show. It's not that at all, it's a rock 'n' roll band.*

"I simply can't understand why he's not a huge star," said **Elton John** of **Iggy,** after witnessing a **Stooges** performance at Richard's in Atlanta. So enraptured was the unpredictable Mr. John that he showed up the next night; this time, however, to climb up onstage wearing a gorilla costume and dance with the amazed and delighted head Stooge. "Elton's a swell guy," gushed Iggy after the incident (**Davey Johnstone,** Elton's guitarist, also expressed admiration for the power playing of Stooges' guitarist **James Williamson.**) Be nice to see this mutual admiration turn into something more concrete. . .

Creem December 1973

Some concerts were excellent, justifying many rock critics' belief that Iggy was one of the most exciting performers around. Ehring feels that Iggy and the Stooges always did much better shows in smaller cities than in Detroit, Los

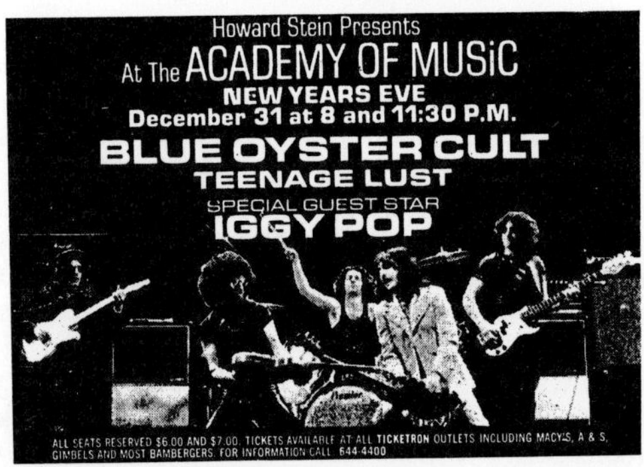

Angeles and New York, where they were better known and where the expectations of both critics and audiences were usually higher:

> *At the important shows, where everyone was backstage, Iggy succumbed to stage fright. It seemed to me that everyone said, "I'm your friend, Iggy. Take some of these drugs." Not, "I'm your friend. Stop. Get it together because you're great." It always happened at the shows that really counted. At the "nowhere" shows, he did brilliant shows. Just brilliant performances!*

# 20 THE END OF THE STOOGES

**There were some good times and some good shows. But what happened eventually was that I got really tired. The shows got violent and too malicious. One day I decided it was too nasty, what I was giving to people. So I just quit. It should have been a hard decision, but it wasn't. I cancelled tours and left music.**

Iggy Pop to John Rockwell, *New York Times*, March 1977.

By early 1974, the Stooges' repertoire of songs had expanded considerably; new songs were written in Los Angeles and while on the road. The latest additions were "Rich Bitch," more or less a jam with some "bar room" piano by Scott Thurston, and "I Got Nothin'," a more delicate song with a slight resemblance to Dylan's "Knocking On Heaven's Door." Also new in their set were "She-Creatures Of The Hollywood Hills" and the Chuck Berry-influenced rocker "Wet My Bed." Musically, some of the tunes written after *Raw Power*, and particularly "Open Up And Bleed," "Cock In My Pocket," and "Wet My Bed," were on a par with the strong *Raw Power* material, but the lyrics were just brief sketches, usually obsessed with sleazy sex. Other tunes such as "Rich Bitch" and "Head On" were just jams of half-developed riffs, usually with improvised spur-of-the-moment lyrics by Iggy. Given time, some songs definitely could have been improved, and given the right circumstances, the Stooges could have recorded a great follow-up album to *Raw Power*.

In February 1974, the Stooges returned to Michigan to play some shows in the Detroit area: Toledo Sports Center, Lansing, and Wayne, where the concert was held at a small club called the Rock and Roll Farm. Ehring describes the place:

*It was a sleazy club — a biker beer bar. Sure to be a riot! It was a very small club and we rolled in there with all these amps. Eric, our equipment man said, "We'll blow this place out! This is impossible." I called our agent and said, "We're not playing here. This is crazy." They just said, "It's a day off and you need the money!" So we played it. Of course a riot ensues. Bikers are pushing each other, slamming their heads on the floor. It was horrible.*

A group of bikers from the Scorpions, a Detroit motor cycle gang were present at the club to initiate a new member into their gang. His initiation rites included throwing eggs and bottles at the Stooges and then punching up Iggy:

*Eggs kept flying up on the stage, and as the set went on I was getting really sick of it. So I said, "OK, stop the show right now!" I'm calling the fucker down, and everybody just clear out. So everybody clears out and here's this guy about six foot three, like 300 pounds, with a knuckle glove on up to his elbow with little studs on it. So I said, well, what the fuck, I might as well get it over with. So I put down my mike and stepped out and it was just like seeing a train coming. Bam! He just got me, but he didn't deck me. He couldn't knock me down. It was real weird. I kept standing up but I couldn't hit him. Finally the blood got to be too much for him so he just stopped and said, "OK, you're cool." I didn't feel so cool. But we went back on and played "Louie Louie."*

Back in Detroit, Iggy went to WABX radio station and challenged the entire motor cycle gang to come to the Stooges' sold-out show at the Michigan Palace a few days later. A lot of extra security was brought in, and just to feel safe on stage, the Stooges brought some guys of their own. Iggy describes the show:

*All the Scorpions came down to the Michigan Palace. They started out with just beer bottles and wine bottles and vegetables and stuff like that. But I had an arsenal backstage and a few throwers, so I had them all come out and whip stuff back at them. It was like a hail.*

Although a lot of trash was thrown onto the stage, fortunately nothing serious happened and no one was injured.

The Michigan Palace concert was recorded on a four-track tape recorder and parts of the show was released in 1976 as *Metallic KO* by Skydog, a small French label. Ron knows the story behind the album:

*That record was my friend Michael Tipton who lives in Detroit. I said it was OK for him to set up his little four-track machine and record the gig for fun. He gave us each a copy. Iggy lost his. James lost his and my brother lost his. I had the only copy because I save everything. So I had the tape and James goes, "I've got this class in engineering and I need a project. Can I borrow your copy that Tipton gave you? I lost mine." I never got the tape back. The next thing I know, Iggy and James booted my tape to Skydog for $2,000. Michael Tipton was furious. He recorded it! They didn't give me a penny.*

Ron's story is contradicted by Iggy who claims it was James alone who sold the tape to Skydog's Marc Zermati:

*Without my knowledge, James sold him the rights to get some quick bread, and Zermati took off to France where he figured I couldn't find him.*

*Metallic KO* is a horrific document of the Stooges live in concert. It is often mistaken to be the concert where Iggy was almost knocked out by a knuckled biker, but that happened at Wayne's Rock and Roll Farm, the concert prior to the Michigan Palace show. Nevertheless, the rowdy and somewhat hostile Detroit audience is very much evident on

Smoking a joint on stage at Toledo's Sports Center, February 1974. (David Koepp collection)

the record; the bottles and debris thrown onto the stage and at Iggy can be clearly heard. The sound quality leaves a lot to be desired, and it does sound more like an ordinary bootleg than an official live record.

The album was originally issued in 1976 by Skydog, run by Marc Zermati in Paris. The rights were then sold to the American label Import Records, and it was released in the States in the spring of 1977. In *Creem*, Billy Altman enthusiastically heralded it as "the last rock 'n' roll concert ever!":

*After side two, you can take all your records and your radio and toss 'em right out the window. After side two, you wanna get into a car and plow down the highway at 90 mph and wrap yourself around a telephone pole. Because you've heard* it *and there is no coming back.*

Nick Kent, writing for *New Musical Express*, felt the album was:

*...on one level, at least, the most vicious, malicious slice of rock ephemera ever made available to the public. Never have wounds been so open — the level of sheer numbing pain that Iggy is so obviously going through — the emotional breaking point at the end as the bottles fly and Pop spits out over the opening bars of "Louie Louie" — "God, I never thought it would get to this."*

After the Michigan Palace show, Iggy and James met up with *Creem's* Lester Bangs, and James was full of enthusiasm for the Stooges' future:

*It's all finally working out like we've always planned; we've worked more in the last few months than in the past two and a half years. We're doing it the hard way, and the right way. I'm not gonna say it's all on the up and up, because it's not. We've got a lot of problems right now: we have a reputation to live down, and we still make mistakes. But our following is getting stronger.*

The band had some time off after the Michigan Palace performance, and they spent it at home in Ann Arbor. A few days before they were about to go on the road again for another tour, Iggy unexpectedly called up Ron to tell him that he had decided to quit:

*We had a few days off. I was at home with my mother, and Iggy suddenly calls me one day and he goes, "Look, I'm sorry Ron, but I have to quit. I can't go on any longer. I just can't handle it any longer."*

**The Stooges' last ever performance, Michigan Palace, Detroit, February 9, 1974.** (Joe Karoly and David Koepp)

Ron thinks the pressures on Iggy had become too heavy and that he couldn't handle the expectations without downers and alcohol:

*There were a lot of things. The Bowie-Iggy link for one thing. Iggy was always in the papers, they wrote about him as the new rock star who was heading for a fantastic solo career. He read about how great he was, and how he could do much better without the Stooges. The shows were often billed just as Iggy Pop. All this created a void between Iggy and the band. ..... He was physically and mentally wrecked. He had driven himself too hard, and he was doing lots of downers. He'd become so nervous and tense that he had to take downers just to relax.*

The Michigan Palace concert in Detroit on February 9, 1974, became the last ever Stooges performance; they never played or performed together as a group again.

In interviews after the split, Iggy has expounded on his decision to quit the Stooges just as they were about to break through:

*We had another tour to go on and I just said stop! Time out! Because I can't stand to go out on stage and not feel proper about what I'm doing. ..... The shows were getting crummy. They were violent, nasty. Attendance, ironically, was picking up. But I thought I should quit. I didn't want to look back on all those shows and think that they had been bad. I thought it was better to take a break, even if it meant that I might never be able to get started again.*

# 21 THE STOOGES – AN EPILOGUE

**Maybe the stuff I did with Iggy is legendary now, but at the time we were living like dogs — hardly ever eating, never sleeping, drugs like you wouldn't believe, burning ourselves out like maniacs. You can't live like that for very long.**

James Williamson to *Bomp Magazine*, November 1977.

(Leee Black Childers)

It is not an easy task, or even a feasible one, to sum up the remarkable and turbulent history of the Stooges. Nevertheless, this book begs for some form of explanation as to why the group never was able to fulfill their potential and achieve stardom: why did the story have to end just as they were being hailed as the "saviours" of high-energy rock 'n' roll, and just as Iggy was becoming known as one of the most exciting contemporary performers? Iggy and the Stooges were constantly lauded by the progressive music critics, even up until the bitter end in February 1974. Lester Bangs, for example, wrote in *Creem* in early 1974:

*I've been sitting in essentially this same place for five years now, counting a couple years layoff, waiting for them to break over the edge they always seem to be pushing toward and make it big.*

His anticipation was shared by many in the music press and business.

Throughout their history, Iggy and the Stooges never made any musical compromises in order to reach a larger audience. They never acceded to record company or management suggestions that they make their music more accessible or smoother. Although CBS/Columbia probably hoped for, or even expected, *Raw Power* to be as commercial as the other Bowie-associated records (Lou Reed's *Transformer* and Mott the Hoople's *All The Young Dudes* ), it was obvious that this didn't influence the Stooges' songwriting in the least. Consequently, they were not fully supported by the record company. Elektra might have had the same expectations in 1971 when a third album for the label was considered, but when performing for the record company executives, the Stooges cranked up their amps and blasted away, totally ignorant of such wishes. In Danny Fields' opinion, the Stooges' type of music was ahead of its time:

*At that time there really wasn't any market for what they were playing. People weren't aware of the trendy European market at the time. When you look at it through the eyes of the late 70's and 80's where things like that are custom-made. Lou Reed, Patti Smith, etc are tailor-made for Europe, but the Stooges broke the ground and no one was aware of it as a marketing effort to do it that way.*

Three years after the break-up of the Stooges, groups like the Sex Pistols, the Clash, and the Damned were playing their own versions of the Stooges' raw high-energy music and effortlessly getting onto the charts.

For all concerned, managers, record company people, promoters, the Stooges were a difficult band to control. Because of their headstrong personalities and arrogance, there was a lack of direction. Their manager in 1968-70, Jimmy Silver says:

*They were too undisciplined. They were too arrogant — in a nice way — a way that I admired. They were just too loose, really. They didn't have anything focused on success, the way you have to do it. There was no one whipping them into shape. No one could really control them and hold all the pieces together.*

Of course, there is the question whether Iggy and the Stooges really *wanted* to make it big, and to what lengths they were willing to go to achieve success. The sentiment of many interviewees for this book seems to be that they never cared for or focused hard enough on popular acceptance; their prime concern was their music and how to get by from day to day. However, it is interesting to note James Williamson's approach to commercial success when interviewed in early 1974:

*If we can make a good solid album, we're alright. If we can't get record sales on this next album, then we're fucked. I think this material's gonna be a lot stronger, and our overall production sound's gonna be a lot better. It's gonna be a very clean album, very commercial album.*

In many ways, Iggy's live performances with the Stooges was the ultimate stage act. He couldn't possibly have changed it or improved upon it in order to remain interesting to a larger audience. Alice Cooper, Black Sabbath, Kiss, and a number of other groups who have emerged since the Stooges have gained enormous popularity by varying Iggy's act and using it themselves. Obviously, they never take it to the same extremes that Iggy did, but their shows nevertheless incorporate many of the attitudes pioneered by Iggy and the Stooges. But compared to times when Iggy expressed his inner self in a genuinely frightening and unpredictable way, these groups are safe play-actors. In a sense, Iggy, whose commitment was *real*, was locked into an orbit of self-annihilation. He reached the conclusion that, to be able to continue making music and performing, he had to quit the Stooges and re-emerge with a new, toned-down approach.

In addition to these problems related to management, record companies, and their music and performances, Iggy and the Stooges had considerable personal problems with drugs. They were forced to stop in 1971 due to heroin addictions, and in 1974, it was, at least partly, Iggy's downer habit that caused him to throw in the towel.

Undoubtedly, Iggy Pop and the Stooges have been an important influence on many artists, both in terms of music and performance. Much has been written and said about their impact on the punk rock movement and their influence on other groups. Therefore, it is needless to elaborate on this subject. Instead, the last words are those of James Williamson; perhaps he summarizes the Stooges succinctly:

*I can't accept this mythology surrounding the Stooges. You've got to look at things as they are: we were just guys playing rock 'n' roll that wasn't accepted. And rightly so: it wasn't timely or commercial.*

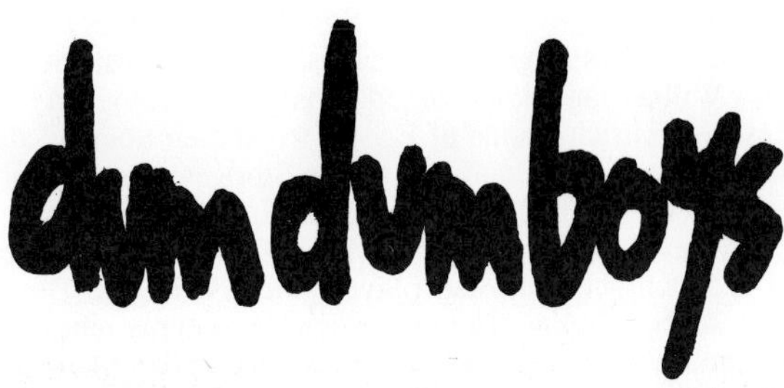


**WHAT ARE THEY DOING TODAY?**

**Ron Asheton** still lives in Ann Arbor where he is fronting a new band called Dark Carnival. He is also involved in film making, and he is a member of Excalibre Pictures. They write, direct and produce low budget horror movies:

*I really love it. They write good characters for me. I'm always some sort of a Jack Nicholson type.*

Ron has acted in several movies, among them *The Carrier* and *Wendigo.*

**Scott Asheton** also lives in Ann Arbor. He plays drums in a group called Steve Morgan and the Funguys. They play frequently in the Detroit area and New York.

**James Williamson** has quit the music business altogether. He is married and lives with his wife and five-year-old son in Orange County, California. He works in the computer field.

**Scott Thurston** is still actively playing rock music. After playing with the Motels for several years, he recently toured with Jackson Browne's band.

**Jimmy Recca** lives in a suburb of Chicago and works at a company that makes circuits for effect boxes for guitars. His wife is a nuclear scientist. Jimmy and Ron are still good friends:

*I see Jimmy a couple of times a year and talk to him on the phone. He has been in a couple of bar bands since the Stooges.*

**Billy Cheatham** lives in Ann Arbor and works as a mason. According to Ron:

*He's 200 pounds, with a crew cut and an Abraham Lincoln beard. He looks really good though, but not like the Billy Cheatham of the Stooges days.*

**Steven Mackay** still plays the saxophone now and then. In recent years, he has played with Violent Femmes.

**Dave Alexander** and **Zeke Zettner** both died in 1975.

# 22 KILL CITY

**I live here in Kill City, where the debris meets the sea / It's a playground for the rich but it's a loaded gun to me / The scene is a fascination, man, and everything's for free / Till you wind up in some bathroom, overdosed and on your knees.**

"Kill City" by Iggy Pop and James Williamson, 1975.

Following the break-up of the Stooges in February 1974, Iggy went to Los Angeles where he shared an apartment with James Williamson. James started playing with Tony and Hunt Sales, the musician sons of US TV comedian Soupy Sales. They had become friendly while the Stooges were living in Los Angeles in 1972-73. Later, Ron Asheton also came to the city, and he began jamming with ex-Stooge Jimmy Recca and K.J. Knight, who had played drums with the Detroit group Amboy Dukes. The two groups took turns rehearsing at the house of former Doors keyboardsplayer Ray Manzarek. Danny Sugerman, Ray's manager, also took over the managerial duties of Iggy, who bounced back and forth between Ron's and James' bands, unable to decide what he really wanted to do. Drinking heavily and doing lots of drugs, Iggy wasn't capable of concentrating on hard work for any lengthy period of time.

On the three-year anniversary of Jim Morrison's death, July 3, 1974, Iggy, now with dark hair, appeared at the Whisky A Go-Go. Backed by Manzarek's band and James Williamson, Iggy did a set of Doors songs, including "LA Woman," to which he improvised some extra lyrics, "Jim Morrison died today, Jim Morrison was more beautiful than any girl in this town, and now he's dead, now I cry." There were plans for an Iggy solo album to be produced by Ray, who said to *Rolling Stone* at the time:

> *With the right backing, Iggy could be really sensational, he's so dynamic on stage. Right now our friendship is at the bare bones beginning. After I produce his album, who knows what will happen? But I'd only add a singer to the band if it made the music better. I'd never get a singer to dance around or a lead dancer.*

Even though Iggy's association with Ray Manzarek was well-publicised, even sparking rumours of a new Doors line-up, nothing concrete came of it.

Iggy's erratic and self-destructive behaviour seemed to culminate one night when he appeared at Rodney Bingenheimer's English Disco on Sunset Boulevard in Hollywood. Improvising a play of his own creation entitled "Murder Of The Virgin," Iggy cut up his chest with a knife in

**Ron Asheton, Iggy and Jimmy Recca in Los Angeles, March 1974.** (Stooges Fun Club collection/Gilles Scheps)

a fit of total madness. Sugerman tried to make the most of the incident, phoning up members of the music press to tell them about "Iggy's most totally committed artistic statement ever."

Later in the year, Iggy did another solo appearance in Hollywood. Together with the New York Dolls, Michael Des Barres, Zolar X, the GTO's, Rodney Bingenheimer (disc jockey), and Kim Fowley (master of ceremonies), he performed at the Dolls' "Hollywood Street Revival And Trash Dance" show, more commonly known as "The Death Of Glitter." Iggy appeared on stage with James Williamson, Ray Manzarek, Nigel Harrison (later in Blondie), and a pick-up drummer, doing a set of non-originals including "Route 66," "Nadine," Dylan's "Subterranean Homesick Blues," and "Everybody Needs Somebody To Love."

Iggy spent the rest of 1974 doing virtually nothing:

*I just wanted to forget everything that had gone before. I was sick, out of my mind. I couldn't sleep, my back had been put out of joint after I'd fallen backwards nine feet off a stage, and I was in constant pain. I had to get myself into a stupor just in order to handle it.*

Iggy's problems with quaaludes, downers and alcohol worsened, and his deteriorating health eventually caused him to consult medical and psychological experts at the Neuropsychiatric Institute (NPI) at UCLA in Los Angeles:

*I said to them, "I've been addicted for a long time to very heavy drugs. Since then, I've come off them, but now I'm a fool who uses pills and slobbers a lot. Would you help me? Would you lock me up here where none of my so-called friends can get at me? I want to learn self-discipline, self-protection and self-control, and try to get myself a direction again." A guy of my own age, Murray Zucker, became my psychiatrist.*

"Murder Of The Virgin" at Rodney Bingenheimer's English Disco, Hollywood, August 11, 1974.
(PN collection)

In March/April of 1975, Iggy recorded some tracks with James Williamson's group which comprised the Sales brothers on bass and drums, and ex-Stooge Scott Thurston on keyboards. Songwriter Jim Webb had donated his home studio for the sessions. Los Angeles rock critic Ben Edmonds, long a believer in Iggy's potential, had heard some of Iggy's and James' new tunes, and he assumed the role of producer and financial backer for the *Kill City* sessions:

*I saw that his new material was good and that his guitar player and piano player were both excellent. There was always a musical incompetence in Iggy's recordings, which meant that conceptually he was wonderful, but for people who couldn't get into things conceptually it didn't hold up very well. The idea for these tapes was to try to put him into a structured and disciplined framework to show what he could really do.*

The new material included "Beyond The Law," "Hats Off," "Lucky Monkeys," "Sell Your Love," "Kill City," "Consolation Prizes," and "No Sense Of Crime." Two songs, "I Got Nothin'" and "Johanna," originated from the Stooges era. Although Iggy had been very involved in the writing of the material with James, many of his vocals were recorded on weekend leaves from the UCLA NPI.

The *Kill City* tape was circulated to record companies and music industry people, but no one wanted to touch the album. The American record companies were reluctant to become involved with Iggy because of all the long-standing Stooges

atrocity stories and accounts of depravity. Even though Ben Edmonds filed an affidavit in music papers, stating that the new Iggy had cleaned up the proverbial act, it was impossible for Iggy to get a record contract and the *Kill City* album languished until 1977.

One of the few people who frequently visited Iggy in the hospital was David Bowie, who had resided in Los Angeles after his break with MainMan and Tony Defries. Despite his phenomenal success with *Young Americans* and "Fame," this was one of the worst periods in Bowie's life. If possible, he was even more mentally and physically deranged than Iggy. For over a year Bowie had been severly addicted to cocaine. His lack of sleep and food often caused him to hallucinate and he had become paranoid and flirted with ideas of black magic and fascism. Nevertheless, Bowie and Iggy were fit enough to do some recordings in May, using the cheap Oz Studios, a small demo studio in Hollywood. Bowie produced, composed and played most of the instruments on the sessions that included "Turn Blue," "Moving On," "Sell Your Love," and "Drink To Me."

In the autumn of 1975, following his final leave from the hospital, Iggy moved to San Diego to escape the drug scene and "friends" in Los Angeles. It was a fairly successful move, and with the exceptions of a few lapses, he was feeling better than he had in a long time. He even toyed around with the idea of becoming a singer in a San Diego bar group:

*I decided to get out of LA. Get out of rock 'n' roll and just play some music. I went to San Diego and I was going to start a bar band with some high school friends of mine. I knew we were going to be the best damned band in America within a year! But instead I ran into David Bowie again.*

◁
**Iggy in Los Angeles, summer 1975.** (Stooges Fun Club collection/Gilles Scheps)

**David Bowie, 1975.** (PN collection)

# 23 THE SECOND COMING

**He was given a second or third chance by Bowie. David helped him a lot, putting the records out, giving him confidence. They lived together in Berlin, a place Iggy really liked and felt was home. It was the first time he ever worked with anybody that made him do anything. He could be very, very lazy. David put him through some rough times — it was hard work. He learned a lot from David and he really enjoyed it.**

Anne Wehrer (co-author of *I Need More — The Stooges And Other Stories*) to Dorothy Sherman, 1982.

Recording *The Idiot* at Chateau d'Herouville, France, July 1976. (Claude Gassian)

In February 1976, David Bowie started his *Station To Station* world tour on the US West Coast. After one of the concerts at Los Angeles Forum, Iggy showed up backstage. The fuse of new mutual musical projects was lit and Iggy became Bowie's travelling companion for the rest of the tour. Their friendship from the previous year and the MainMan days of 1971-73 was restored:

> *We got to know each other pretty well. A lot of travelling, a lot of long nights. And he got my confidence. ..... He seemed very concerned with doing some work. And much to my credit I trusted him, which is to my everlasting benefit because he's a trustworthy person.*

Besides admiring Iggy's records and performances with the Stooges and his unparalleled ability to improvise lyrics at the top of his head, Bowie valued Iggy's high intelligence and articulateness. But Iggy was also impressed with Bowie:

> *I had never ever seen anybody work that hard! He was getting up at eight in the morning to travel by car — he didn't fly — to the gig. Gets to the town, does a couple of interviews, catches a half hour of sleep and he's on stage doing the show. Then, after the show, the guy won't stop! He's out checking out whatever band is in town. I was exhausted just watching him. He really knows what it is to work hard. No wonder he was doing so well and I was not.*

After the final *Station To Station* concert, in Paris on May 18, Bowie and Iggy went to the Chateau d'Herouville outside Paris to relax and start preparations for the making of an Iggy record. Initially only "Sister Midnight," written by Bowie's guitarist Carlos Alomar and with lyrics by Bowie and Iggy, had been intended for a one-off single, but Bowie had come up with more tunes along the tour. Further songs, including "Tiny Girls" and "Dum Dum Boys," a song about the Stooges guys, were written at Bowie's new Swiss home in Vevey, near Montreaux, during a break in the tour schedule. Gradually the project grew into an album.

During June and July of 1976, they recorded Iggy's comeback album at Chateau d'Herouville. In August, as they could not lengthen the sojourn — the studio being booked by other artists — they decided to carry on with the album at Munich's Musicland Studios. Bowie wanted Tony Visconti, a long-time friend and producer of several Bowie albums, to mix the record but he wasn't available. Instead, the Chateau engineer was flown to Munich. The mixes didn't please Bowie and Iggy, so they waited until Visconti was free and they mixed Iggy's album at West Berlin's Hansa Tonstudios, commonly referred to as Hansa by the Wall because of its proximity to the Berlin Wall. Bowie was responsible for most of the music, while the lyrics were Iggy's. Besides producing the record, Bowie also played keyboards, guitars and saxophone. Session guitarist Phil Palmer added some solos while the bass player and drummer remain unidentified.

The new model Iggy took up residence in a small apartment (with Bowie as his upstairs neighbour) in Schöneberg, West Berlin with his girlfriend Esther Friedmann, the daughter of an American diplomat. He was free of all drug addiction and he enjoyed the fact that he could live in virtual anonymity. Frequently, Iggy and Bowie attended the clubs and bars in the city and took in museums and local art exhibitions. Iggy enjoyed the low-key life and the Berlin period enabled him to take refuge and plan out the next stage of his career. He spoke of Berlin and Germany in interviews:

> *I've always wanted to come to Germany. Even when I was a kid, I read everything about it. I always knew I wanted to come here, just like some guys always knew they wanted... to wear a dress! ..... Berlin is a green and pleasant city. I love the air, I love the streets, I love the people. I aspire to be German some day, quite completely.*

West Berlin was an ideal city for Iggy's recuperation and artistic renewal because it lacked the intensity and overt sensationalism of his previous home in Los Angeles. Isolated from East Berlin since 1961 by the Wall and surrounded by communist East Germany, West Berlin is not constitutionally part of West Germany, although the city is tied to it economically, judicially and financially. The supreme authority is still in the hands of the western powers (France, England, United States).

On the strength of his past record with RCA Records, Bowie managed to get Iggy a contract with the label. RCA agreed to release three Iggy Pop albums with the option to renew the contract if they so desired. The album, entitled *The Idiot*, was released in March 1977. The cover of the album, which featured an eerie black and white photograph of Iggy taken by Bowie in Berlin, was fashioned after a painting by Erich Heckel called "Roquairol." Those who had expected the arrogance and vehemence of Iggy's recordings with the Stooges were surprised. Bowie's influence was very strong; it was recorded prior to his own *Low* and it clearly pre-dates Bowie's move towards synthesized technorock. The reception was somewhat mixed; the American critics, particularly, were put off by the record's gloomy mood. But *The Idiot* was a very strong comeback album and some of the songs have become classics: "China Girl," "Sister Midnight," and "Nightclubbing." It remains as one of Iggy's finest achievements and he concluded that *The Idiot*:

*...is my album of freedom. I'm not saying that it's a great*

**NEW MUSICAL EXPRESS October 9th, 1976**

IGGY STOOGE phoned from Paris to say he's finished recording (with David Bowie producing), and that the album will be released in January. He says it's a cross between "James Brown and Kraftwerk".

Iggy sounded in control, said that he looks "fifteen", and admitted to yet another hair color change. (No more the platinum blond as depicted left, it's a dark brown now, and very short.)

Asked whether he felt Bowie had "rescued him", Iggy replied, "Well, not really. . . because I know what I'm worth. But David did take a chance on me when most other people in this business gave up.

"Of course," he added, "you know what I think of this business. . .

"For a long time, David and I have talked of working together. At first we just had plans to do a single, but when we liked what came out of that, the album happened.

"Although a lot of people made remarks, I wasn't surprised when David came to the U.S. for his tour and took me on the road with him. I'm really at the point where I just don't give a damn what people think.

"I was just happy to make some music. It's as simple as that."

Iggy said he missed performing, and plans to go back out to do conce-ts in January. He's been checking out musicians in New York and Detroit, and said it was "possible" that he would continue to work with James Williamson again, but that they hadn't really talked about it yet. He had a lot of kind words for Carlos Alomar; saying a lot of people thought he just played in one, funky style, but that he was really very versatile.

"I don't see any need to change the way I perform at all," said Iggy when asked what he planned to do onstage. "Surprised? Some of my friends have asked me, 'What are you going to do onstage this time?', as if I would have a big spider come down from the ceiling. . .

"It's lovely to be a spectacle, but I refuse to live my life to adapt to being a spectacle. I am the way I am. I couldn't go out and put on a monkey suit."

For Iggy, this is another chance. For Bowie, it is quite possibly a long-time wish fulfilled. When he first came to America in 1971, he told me that his idols were Lou Reed and Iggy. He's since produced albums with both.

*album or some fantastic work of art, but I love it and it means a lot to me.*

Joined by a low-profile Bowie on keyboards as musical director, Iggy went on his first solo tour in March 1977 to promote the new album. Besides Bowie, the backing group consisted of Hunt and Tony Sales and Scotsman Ricky Gardiner on guitar. Bowie's presence on stage with Iggy stunned both audience and press alike but Bowie steadfastly refused to give interviews throughout the tour. Clearly, this was Iggy's show. Bowie was content with his position as one of the boys in the band, surrounded by his keyboard equipment, chain-smoking cigarettes, periodically casting a sly glance at the awestruck audience. Starting at Aylesbury Friars , Iggy played theatres in England and North America. It was a new toned-down Iggy that the audience saw; there were no more self-destructive routines or audience confrontations. Instead, Iggy put on a professional and energetic show:

*I knew exactly what was on the line so I gave them an Iggy Pop who was safe, professional, fast, dependable. A responsible entertainer who was going to give all the paying customers a good disciplined rock show, with a little extra that is uniquely mine.*

Reviewers celebrated Iggy's resurrection and audiences packed houses.

Bowie finally broke his vow not to permit interviews when he and Iggy appeared on Dinah Shore's *Dinah!* show towards the end of *The Idiot* tour. It was apparent that Bowie's intention was to counter a number of snipes made by the press for the length of the tour that Iggy had, in essence, been reduced to "David's boy" and that *The Idiot* was just another Bowie album. However, Bowie made it clear that he held Iggy's creative processes in high regard, stressing that he merely enhanced the already inherent genius of Iggy:

*Jimmy and I collaborated because I was intoxicated with what I thought he stood for, and I never want it to be thought that I'm some kind of hand manipulator or Svengali behind what Jimmy's doing now because he's getting popular now. It's only because he was six years too early with what he was doing with the Stooges!*

IG AND SUPER IG

Record Mirror, March 12, 1977

Iggy does it his way (and Bowie's)

PIN UPS

Words: NICK KENT
Pics: CHALKIE DAVIES

God, I never knew it would get to this

IGGY SAID IT. IGGY HAD THE POWER, IGGY HAD THE DISEASE

ALBUMS

Buried but not dead

Melody Maker

MARCH 12, 1977

Springsteen back in town?

ELP What we've been up to for the last few years —page 26

CARS RACE TO LONDON

Barry White talks on the eve of his British tour —page 36

The return of THE WORLD'S FORGOTTEN BOY

Iggy Pop by Giovanni Dadom

Iggy and Bowie on *The Idiot* tour, March 1977.
(Jacquie Deegan and PN collection)

After *The Idiot* tour and a short holiday of Japan, Iggy and Bowie headed back to Berlin. Using the tour band plus Bowie's guitarist Carlos Alomar and with Bowie once again producing, Iggy recorded a new album in only 13 days at Hansa by the Wall studios:

> *Three of the songs were written while we rehearsed for the last tour ["Some Weird Sin," "Tonight," and "Turn Blue"] but the best of the stuff was written in about one and a half day. That was the way I wanted to work on this album. To achieve the immediate effect that I wanted I had to work hard, much harder than everybody else in the band. A six-to-eight-hour session involved 12 hours of work for me because I was taking the tapes home with me and just kept on working.*

Although he contributed the music to seven of the nine songs on the album, entitled *Lust For Life* , Bowie played a less influential role than on the predecessor. Much of the difference between the two albums can be attributed to Iggy's determination to remain one step ahead of everyone else in the studio.

*Lust For Life* tour, September 1977. (PN collection)

While *The Idiot* was still a current item in the music stores, *Lust For Life* was released in September 1977. It is a highly enjoyable record and, true to its title, it is very spontaneous and more positive than *The Idiot.* Even though the contents of the album sometimes harkens back to the attitudes of the Stooges days with such narcotic infested tunes as "Turn Blue," "Tonight," and "Neighbourhood Threat," Iggy manages to inject a new vitality into his music with cuts like the title tune as well as "Success" and "The Passenger," possibly one of Iggy's most popular songs.

Coinciding with the release of *Lust For Life*, Iggy went on a new tour, presenting his first ever shows in Europe (outside of England), where his cult reputation was enormous. He was especially popular in Holland, where a single of "Lust For Life" became a Top 10 hit, and in Germany and France where independent fan clubs had been established in 1975-76. Bowie stepped aside to do some projects of his own and his place was taken by ex-Stooge Scott Thurston. Canadian guitarist Stacey Heydon (Bowie's guitarist on his *Station To Station* tour) replaced Gardiner. For the most part, the concerts were well received. The emerging punk rock movement heralded Iggy as the undisputed "Godfather of Punk" and his audience was larger than ever.

Jamming with the Outsiders at London's punk temple, The Roxy, September 29, 1977. (Melody Maker)

Towards the end of the *Lust For Life* tour, in November 1977, *Kill City* was released. The tapes had been in James Williamson's possession since the recordings were made in 1975. He had remixed the tracks and offered them to the small Los Angeles-based Bomp Records. In James' opinion, it was the best music he and Iggy ever recorded:

> *One of the reasons why I wanted to put out the album is that I think it's a good documentation of what the Stooges were doing — it's probably, as far as I'm concerned, the best album we ever did.*

However, Iggy wasn't too pleased with the release:

> *It wasn't a finished product and I wished James would have waited. I wasn't happy with it; it should have been finished off. It's the closest I've come to mediocre work. I wouldn't advise anyone to buy it.*

When it was released, *Kill City* was seen as the missing link between Iggy's new solo albums and *Raw Power* ; it contains the seeds of Iggy's new subtlety, but retains the demonic intensity of all classic Stooges recordings.

With the three albums and two extensive tours, 1977 was Iggy's triumphant return to the rock world. The Bowie-link and the punk rock movement finally gave Iggy the recognition and respect he had long striven for. Much like Iggy's records with the Stooges, punk was simple and aggressive high-energy music. It explicitly opposed hippies, artistic and musical complexity, and the entire rock establishment. The foremost groups were English: the Clash, the Damned, the Sex Pistols, 999, Chelsea, Slaughter and the Dogs, etc. The punk rockers adopted Iggy as an icon; they covered his songs and aped his stage behaviour and attitudes. In many ways, Iggy achieved mythological asylum. In the future, he would always be excused benevolently for his remarkable inconsistency.

In May 1978, Iggy brought Fred "Sonic" Smith's Detroit-based Rendezvous Band to Europe for a tour in May-June. Besides Smith, once with the MC5, on guitar, the group consisted of Gary Rasmusen (bass), who had played with the Up, contemporaries with the Stooges and the MC5, and Scott Asheton on drums. In addition, Scott Thurston played keyboards and guitar. In conjunction with the European tour, *TV Eye 1977 Live* was released as a document of the 1977 tours. The sound quality is occasionally very poor and the record is generally considered to be a disaster. Iggy explained the reasons for releasing the album, his last for RCA:

> *I made that record because I was short a few bob and wanted to make as much money in as short a time as possible — bleed the record company like they bled me. The best thing about the record is that the budget was $75,000 and I spent $5,000 making it! I lived a while off the money, and I did it to get off RCA.*

Live in Europe on the *TV Eye* tour, May 1978. (Pressens Bild) ▷

# 24 LOOKING FOR ONE NEW VALUE

**I've got a hard-assed pair of shoulders / I've got a love you can't imagine / Yeah, and what I've got I double / I swear I'm keeping out of trouble / I'm looking for one new value / I'm looking for one new value / But nothing comes my way.**

"New Values" by Iggy Pop and Scott Thurston, 1979.

Iggy in early 1979. (Claude Gassian)

Back in Berlin, Iggy spent the best part of 1978 practicing guitar and writing new material:

*I said to myself, "I want to write my next album," so I picked up a guitar, went out and got some diet pills, and sat for eight or nine hours a day learning how to play the guitar. And then I wrote some songs. I didn't like to have to depend on other people so that's the way I wanted to do it.*

Meanwhile, Iggy's manager Peter Davies, who had been lured away from RCA, scouted around London for an attractive record deal. The English division of Arista was interested and in late 1978, Iggy signed with the label. Arista was an American record company started by Clive Davis, the man who signed Iggy to Columbia in 1971. He still had some reservations about Iggy so he remained without a record contract in America until the autumn of 1979.

In early 1979, Iggy flew out to Los Angeles to team up with James Williamson, who would produce the record. At first, Iggy wasn't too enthusiastic about recording in the States again:

*I only went there because they're so good with costs. I felt it was important that every dollar spent on this album went directly into the studio and onto the record, rather than being spent on silly extras. America is the best place for getting something done very correctly.*

The album, *New Values*, was recorded with the basic nucleus of Scott Thurston on guitar and keyboards, Jackie Clarke on bass, and one-time Tangerine Dream drummer Klaus Kruger, whom Iggy had met in Berlin. James Williamson only contributed a guitar solo on "Tell Me A Story" (originally titled "Lucky Guy"). 15 tracks were laid down at Paramount Recording Studios in Los Angeles. Three songs were left off the album, while no less than seven of the album tracks were written by Iggy. Four songs were collaborations with Thurston, including "Angel" and "Curiosity" which they had written in 1974. One of the best tunes, "Don't Look Down" was penned by Iggy and James Williamson.

To a large extent, Iggy's lyrics were autobiographical and he took a great deal of precision and care to express himself

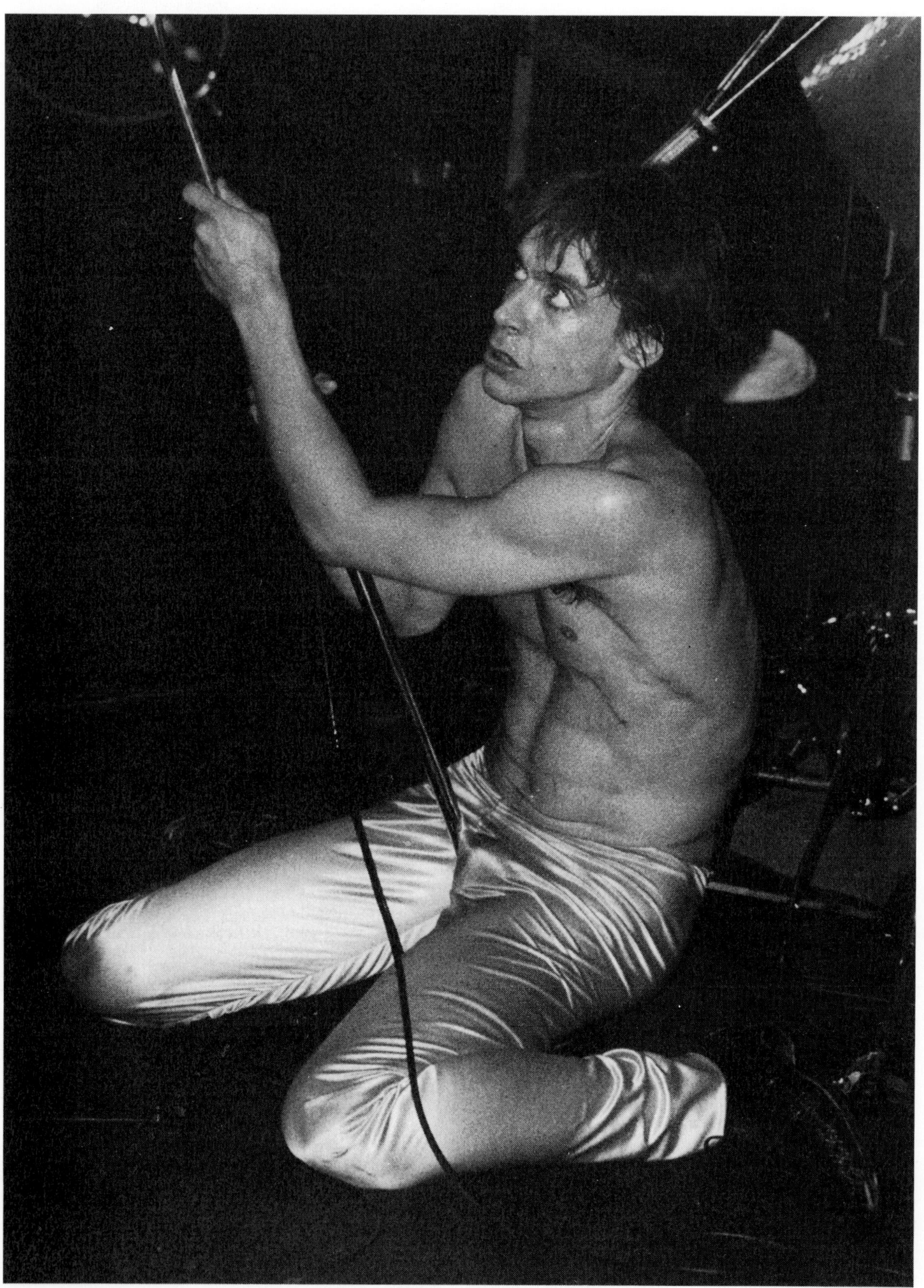

clearly:

*James Williamson, who knows me best except for one or two people in this world, had a lot to do with the lyrics. We started with my usual "blurting" at the beginning of the process. Once a song was created, we stopped there. I took a long vacation in Mexico, came back to LA and James and I sat down with paper and pencil together and tried to refine the content of what I'd said so that the people would understand it. I tried to be very explicit on this album.*

Released in April 1979, *New Values* was almost unanimously praised by the press. With strong, well-crafted rock tunes such as "Five Foot One," "Don't Look Down," "New Values," and "I'm Bored," the album is a worthy successor to the two Bowie-produced records. Its commercial appeal was evidenced by its immediate appearance on UK LP charts.

A two-month UK/European tour was lined up to promote *New Values*. This time, Iggy played smaller venues — mostly universities and clubs. The backing group included Jackie Clarke on guitar to make way for ex-Sex Pistol Glen Matlock on bass, Scott Thurston on keyboards and guitar, and Klaus Kruger on drums. The tour over in June 1979, Iggy decided it was time to record a new album. Retaining Matlock and Kruger, Iggy went to the Rockfield Studios in Wales. Scott Thurston left to join the Motels. Steve New from the Rich Kids, XTC-member Barrie Andrews, and Ivan Kral from Patti Smith's group completed the new wave band. James Williamson was flown over from California to produce the album.

However, the sessions with James ended after only two weeks. Iggy got frustrated with James' over-ambitious recording process and he objected strongly to the commercial sound James wanted to achieve. According to Ivan Kral:

*We were in the middle of the sessions when Iggy decided enough is enough with James. James wanted to go for the big production. He wanted to transfer the 24 tracks onto 48 tracks. Iggy didn't like many of James' new production ideas, "What are you doing with my tape? Who are you, Phil Spector? This is my album!" That was the end of their collaboration.*

Iggy fired James and the sessions were carried on with studio engineer Pat Moran as producer. Iggy wrote five of the songs by himself, while three were co-written with Glen Matlock. Guests in the studio and on the record included Simple Minds and Bowie, who co-wrote "Play It Safe" with Iggy.

In October 1979, the American division of Arista eventually released *New Values* and Iggy toured throughout the autumn/winter there with an impressive back-up group that included Ivan Kral, Brian James of the Damned on guitar, Matlock on bass, and Kruger on drums. After barely pausing for breath, Iggy was back on the road again in February 1980, promoting *Soldier*. Once again the reception was overwhelming and the critics were full of praise for Iggy's new-found lyricism. More aggressive than *New Values*, *Soldier* is a fine album which contains some of Iggy's most witty lyrics.

Only Kral and Kruger remained from the *Soldier* album line-up for the short UK *Soldier* tour in February 1980. Billy Rath, who had played with Johnny Thunders, came in to replace Glen Matlock, while Rob Duprey, whom Iggy had discovered in a New York club, handled the guitar duties. The tour continued in the States, but after only three shows there, Rath and Kruger were fired. According to Kral:

*The German drummer Klaus had just had it. He didn't like the rock 'n' roll scene. He wanted to be by himself a lot and he would never go out with us. Also, he didn't like how Iggy treated women. I think he was depressed. He threw a chain against a wall and yelled, "I can't stand it anymore!" Iggy just said, "OK, you don't like it — you can split." After he told Klaus, he fired Billy too.*

Billy Rath was a heroin addict and it was impossible to work with him. Kral went to New York to recruit a new drummer and bass player for the band:

*I hired Michael Page and Douglas Bowne. I had seen Douglas on drums with John Cale and I thought he was tremendous. I auditioned several bass players, including Kenny Aronson who used to play with Wayne County, until I found Michael Page. I remembered him from the Dolls. He was a sweetheart. He was really incredible — a very nice and generous guy.*

Promoting *Soldier* in Europe, May 1980.
(Jaime Gonzalo/Ruta 66 archive)

◁
Live action at Paris Palace, France, May 15, 1979.
(Claude Gassian)

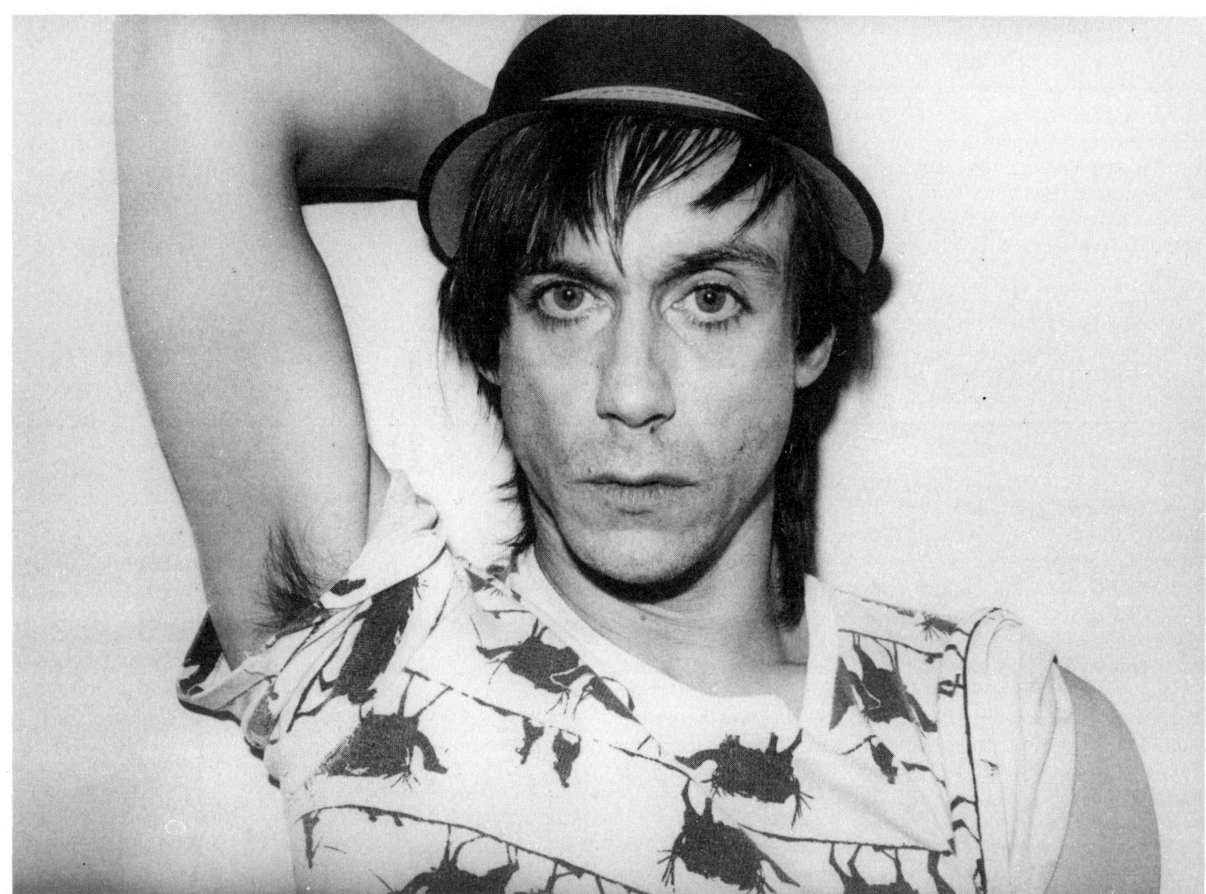

**Iggy in 1980.** (Marcia Resnick)

From March until June of 1980, Iggy toured extensively all over North America and Europe. Another American tour, called the *Nightclubbing* tour because of the venues being mostly small clubs, followed later in the year. The line-up with Kral on guitar and keyboards, Duprey on guitar, Page on bass, and Bowne on drums, played over 110 concerts during 1980. Even though it wasn't Iggy's best band, it was probably one of his most homogenous and harmonic group:

*I'm working with an American band and these guys are so fucking great they keep me laughing 24 hours a day, out of my mind. I haven't been so happy since the original edition of the Stooges.*

Arista put very little effort in promoting *Soldier* and the tours were not financially backed by the record company. Instead, Iggy had to borrow money from the booking agents for the first few weeks of concerts, before being able to finance the tours.

The gruelling tours were exhausting and caused Iggy to revert to his former habits of alcohol abuse:

*To preserve my mental vision in a pristine state, I abused my body and my ability to relate to other people or judge reality objectively, with alcohol. I didn't have to waste my time associating with dealers of illegal substances.*

Rob Duprey said of the self-indulgent lifestyle on the road:

*Rock 'n' roll to me is like a travelling carnival. It's a shame to see it get so sophisticated. Groupie-ism is phenomenal. It's disposal. All the girls fuck the guys in the band and the next day you're gone. You don't have to deal with their crappy boyfriends.*

Although he was very excited to be playing with Iggy, Kral saw how badly people were being treated and how destructive the excessive rock 'n' roll lifestyle was:

*Iggy would drink a lot. So would I. He would eat for three people, then he would go back to the hotel and sleep until the gig. Then, he wouldn't eat, just drink early in the morning. I saw people for the first time on tour with him. They would get sucked into that lifestyle, even though they had no experience on the road. They'd say, "Oh yeah, party time!" and after a week they would be dead. They couldn't keep up. ..... A lot of times, Iggy was like a baby or a little kid. Sometimes he would be very calm, gentle and intelligent. But other times there was total meanness in his eyes and he would say horrible things. I remember a lady who came backstage once. She wasn't that young anymore. Iggy took one look at her and said, "You're old. Look at you. Just look at you!" She started crying and screaming. Iggy just said, "Get her out of here!" He would just rip anybody apart!*

**Rob Duprey, Iggy and Michael Page at Ritz, New York, December 7, 1980.** (Steve Macanka)

# 25 ROCK AND ROLL PARTY

**I was feeling that I was on the dead-end circuit from 1980 to 1983, but I didn't know what else to do. I remember doing a show in some college town, in a tiny club, and afterwards some fans came back. I thought I had done a good gig and they were going to tell me that. But they looked at me very seriously and were shaking their heads, and they said, "Iggy, you deserve better than this. You shouldn't be here." And I wasn't so stupid that I didn't realize the implications of what they were saying.**

Iggy Pop to Lisa Robinson, *Interview*, November 1986.

Iggy and Ivan Kral, collaborators on *Party*. (Steve Macanka)

Although *New Values* and *Soldier* were fairly good sellers, particularly in England and Europe, Arista wanted the next album to be a strong commercial proposition. In the summer of 1980, Iggy got together with Ivan Kral to write new material at the Iroquois Hotel in New York. Most of the tunes were based on Kral's riffs and chord sequences to which Iggy made up lyrics. Working with Iggy was never boring:

*I loved it! Some days he'd feel really creative and we would work until five in the morning. Other times, he'd say,"Fuck it, I can't even get up today. There's nothing there." We were like stepping over each other trying to get ideas. He was making up words all the time. Sometimes I would suggest lines and he caught on to it. He came up with "Eggs On Plate." It started as "Eggs On My Plate" — I wrote it for Patti Smith a long time ago.*

In August 1980, Iggy and his touring band (Kral, Duprey, Page, Bowne) went into New York's Record Plant studios with Tom Petty's engineer Thom Panunzio as producer. A dozen tracks, all penned by Kral/Pop, were recorded, but Arista's Managing Director, Charles Levison, wasn't completely satisfied with the material; he felt it was too uniform in sound. On Levison's suggestion, Iggy agreed to work with Tommy Boyce of Monkees production fame. The record company wanted to include some accessible cover versions of well-known pop songs on the album. However, Kral played Boyce a tape with "Bang Bang," a new song he had written with Iggy:

*We needed some commercial stuff and I started playing "Bang Bang." Boyce was immediately interested, "What's that? It's great! Let's do it, it's danceable." I gave Iggy my lyrics but he changed it to his own. Originally it was very non-Iggy — a song about the emancipation of women. ..... Boyce really gets the work done. He was excellent. I really like the sound he got on "Bang Bang" and the covers.*

Arista promotion shot, 1981. (Arista)

The album, entitled *Party*, was released in June 1981 (August in the States). Despite its commercial intentions, it failed to sell in anything like the quantities expected by Arista. Many critics were disappointed in the record's dull sub-heavy metal riffings and Iggy's hedonistic lyrics, obsessed with superficial buddy relationships and frantic pleasure seeking. Most reviewers were of the opinion that *Party* was the third album in a declining series that began with *New Values*. However, it does contain a few strong stand-out tracks, among them "Eggs On Plate," "Pumpin' For Jill," and "Bang Bang," which Bowie covered on his 1987 *Never Let Me Down* LP.

The hectic touring pace of 1979/80 continued in 1981. In June/July, Iggy made a one-month European tour to promote *Party*. Richard Sohl, Patti Smith's keyboardsplayer, was added to the line-up of Kral, Duprey, Page and Bowne. After three shows at Ritz, a New York club, to start off the subsequent American *Party* tour, Ivan Kral unexpectedly quit the group:

*I felt like I couldn't grow as a human being anymore. I felt like I was trapped. I like parties and going out, but there's a point... it's not the same as when you were 18 or 25 years old. I was simply tired of the entire rock scene.*

Iggy took Kral's decision very hard. According to Kral:

*I guess nobody has ever left Iggy. He always fired people and he always had a new band. Maybe I was the first one to leave him and that's what got him. Later I ran into David Bowie and Iggy. David came up and said, "You owe Jim one." I was crushed. Anyway, I hope we'll work together again some day.*

Kral started playing with John Waite who had left the Babys. Gary Valentine, a friend of Rob Duprey who had previously played with Blondie, became a last-minute replacement for Kral.

After the final dates of the *Party* tour, at New York's Savoy club in September, Richard Sohl was fired by Iggy. According to Duprey, Iggy wasn't satisfied with Sohl's stage presence:

*Iggy felt that Sohl didn't contribute enough in the way that was called for. He wanted a real kind of upfront, bash out "I gotta boner" type of guy.*

At the same time, Douglas Bowne left the group in order to play more jazz-oriented music. For the next American tour, Bowne's place was taken by Clem Burke, another Blondie-member. Carlos Alomar, Bowie's right-hand man and guitarist, was also added to the line-up. During the tour, which was dubbed *Follow The Sun* tour, Iggy picked up the idea of wearing women's clothes on stage. According to Sal Lupo, Iggy's "lighting designer" on many of the American tours:

*He had a collection of things that he'd been wearing at home. It had nothing to do with transsexuality. For him it was total comfort. He felt he was so comfortable in them that he started wearing them on stage. Some of them were skirts with tops — others were dresses.*

Towards the end of the tour, Iggy played two dates opening for the Rolling Stones at the Pontiac Silverdome, an 80,000-capacity stadium north of Detroit. It was a prestigious event for Iggy and he chose not to wear a dress on the first night:

*The first night, I wore trousers and did a 23-minute set. The second night, I wore a mini-skirt. And apparently it was a bit revealing under the lights. I still have a lot of the stuff that was thrown at me that night. There was a definite mixed reaction that night. At least half the people liked what I did. The other half—fuck them. There was definite booing.*

*Party* was not the commercial success Arista had wished for, and in 1982, Iggy's contract was terminated, once again leaving Iggy without a record deal. Having left Berlin for the States in 1980, Iggy moved to Brooklyn, where one of his friends was Chris Stein of Blondie:

*Then a rumour started that he was forming Animal Records and I was going to be on it. When I returned from my tour I saw Chris and he laid it on the line, "Look, I'd like to record you. It's a rumour now anyway, we might as well go ahead!"*

Iggy chose to record an album for Stein's Animal Records because he wanted to do a small unemcumbered one-off project that didn't involve the complications and record company pressures of a three-album contract.

Iggy's new musical collaborator after Ivan Kral was Rob Duprey, who had been in Iggy's back-up groups since 1980. The two of them worked closely on the album, *Zombie Birdhouse*, during January-May of 1982. Duprey had been making demo tapes at home with a little tape recorder:

*I just made recordings for the love of doing it. Not for any real direction or purpose. It wasn't particularly commercial, just quirky. I gave Iggy the tapes and he was very interested.*

Iggy and Duprey were able to get some money in advance from Animal to buy a four-track tape recorder. The writing and arrangements were mostly done in Duprey's spare bedroom:

*We worked at length on this album before we went into the studio. I felt that, particularly on my last two albums, I was losing the articulation of what I wanted to be saying.*

Produced by Chris Stein, the album was recorded for $30,000 at the 16-track Blank Tapes Studio in New York. Rob Duprey handled all guitars and keyboards, while Clem Burke played drums and Stein played occasional bass.

Having completed the record by June 1982, Iggy went to Haiti for a few weeks of rest and to take some pictures for the album cover. Anne Wehrer flew out to join him to complete the manuscript for *I Need More*, a book about Iggy's life she was writing with Iggy. She was dismayed when she saw the state Iggy was in:

*He was thrown out of all clubs because he was drunk all the time. He often got mad and started screaming at people. It was so distressing and you can't help but want to help him, yet you can't do anything. He wants attention but he doesn't want help. ..... Haiti was the wrong place to go to: you can buy any drug you want from the drug store without a prescription. At a certain point, I said, "Look, you're not working on the book. I've got to get back or else I'm going to blow the publishing contract."*

Clearly, Iggy was in bad shape after being on the road so long. After three years of exhausting tours, he had become an insomniac and after an automobile accident, he ended up in the hospital with broken ribs and pneumonia. He had to cancel several benefit appearances in the summer of 1982 because of his poor health.

At a record store in San Antonio, Texas, November 1981. (Steve Bartels)

Iggy on stage with Johnny Thunders and Wayne Kramer, New York, summer 1982. (Marcia Resnick)

Despite all the problems, *I Need More — The Stooges And Other Stories* was published in October 1982. The book is a highly entertaining collection of episodes and stories from Iggy's life. According to Wehrer, Iggy wanted to make the book because he wanted to diversify his activities:

*He said to me, "I'm getting older. I can't be a rock 'n' roll star forever. I really have to expand and do other things like David does. Get into movies." He's certainly intelligent enough to do a number of things instead of putting out records and going out on tour.*

Iggy commented on the book:

*In the end, I think the book became a kind of an autobiography, but what I wanted to show was that the most interesting thing about rock 'n' roll are the homemade things, before the band even gets its recording contract.*

Coinciding with the publication of the book was the release of *Zombie Birdhouse*. There were no pressures from Chris Stein and Animal Records to commercialize the album and it is Iggy's most experimental and pretentious record. Consequently, the sales were miserable, and Iggy had to work hard, playing all over the States, to survive. Although Wehrer estimates that Iggy had made about $400,000 from his 1980-81 tours, the money had all been spent.

Iggy put together a new band for the concerts. It consisted of another ex-Blondie member, Frank Infante, on guitar, Rob Duprey on guitar and keyboards, Michael Page on bass, and Larry Mysliewicz on drums. After a three-month American tour, entitled *The Breaking Point*, in early 1983, Iggy went to Japan and Australia for his first ever concerts there. These concerts, in the summer of 1983, became Iggy's last for over three years. He obviously felt that he had reached the end of the road and come to a standstill in his career as a musician and performer. According to Wehrer:

*He was very, very concerned. The whole thing about calling the tour* The Breaking Point *was that he was either going to drop dead or he was going to go to other things. It was the time to change. At one point, he said to me that he didn't think he would make it into 1984!*

# NOT JUST A STOOGE

**WHEN 'New Values' debuted in 1979, Robert Christgau (a critic who likes and understands Iggy Stooge / Pop on several levels) remarked rather acidly on the amount of people "who consider Iggy a font of natural wisdom."**

And last week's publication of Pop's first book, *I Need More: The Stooges and Other Stories* ("by Iggy Pop with Anne Wehrer") isn't likely to lessen those numbers who have always followed the I-crawled-on-glass-and-lived side of the stooge schtick.

But for admirers of the Pop oeuvre who are a little less solemn about his career (accomplishments? exploits? survival?), *I Need More* will be of justified interest. The real subject of the book is not Iggy at all, but thought — and also because a comfortable kind of honesty permeates the proceedings.

*I Need More* is explicit, unrehearsed, straightforward, and opinionated. Sample, on the Stooges' legendary heyday:

"Sometimes we'd have to practice in parkas and mittens, but it didn't matter. We were fanatics. Each obstacle became more of a laugh. Through all this I was very calculating — I was the smart one in the band — I was concerned very much with where we could gain points with a DJ and how much we'd lose."

The book covers exactly what its list of 'Contents' promises: it tells you Something About Myself, We Got Lucky, First Musical Impressions, Why I Do What I Do, Dairy Queen and Decline, Capitalism Versus Rock, Getting Over Feeling Bad, The Right Stuff, Who's Who In Parasites and 38 other dissertations. (The lyrics to 16 of the songs Pop has written are also included and the volume is bookended by a pair of poems).

'I Need More' has been sponsored by New Jersey's Karz-Cohl, Inc, who according to Iggy "publish Polish poets". The impressive layout was overseen by its author and many of the not-seen-before photos come from his family, girlfriend, and associates.

The important thing about *I Need More*, perhaps, is that it succeeds not as "some fan thing" (which is how Iggy fears it may be taken), but in its chosen format — as literature. The colloquial side of American art (that side which values experience more than 'civilisation') has always been the truest yet also the most difficult turf for American artists — performers, painters *or* writers.

And, progressively, it has become even more mis-apprehended, mis-represented, and mis-used. Since this is the territory so explicitely stalked by the Stooges, and so aggressively explored since by their founder, it's satisfying to see *I Need More* deliver some perspective along with its anecdotes:

"You know something, we're caught in a big bad world where one car alone can be painted yellow, black and red and hubcaps get stolen, you know, and musicians come and musicians go, they all have their price.

'Girls fight over men. People gorge on images, and I just can't trust it. I mean, whatever happened to when a guy just wanted to play some honest music for his peer group? What is it about this rock and roll? Well, it's the thing that shakes you out of your marriage. It's the thing that disarranges your kidneys. It's what sells McDonalds. It's a gathering place."

Altogether, Iggy's book is a rambling prose poem — the poetry of both experience and ideas, leavened with a lot of laughs. Or, as fellow Ann Arbor author Donald Hall would put it, it's "the poetry of a man in the world, responding to what he sees: with disgust, with pleasure, in rant and in meditation."

If you fancy a copy, you can order it from Karz-Cohl Inc at 320 West 105th St, New York, New York 10025 USA, for the equivalent of $9.95 plus $2 p&p (surface mail only).

**Cynthia Rose**

# 26 THE QUIET YEARS

**I grew increasingly curious as to what it would be like to be very sober. I thought, "Christ, how would that feel? Could I do that?" What would it be like to write a song without sort of conceding that moment of panic, when you say, oh hell, down a couple of quick beers and then it'll come out, or smoke this joint and my thoughts will expand. I also found myself suspecting that my promiscuity, sexually, was getting in the way of my music, because it didn't allow me a home life. I thought that with a home life, perhaps I'd have a better foundation for harder and better work.**

Iggy Pop to Barney Hoskins, *New Musical Express*, October 1986.

Between 1981-1983, Iggy had seen the quality of his life diminish; his records sold less and less and his concerts were often disasters. The turning point came in the summer of 1983, when David Bowie released his version of "China Girl," originally recorded for *The Idiot* and co-written by Iggy and Bowie. It was culled as a single from Bowie's best-selling *Let's Dance* LP and, accompanied by a spectacular promotion video and Bowie's *Serious Moonlight* tour, it became a worldwide hit. That meant royalties for Iggy and for the first time in years he could support himself financially without being forced to go on the road. Iggy decided that the Australian tour in the summer of 1983 would be his last stage work for considerable time.

Determined to once and for all come to terms with his reliance on alcohol and various drugs, Iggy went on a detoxification programme at a clinic in Los Angeles where he temporarily lived. He worked hard on self-improvement; his quest was to make order out of chaos:

*The first steps were just very basic — let's see if we can manage getting up in the morning, getting through the day, starting to do basic things to set up a small household. I learned to keep books, learned to balance a cheque book and a bank account, pay taxes, leased an apartment — first time for everything!*

During the stay in Los Angeles, Iggy recorded the title track to Alex Cox's film *Repo Man*. It was made in collaboration with ex-Sex Pistol Steve Jones. Having faced many of the same problems as Iggy with drugs and alcohol, Jones had become a militant crusader against intoxification as a way of life.

Later in 1983, Iggy with Japanese girlfriend Suchi (she had been at Iggy's Tokyo concerts in June 1983), and David Bowie and Coco Schwab (his personal assistant and close friend) went to Bali for a holiday. The visit inspired a new Bowie/Iggy collaboration, "Tumble And Twirl," and in the spring of 1984, Iggy worked closely with Bowie on his follow-up LP to *Let's Dance*, entitled *Tonight*. This time, Bowie included no less than five songs that Iggy had had a part in writing: "Neighbourhood Threat" and "Tonight" from *Lust For Life*, "Don't Look Down" from *New Values*, and two newly written compositions.

After years of non-stop touring and precarious itinerant living, Iggy moved to a spacious Manhattan apartment in 1984. He settled down to a quiet life with Suchi, whom he married:

*We did it to please the US government. We just had so much trouble getting through customs that we thought we'd better. She's been very good to me and has repeatedly in times of crucial moments urged me to curb my anger.*

To many people's amazement, Iggy settled comfortably into domestic bliss:

*When some problem has peaked, and my thinking isn't getting me anywhere, I like to pull out the vacuum cleaner and vacuum the house. One of the first things I like to do when I wake up in the mornings is to clean something. I don't really care what it is. That feels real good. Suchi's the bed maker. I throw out the garbage. Suchi does the dishes, but I'm on general trash patrol.*

One of the main motives behind Iggy's strenuous efforts to lead a responsible and organized life was his son, Eric. Born out of wedlock in 1970, he grew up with his mother, Paulette Benson, in Los Angeles. Iggy felt a genuine affection for his son and had stayed in contact. In 1982, Iggy was contacted by Paulette who was having difficulties with the boy. She wanted Iggy to take responsibility for Eric from there on. Despite many ups and downs in their relationship and Eric's somewhat unstable upbringing, Iggy has remained very close to his son. In an interview with Nick Kent in *The Face*, he talked candidly and with pride about Eric:

*He lives in Philadelphia where he's got his own apartment. He's studying accountancy, basically in order to find a way to make large sums of money. That's his thing currently. Now I can afford to support him financially in his efforts at self-improvement. I wanted most of all for him to have a person in his life, a paternal friend he could communicate with. I've finally established a successful rapport with him. I feel good about it.*

As he learned to live and work without stimulants, the two-year hiatus in 1983-85 enabled Iggy to regain his physical and mental strength. Even though he wasn't in the music papers or in the public's eye, it was a very creative period for Iggy. Intent on making more melodic songs, he practised doing melodies and tried to develop his voice as an instrument. At the same time, he indulged himself daily with writing essays, poetry and song lyrics, often lugging his typewriter to Washington Square Park for inspiration. His writing ambitions in the future include doing some screenplays and another book to follow up *I Need More*. He also got back into painting, a pastime he had picked up from Bowie back in their Berlin days.

Sparked by performances of Sam Shepard's *True West* and other plays, Iggy started taking acting lessons and auditioning for theatre and film roles:

*It was a good opportunity to take off my armour and perform in just a bare room with a few people who had no clippings on me. ..... I admire the discipline of the people in the theatre. They work hard. It was a good way for me to stay on my toes. If you know that anytime the phone rings, you might get a call that says there's a great script with a part for you coming over, you can't be stoned, out romancing or whatever. You have to be poised. I couldn't be in a musician's mode where if I wasn't working I could just light up a spliff and stare at the sun.*

Although he didn't consider acting as an alternative vocation, Iggy got three small film roles. In Martin Scorsese's acclaimed *The Color Of Money*, he played one of the pool players that Tom Cruise's character met on the road. In Alex Cox's *Sid And Nancy*, a film about the dead Sex Pistol Sid Vicious and his girlfriend, Nancy Spungeon, Iggy played a straight guy checking into the Chelsea Hotel. He also played the manager of an S&M bar in *Miami Vice*, but Iggy's part was edited out of the show and never broadcast.

By June of 1985, Iggy had saved about $40,000 from publishing income, and he felt confident enough to attempt another record. He took off to Los Angeles where he rented a house with Steve Jones. They spent four months there, recording demos at an eight-track studio in the bedroom of Olivier Ferrand, a Swiss photographer and musician. Steve Jones and Ferrand played all instruments and 11 tracks were laid down, including versions of Jimi Hendrix's "Purple Haze" and Sly and the Family Stone's "Family Affair," as well as new tunes such as "Cry For Love," "Winners And Losers," and "Fire Girl."

**Iggy in New York, 1984.** (Larry Williams)

In October, Iggy was back in New York again. At the same time, Bowie arrived in New York to work on his *Labyrinth* soundtrack. Iggy went up to see him at his hotel suite, and they played each other their new demos:

*He was sceptical at first; I think he didn't want to put the tapes on because he probably thought that I was out in California doing Stooges retreads. And he heard the tapes and his jaw dropped! I was really proud that he and Coco really liked them. I was able to show them that I had not been wasting my time, or wasting the money that I'd made off his records.*

At first, Iggy had no intentions of asking Bowie to produce the album for him. But Bowie was excited by what he heard and he volunteered to help write additional material and to produce the record at the Montreaux Studios near his Swiss home.

Another period of songwriting followed, this time with

Bowie. New songs were written in the Caribbean over Christmas 1985 and in Switzerland during January-March 1986, after which Iggy returned to New York to work on and refine the lyrics:

*I was keen to make them as good as I could, but I was terribly afraid of the trap where the artist sits in his garret all alone and there's no real deadline. I was afraid that I would overthink them and start wadding up perfectly good pieces of paper, tossing out the baby with the bathwater.*

When it came to record the album (which became *Blah Blah Blah* ), simplicity, discipline and perfection were the rule. Using British guitarist Kevin Armstrong, who had played in Bowie's Live-Aid backing group, and Turkish multi-instrumentalist Erdal Kizilcay, the tight little group managed to cut 10 tracks in two weeks. Steve Jones couldn't make the sessions because he was busy with ex-Duran Duran Andy Taylor's solo album. Co-producing the album with Bowie was Queen's engineer David Richards. Work was intense and Iggy and Bowie were fervently searching for the right commercial sounds. To achieve the state-of-the-art drum sound that permeates the record, they combined drum chips borrowed from Queen drummer Roger Taylor with live percussion. For the snare drum sound alone, they played the records of Prince, PIL and Bruce Springsteen to try to find a sound that was even better.

Back in New York again, Iggy started circulating the completed *Blah Blah Blah* tape to the record companies' A&R departments:

*I knew there was this perception of me as a flake that was making it difficult for me to be taken seriously. So I combed my hair, put on a suit and went and sat down with every record company president who seemed suitable and talked to them until they were convinced that I was serious.*

Several labels expressed interest in signing Iggy, and after meeting with A&M Records' chairman Jerry Moss (the "M" in A&M), a recording deal was struck with the label. Having successfully steered himself away from being just another disorganized broken-down rock star, Iggy was ready to return to the rock scene once again:

*Being a survivor, that's one kind of accomplishment, but I also want to be appreciated for the work I'm doing now. I need to prove to myself that I can achieve this transition from "God's garbage man" to someone who can offer the public more than a warped celebration of sex, drugs and dissipation.*

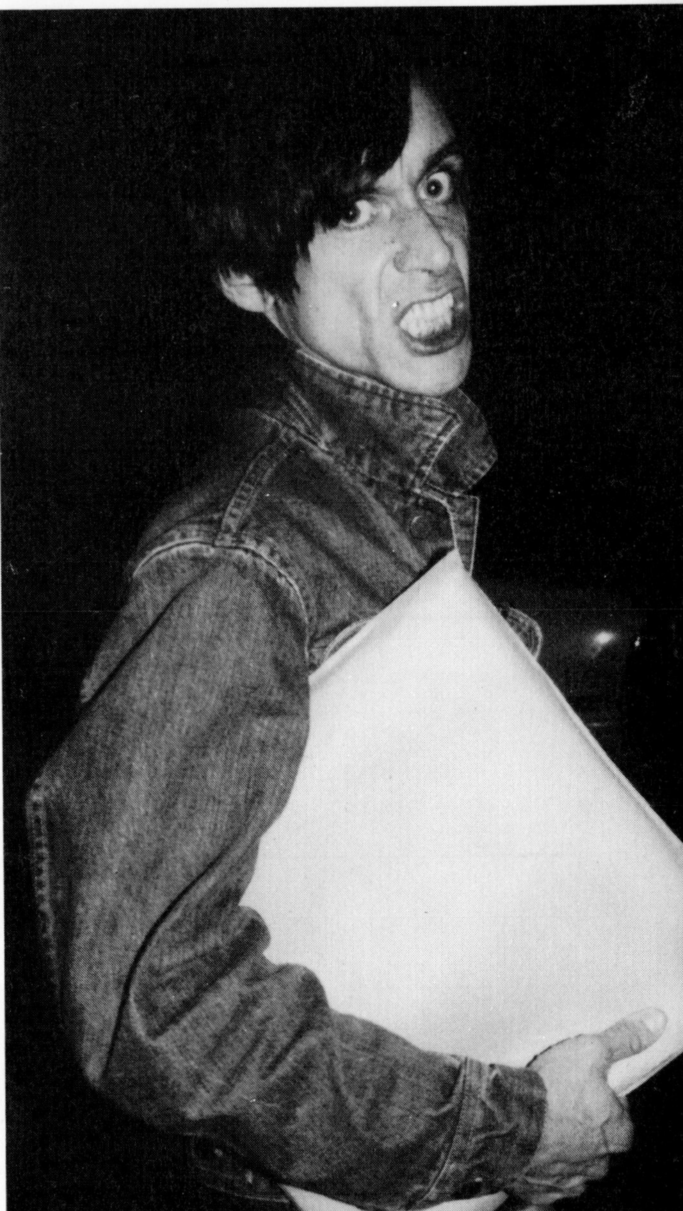

**In New York City, 1984.** (DLS collection)

# 27 HERE COMES SUCCESS

**I have no desire to continue being a failure. I have achieved failure so I want success. I want badly to be a very, very good artist and I don't think I'm all that great. So I've got a lot of work to do to be as good as I want, which is why I've never given up.**

Iggy Pop to Mark Cooper, radio interview, 1986.

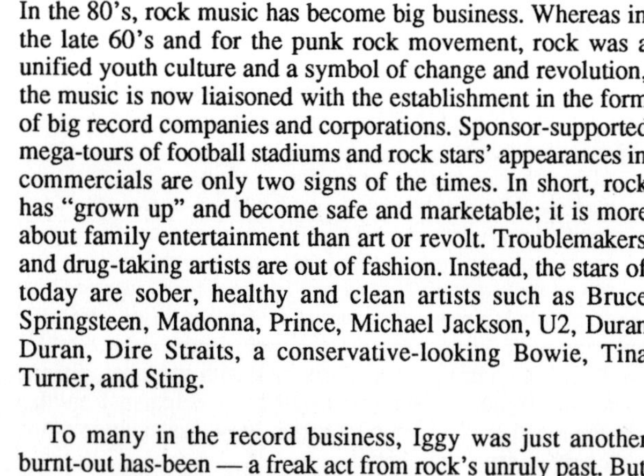

In the 80's, rock music has become big business. Whereas in the late 60's and for the punk rock movement, rock was a unified youth culture and a symbol of change and revolution, the music is now liaisoned with the establishment in the form of big record companies and corporations. Sponsor-supported mega-tours of football stadiums and rock stars' appearances in commercials are only two signs of the times. In short, rock has "grown up" and become safe and marketable; it is more about family entertainment than art or revolt. Troublemakers and drug-taking artists are out of fashion. Instead, the stars of today are sober, healthy and clean artists such as Bruce Springsteen, Madonna, Prince, Michael Jackson, U2, Duran Duran, Dire Straits, a conservative-looking Bowie, Tina Turner, and Sting.

To many in the record business, Iggy was just another burnt-out has-been — a freak act from rock's unruly past. But Iggy had spent his time well. Having completely cleaned up his act, he returned with a vengeance with *Blah Blah Blah*, released in October 1986. Easily his most commercial and accessible album ever, it is a slick, tuneful and well-crafted record. Iggy has channeled the energy of his past work into articulate reflections; the album finds him playing the role of yearning romantic and sharp social observer, rather than the angry nihilist of Stooges days. Even though Bowie's melodic and musical influences are obvious on songs like "Shades," "Baby, It Can't Fall," and "Isolation," Iggy never sounds contrived. The production is superlative and Bowie and Richards have achieved a truly modern and powerful sound.

*Blah Blah Blah* was an unabashed attempt by Iggy to become more commercial:

*Radio neglect in the past has hurt me more than anything else. I've written some great songs, and I know if more people had heard my music back when... which sort of brought me around to the idea of using a "name" producer. I realized it's very important that this record sound as polished, as competitive as possible. I didn't want there to be any obvious reasons why it shouldn't get on the radio.*

(Magnus Lewin)

As could be expected, some critics complained of a "sell-out," while others claimed it was a David Bowie album disguised as an Iggy Pop record. But, on the whole, the reception was very enthusiastic and most reviewers agreed that it was an impressive work. *Rolling Stone's* David Fricke commended the album and Bowie's contribution:

> *There is a vital edginess to Iggy's singing that elevates* Blah Blah Blah *way above recent Bowie ham like 1984's* Tonight. *In fact, although he doesn't sing or play a note here, this is one of Bowie's most dynamic outings — in terms of content, spirit and sheer crackling energy — since* "Heroes."

*Creem's* reviewer Richard Riegel was more indifferent:

> *It comes across as something of an Iggy-flavoured Bowie album: Ig's vocals are as lean and mean as his body in the cover photo, and his lyrics do their usual provocative-and-remote-as-a-trailer job. But what the public will take to heart from* Blah Blah Blah *are the swelling, booming, orchestral, fatally Bowie-esque choruses which distinguish each song.*

The English reviews were somewhat mixed. John Wilde, writing for *Sounds*, was ecstatic:

> *These are Iggy's wanton instincts gathered up, back to his narcissistic, real gone best. These are ominous, boundless rhythms thundering outside your front door and, yup, Iggy Pop is back with a slam. The last hero.*

Within months of release, *Blah Blah Blah* became Iggy's best selling album ever. The album brought him a new and younger audience that for the most part hadn't even heard about the Stooges. In several countries, the album reached the Top 10 in the album charts, including Sweden where it went to number two. In Canada it earned Iggy his first ever gold record. The first single chosen from the LP was "Cry For Love," co-written by Iggy and Steve Jones. Even though the video was played a lot, the record didn't do too well. However, the second single, the better-chosen "Real Wild Child," a fast, rocking blues song originally done by Buddy Holly and covered by Albert Lee, became a hit in many countries. In England it reached number 11 and became Iggy's first ever hit there. He even got to perform it on *Top Of The Pops*. Two further singles were issued in 1987: "Shades" and "Isolation," both penned by Iggy and Bowie. Iggy also collaborated with Japanese musician Ryuichi Sakamoto on a track called "Risky."

Amid a blaze of publicity (front pages on *The Face, Sounds, Melody Maker, Spin*), Iggy arrived in London in October 1986 to do promotional interviews and assemble a new band for his first live work in three years. For the first time, he chose to work exclusively with British musicians:

> *I couldn't go on playing music with idiots who play their hair-dryers more than their instruments. ..... Again and again, I find myself working with the British. For some reason, I tend to have more in common with the people I meet in London than with American musicians. The American bands I've had usually want to score girls and drugs more than they want to make really good music. Britain is a poor country with a lot of very talented people, so you meet all sorts of very hard-working, hustling guys here.*

Guitarist Kevin Armstrong became band-leader and he hand-picked the musicians for Iggy. Shamus Beghan, who had

Back on stage again, Iggy in Stockholm, Sweden, July 1, 1987. (Paul Quant)

played with Madness, played keyboards and occasional guitar, Phil Putcher played bass, and Gavin Harrison drums.

The *Blah Blah Blah* tour started on the US West Coast in late October. After a two-week American tour of clubs, Iggy played concert halls and theatres in Europe, winding up the tour in London before Christmas. Having trimmed away some of the sillier and negative elements from his concerts, Iggy felt and looked a new performer. Concentrating on material from the new album, *The Idiot*, *Lust For Life*, *Fun House*, and *Raw Power*, Iggy's new live shows earned him rave reviews. *Hollywood Reporter's* Jeffrey Ressner wrote of Iggy's Los Angeles shows:

> *Iggy has weathered incredibly well, considering how much he's abused himself with the excesses of rock life over the years. He's cleaned up his act, he looks good, and his vocals are as fiery as ever.*

Checking out his New York concerts at Ritz were, among others, David Bowie and Mick Jagger. *New York Newsday's* Wayne Robbins was impressed:

> *90 minutes of gyrations, culminating with a sensous accounting of the punk anthem, "Lust For Life." Pop, naked from the belt line, slung low, to the tip of his head, has further perfected his sense of self-choreography as he spins and grovels and gyrates. This is primal performance art, and Pop is the raging bull of rock, shadow-boxing on stage like an undernourished Jake La Motta.*

The two concluding shows, at Brixton Academy south of London, were among his best on the tour. Chris Roberts, writing for *New Musical Express,* raved about Iggy's return to the stage:

> *Muscles and guts like Iggy's make it a sin to extract highlights from this bodily rush of a performance. It's a steamroller stream of consciousness, and you can forget anything you ever read or thought or twitched about rock 'n' roll before because this is where it was and this is how it is. ..... Iggy Pop is pop in its purest and filthiest form.*

After a one-month break over Christmas and New Year, when Iggy visited his parents who have moved from Ypsilanti to Myrtle Beach, South Carolina, he was back on the road again in January 1987. Opening for the Pretenders, Iggy played arenas in the States and Canada, before going to Japan for concerts there in April. Once again, Iggy got excellent reviews; many critics felt the Pretenders/Iggy show was one of the most exciting of the year. In June 1987, Iggy returned to Europe for open-air dates at various festivals and a tour of UK theatres.

Immediately after the tour, Iggy began writing songs for the follow-up album to *Blah Blah Blah.* This time, he decided to write the majority of the material by himself:

> *Not having a band made* Blah Blah Blah *a static record, although I'm proud of it when I hear it. But I did want to do something that's a little more natural this time, where the primary force of the words and music came strictly from me. If I'm gonna put my name and face on a record, it ought to have more of my music.*

By early 1988, he had enough songs to start recording the LP. Iggy recruited buddy Steve Jones to play guitar, Shamus Beghan (keyboards), veteran of the 1986/87 tours, Leigh Foxx (bass), formerly of Boston's Sidewinders and recommended by Chris Stein, and Paul Garisto (drums), ex-Psychedelic

Iggy in 1988. (A&M)

Furs. The versatile Bill Laswell, known for his work with PIL, Motörhead and Was Not Was, was enlisted as producer:

*Bowie had always thought Laswell was good. He said, "You should meet this guy. He can give you a great sound and still get that heaviness." Then Bill asked me to do a cut on Sakamoto's* Neo Geo, *and I really got to like him.*

Recorded in New York, the album took just three weeks to make.

NEW YORK POST **WEEKEND** FRIDAY, JULY 22, 1988

## Iggy pumps out energy

By JIM BESSMAN

TO describe Iggy Pop at the Ritz Wednesday night, you need only recall the title of his 1973 album "Raw Power," then add it to his new album's title, "Instinct." Now over 40, the forefather of punk runs on instinct and still puts out more raw power than any of the thrashiest metal bands which descended from his seminal '60s rock band, The Stooges.

How does he do it? Superb conditioning, apparent in his grotesquely wiry arms and a muscularly defined torso stolen from a teenager. Plus a jackhammer four-piece band, overdriven by ex-Hanoi Rocks guitarist Andy McCoy.

The combination of Pop and the band's high-energy assault even made the lesser songs from his new album catch fire, and — for once — made the Ritz's typically heavy jump-cutting of the show on its video monitors a hit rather than a hindrance.

Pop brought out all of his trademark moves — twirling the mike stand like a baton and flinging it over his shoulder, lying on the floor and rolling around so those up front could stroke his hair.

But the best came last, after the first encore song (and current single) "Cold Metal" (with ex-Sex Pistol guitarist Steve Jones sitting in) and the Stooges' alienation classic "No Fun," when Pop pulled out all the stops on that group's bestiality classic "I Wanna Be Your Dog."

**ROCK** *review*

Besides obscenely acting out the lyrics, Iggy doused himself with water, ludely lolled his tongue, then got down on all fours — truly rock's top dog.

Kevin Mazur/London Features

**IGGY POP**
*Forefather of punk.*

The album, aptly titled *Instinct*, was released in June 1988. Six of the 10 songs are written by Iggy, including four of the strongest tracks: "High On You," the partly autobiographical "Instinct" and "Cold Metal," which was picked as the first single, and the impressive "Lowdown." Steve Jones, whose relentless power chords run throughout the album, co-wrote four songs with Iggy. Compared to the highly accessible and commercial predecessor, *Instinct* is a return to basics; while still maintaining a clean sound, it is a raw and uncompromising album. Lyrically, *Instinct* is a continuation of Iggy's articulate and biting observations on life and mature romanticism first displayed on *Blah Blah Blah*. Even though some critics complained that the album was monotonous and an ill-fated venture into heavy metal, the press reception was generally very positive. Many reviewers welcomed the return to the energy and "raw power" of the Stooges LPs. In *Melody Maker*, the album was hailed as "an astronomical success," and "another masterpiece from the man Jesus Christ calls 'Sir.'" *New Musical Express*' Jane Solanas thought the album was "excellent," even though she felt Steve Jones' "mad axe-merchant antics" were "way over the top." Roy Wilkinson in *Sounds* also enthused about the album:

*It's a shamelessly direct, visceral record. It's a very resonant, dignified album, emphasized by the way it sometimes draws near to self-parody. The way it balances on this tightrope without falling adds to its poignancy.*

Many reviewers also praised the lyrics and, without doubt, Iggy is increasingly gaining credit as a lyricist.

On July 8, 1988, Iggy kicked off a new world tour in support of *Instinct*. The tour included his first dates in South America and Tel Aviv, as well as a bill-topping appearance at the Reading Festival in England. Iggy's new band included former Hanoi Rocks guitarist Andy McCoy, bassist Alvin Gibbs, formerly with UK Subs, Paul Garisto on drums, while Shamus Beghan remained on keyboards and rhythm guitar. The concerts naturally featured several songs off *Instinct*, but Iggy also acknowledged his past by playing many old numbers; half of the set was made up of Stooges classics such as "1969," "1970," "Scene Of The Crime," "Penetration," "Your Pretty Face Is Going To Hell," and "Johanna." Witnessing Iggy's show at Whisky A Go-Go in Hollywood, 15 years after the Stooges' legendary five-night-stand at the club, *Los Angeles Daily News* reporter Craig Rosen wrote:

*No peanut butter or broken glass, but Iggy was up to some of his old tricks. During "Tuff Baby," he climbed upstairs only to hang upside down from the railing over the crowd. And at the end of "Five Foot One," he suddenly dove into the audience!*

Whatever may happen in the future, Iggy's place in the history of rock is secure. Through three ground-breaking albums with the Stooges and an inconsistent but sporadically brilliant solo career, Iggy has set rarely-approached standards for the rock artist's involvement with his work, at his best, delivering performances and records that are harrowing, revelatory, entertaining and utterly personal. Few other artists in rock have been as influential. Iggy's music and performances have been forerunners for hundreds of heavy metal, punk and new wave bands, and countless theatrical/"outrageous" acts owe a debt to Iggy for his lessons in shock theatrics. Now 41 years old, healthy, stable, optimistic, joyful, self-assured, ambitious, and, for the first time, solvent, Iggy is happy about his sheer survival and he is quite excited to be recording and performing:

*The things that moved me back in the days of Iggy and the Stooges still move me. But the difference is — I'm sober now. I'm still committed to rock 'n' roll. I still want to get up on stage and get it going. I still want the music to take me somewhere. ..... Basically, I'm in a state of high excitation... very excited and quite alive!*

# 28 JIM OSTERBERG

**I've *always* been a regular guy. I've never really had my head up my ass.**

Iggy Pop to Harold De Muir, *East Coast Rocker*, October 1986.

The disparity between Iggy Pop, "Godfather of Punk" and living legend, and Jim Osterberg, the private man behind the public image and myths has often been noted by interviewers and close associates of Iggy/Jim. The rock media tends to portray Iggy Pop as a self-destructive, outrageous and intense performer, with the chest-cutting and boiling wax incidents of the past usually overly emphasized. Expecting a weird and depraved madman, many interviewers have found Iggy to be a wary, cautious subject to interview; playful, outspoken and more clever than most. Contrasting with the rather one-dimensional picture of Iggy as a wild and aggressive person, his friends and musical colleagues view him as an articulate, charming and highly intelligent man.

In an attempt to describe the Jim Osterberg persona behind the often warped picture in the music media, we have compiled the following opinions expressed by people who know or have known him well, and by journalists who have conducted in-depth interviews with him.

**David Bowie (musical colleague, collaborator and close friend):**
Jim is my friend. Also he is my American friend. At times in our conversations, he encapsulates the elements of Bukowski, Sal Paradise, Sam Shepard and the kid brought up in a trailer park outside Detroit. Although opposite sides of the same coin, we've gone through a lot of the same problems in relation to our craft. We also both share the same affection for long stretches of solitude in foreign climes. But what makes our friendship so durable and, in the final analysis, so humorous is the insurmountable differences between us. He's red and I'm blue.

**Danny Fields (the Stooges' discoverer):**
I couldn't sum him up in 25 words or less. I can only give some adjectives that describe him. He's brilliant. As intelligent as anybody I have ever known. He's very charming and vivid, intense, and a powerful person. In fact, I think he is so intelligent that he goes over most people's heads. It's hard for him to give interviews because he usually flies away and the interviewers are just sitting there with their tongues hanging out. I've seen that happen.

**Wayne Kramer (musical colleague):**
The things that motivate him are deep. They're not thin, "I want to be a pop star" type motivations. He's got these demons in him and he exorcizes them by being a singer, writing songs and making records.

**Leee Black Childers (MainMan employee who lived with Iggy and the Stooges for five months in 1972-73):**
I lived with them in the Hollywood Hills mansion. Iggy and I used to sit in the huge living room by a giant fire place. When we'd talk, he'd be so much wiser than me. So much wiser in the ways of the world, the way people are and in the state of being and mankind. He'd go on and talk all night. I'd just sit there quite entranced.

**Jimmy Silver (the Stooges' manager 1968-70):**
Iggy and I are a lot alike. One of the ways in which we're alike is that we retain almost everything that we ever see or hear. I felt a strong bond or commonality with Jim. He did things that intrigued and excited me. ..... He has a good sense of humour although it's more biting and vindictive than most people in his position are supposed to have. He has a "fuck you" sense of humour. ..... In terms of intelligence, I think Jim's got a tremendous amount.

**Scott Isler (music journalist):**
The first thing that usually strikes people who meet Osterberg is how small he is; it's a testimony to his aggressive on-stage dynamism. The next surprise is his articulateness. As opposed to the monosyllabic Iggy on stage and disc, Jim Osterberg is a quite fluent and funny conversationalist. The temptation is to construct a Jekyll-Hyde theory around nice Jim (who even wears glasses) and monstrous Iggy. Osterberg's occasional moodiness no doubt encourages such ideas, but truth is never that simple. Iggy is very much a conscious creation, the "world's forgotten boy" (of "Search And Destroy") who slashes himself with broken glass and throws up on stage — the self-described "king of failures." Osterberg strives to give the impression of always being in control, knowing exactly what's going down. He is brash and contradicts himself fearlessly.

**Chris Brazier (music journalist):**
I'm not usually inclined to pity the poor superstar, but I begin to understand the special loneliness a genuinely sensitive star must feel, knowing that everyone he communicates with can't help but respond as much, if not more, to the legend, the image, as to the real person. ..... I thought about him as I went to bed. Wild? Depraved? Not so far — just intelligent and impulsive. I figured the key to his personality might lie in that insistently recurring phrase "d'y'unnerstan'?"

**Nick Kent (journalist and long-time Iggy follower):**
The characters — one the Mighty Pop, hard-assed, loud-mouthed megalomaniac, and the other, charming, compassionate Jim Osterberg, are two very different people. It is not a case of schizophrenia, nor is there any confusion as to how and when each role takes over. Our subject is totally in command of his personae and is deeply proud of them — if for nothing other than the fact that they complement each other in the furtherance of his vocation with perfect balance.

**Hugh Padgham (co-producer of Bowie's *Tonight* LP on which Iggy worked in 1984):**
Iggy wasn't like anything I imagined him to be. He was very quiet. I think most people's conception of him is being a complete lunatic who is just out to lunch and running around like a madman all the time. When he came in, he had these big glasses on and he just used to sit in the control room and read. My idea of Iggy now is that of an intellectual.

**Rob Duprey (musical colleague):**
He's fundamentally different from most people you meet. There's an independent streak in him. It just had to be there from the crib. I've never met anyone like him. As much as an exhibitionist that he is, on a private plane he keeps very much to himself.

**Michael Davis (bass player for the now defunct MC5):**
I admire him a lot for the things he has done and the things he's going to do. I admire him for hanging in there. I can see now that there is no end to his thing. He's a totally adaptable artist. He responds to himself, to his own instincts. He's not just going to quit. He can just keep going. He has always had this good spirit going for him, and I'm not just saying positive things about him just to say it. I can picture Iggy on stage well into the future. He could keep doing it forever. He always leaves that crack in the world for people to see that the ground isn't all that solid and for that, he's got immortality.

**Anne Wehrer (journalist):**
He's a smart dude — very well read. He's an incredible historian and he's read a tremendous amount of philosophy. He wanted to study anthropology and he went to the University of Michigan but they were taking too long to get to the point. So he went and got the reading list and read all the books instead of taking the courses. He considers rock 'n' roll a social anthropology.

(Magnus Lewin)

Much has been said about Iggy Pop within the pages of this book, but the last words are those of Iggy/Jim himself.

**On American audiences:**
The American public has always had a taste for the morbid, ghoulish entertainment, and a whole vein of humour based on self-deprecation.

**On his fans:**
I've always liked the people that come to my shows. I get a good mix — a really spunky bunch of very intelligent people. A lot of smarties and sensualists come to my shows. And my fans usually don't like other records.

(Ron McPherson)

**On rock 'n' roll:**
I realized that music has been bought and the rewards are too large. It's been made into something like golf. Just another American sport with an expensive set of apparatus you have to buy in order to play.

**On David Bowie:**
He's been my closest friend, and I love him very much. We've remained friends all through the years even though we haven't always worked together. He was the first person from the professional, "adult" music business to treat me with dignity, and treat my ideas with respect instead of going, "This dangerous lunatic!" For that I'm grateful. When I was penniless, he opened his home for me. Also, he's taught me a lot about life in general. He has a very big heart — he's extremely generous with his ideas.

**On TV:**
TV has sucked the insides out of most people in my country. That's why I started painting — as a reverse TV. Instead of sitting in front of a screen and having all this schmaltz poured over my head till I'm paralysed, I became the television and shot my insides out onto a blank canvas, to reactivate the animation of what's inside me. TV's one of the instruments by which people lose the ability to live. If you're gonna actually let thoughts be your thoughts, it becomes a problem. I'd rather eat brown rice than sip Coca Cola; at least you have to digest it.

**On his temperament:**
My anger hasn't done me any good. It gives me will power sometimes but when I used to have bad attacks of it, it never did me any good. It's better to take a calm step backwards and hit the mark. Dispassionately, if possible.

**On his image:**
My image is very inaccurate. As much so as I can make it. It's not an advantage in life to have people knowing you if you don't have the chance to know them back.

**On his art:**
It's a dream I had a long time ago and I've given myself to it, and I've discovered in this modern world of finance and industry and fashion and style and media and image, it's a very difficult thing to be allowed to continue your art. Everything I do is aimed towards the survival of my art.

# 29 APPENDIX

## TOUR INFORMATION

### Tour schedules 1977-88

***The Idiot*** **tour 1977**

1 Mar Friars, Aylesbury
2 Mar City Hall, Newcastle
3 Mar Apollo Theatre, Manchester
4 Mar Hippodrome, Birmingham
5 Mar Rainbow Theatre, London
7 Mar Rainbow Theatre, London
13 Mar Le Plateau Theatre, Montreal
14 Mar Seneca College, Toronto
16 Mar Harvard Square Theatre, Boston
18 Mar Palladium, New York
19 Mar Tower Theatre, Philadelphia
21 Mar Agora Ballroom, Cleveland
22 Mar Agora Ballroom, Cleveland
25 Mar Masonic Auditorium, Detroit
27 Mar Riviera Theatre, Chicago
28 Mar Mantra Studios, Chicago
28 Mar Aragon, Chicago
29 Mar Leonia Theatre, Pittsburgh
30 Mar Agora Ballroom, Columbus
1 Apr Oriental Theatre, Milwaukee
4 Apr Paramount Theatre, Portland
7 Apr Gardens, Vancouver
9 Apr Paramount Theatre, Seattle
13 Apr Berkeley Theatre, San Francisco
15 Apr Civic Auditorium, Santa Monica
16 Apr Civic Auditorium, San Diego

***Lust For Life*** **tour 1977**

14 Sep Doelen, Rotterdam
16 Sep Antwerp
17 Sep Markthalle, Hamburg
18 Sep Berlin
19 Sep Daddy's Dance Hall, Copenhagen
20 Sep Konserthuset, Stockholm
23 Sep L'Hippodrome, Paris
25 Sep Apollo Theatre, Manchester
26 Sep City Hall, Newcastle
27 Sep Odeon, Birmingham
28 Sep Colston Hall, Bristol
30 Sep Rainbow Theatre, London
1 Oct Rainbow Theatre, London
4 Oct Palace, Waterbury
6 Oct Palladium, New York
8 Oct Le Plateau Theatre, Montreal
9 Oct Toronto
10 Oct Hamilton
12 Oct Philadelphia
14 Oct Boston
15 Oct Civic Center, Baltimore
17 Oct Toledo
18 Oct Akron
19 Oct Cleveland
20 Oct Cobo Hall, Detroit
21 Oct Aragon, Chicago
22 Oct Milwaukee
24 Oct Madison
26 Oct Uptown Theatre, Kansas City
28 Oct Dallas
29 Oct Corpus Christi
30 Oct Austin
31 Oct Houston
4 Nov Portland
5 Nov Seattle
11 Nov San Francisco
13 Nov Phoenix
16 Nov State University, San Diego
17 Nov Santa Barbara
18 Nov Civic Auditorium, Santa Monica

***TV Eye*** **tour 1978**

10 May Salle Vitrolles, Marseille
12 May Pau
13 May Halle aux Grains, Toulouse
16 May Pabellon del Juventud, Badalona
19 May Jaap Edenhal, Amsterdam
24 May Domino, Stockholm
25 May Chateau Neuf, Oslo
27 May Brunnsparken, Örebro
29 May Det Ny Teater, Copenhagen
30 May Kant-Kino, Berlin
31 May Kant-Kino, Berlin
12 Jun Music Machine, London
13 Jun Music Machine, London

*A few European dates missing.*

***New Values*** **UK/European tour 1979**

20 Apr Factory, Manchester
21 Apr Eric's, Liverpool
22 Apr Top Rank, Sheffield
25 Apr Music Machine, London
27 Apr Pavilion, West Runton
28 Apr University, Leicester
29 Apr Coatham Bowl, Redcar
30 Apr Tiffany's, Edinburgh
1 May Apollo Theatre, Glasgow
4 May Barbarella's, Birmingham
5 May Essex University, Colchester
6 May Pavilion, Hemel Hempstead
8 May Locarno, Bristol
11 May Mayfair Ballroom, Newcastle
12 May University, Leeds
13 May Lyceum, London
15 May Palace, Paris
16 May Palace, Paris
18 May Paradiso, Amsterdam
19 May Stokuishal, Arnhem
22 May Circus Krone, Munich
24 May Neue Welt, Berlin
25 May Rotation, Hannover
26 May Markthalle, Hamburg
28 May Palasport, Parma
29 May Palalido, Milan
31 May Pabellon del Juventud, Badalona
6 Jun Top Rank, Brighton
8 Jun Hammersmith Odeon, London

*A few European dates missing.*

***New Values*** **North American tour 1979**

27 Oct Showplace, Dover
29 Oct Hot Club, Philadelphia
30 Oct Great American Music Hall, New Haven
31 Oct Palladium, New York
2 Nov Paradise Club, Boston
3 Nov Paradise Club, Boston
4 Nov My Father's Place, New York
5 Nov My Father's Place, New York
6 Nov Paradise Club, Boston

8 Nov Le Plateau Theatre, Montreal
9 Nov Music Hall, Toronto
10 Nov Music Hall, Toronto
12 Nov Agora Ballroom, Cleveland
13 Nov Michigan Theatre, Ann Arbor
14 Nov Masonic Auditorium, Detroit
17 Nov Park West Theatre, Chicago
18 Nov Beginnings Club, Chicago
19 Nov Oriental Theatre, Milwaukee
20 Nov Longhorn Saloon, Minneapolis
23 Nov University of B.C., Vancouver
24 Nov Showbox Club, Seattle
26 Nov Old Waldorf, San Francisco
27 Nov Old Waldorf, San Francisco
28 Nov Old Waldorf, San Francisco
29 Nov Old Waldorf, San Francisco
30 Nov Stardust Ballroom, Los Angeles
4 Dec Tempe
9 Dec Hurrah's, New York

**_Soldier_ UK tour 1980**

2 Feb Friars, Aylesbury
4 Feb City Hall, Newcastle
5 Feb Capitol Theatre, Aberdeen
6 Feb Odeon, Edinburgh
7 Feb Apollo Theatre, Manchester
8 Feb Odeon, Birmingham
10 Feb Locarno, Bristol
12 Feb Hammersmith Palais, London
14 Feb Electric Ballroom, London

**_Soldier_ North American tour 1980**

16 Feb Old Man Rivers, New Orleans
17 Feb Old Man Rivers, New Orleans
18 Feb Old Man Rivers, New Orleans
29 Feb Rutgers University, New Brunswick
1 Mar Emerald City, Cherry Hill
2 Mar Fast Lane, Asbury Park
4 Mar My Father's Place, New York
5 Mar Irving Plaza, New York
7 Mar Orpheum Theatre, Boston
8 Mar Stage West, Hartford
9 Mar Great Gildersleeves, New York
11 Mar Bayou, Washington D.C.
12 Mar William Paterson College, Wayne
13 Mar Hole in the Wall, Rochelle Park
14 Mar Factory, New York
15 Mar Norris Theatre, Norristown
17 Mar Agora Ballroom, Columbus
18 Mar Agora Ballroom, Columbus
19 Mar Centerstage, Canton
20 Mar Motor City Roller Rink, Detroit
21 Mar Riviera Theatre, Chicago
22 Mar University of Illinois, Dekalb
23 Mar Grand Ballroom, Minneapolis
26 Mar Opry House, Lawrence
27 Mar Caines Ballroom, Tulsa
28 Mar Boomer Theatre, Oklahoma City
29 Mar Armadillo World Headquarters, Austin
30 Mar Uncle Sam's, Houston
31 Mar Dooley's, Tempe
2 Apr Roxy, San Diego
4 Apr Palladium, Hollywood
5 Apr Warfield Theatre, San Francisco
8 Apr Agora Ballroom, Fort Lauderdale
9 Apr Agora Ballroom, Fort Lauderdale
10 Apr Agora Ballroom, Tempe
11 Apr Agora Ballroom, Atlanta

**European tour 1980**

24 Apr Markthalle, Hamburg
26 Apr Rotation, Hannover
27 Apr Metropol, Berlin
28 Apr Aladdin, Bremen
29 Apr Sheeta, Bielefeld
30 Apr Satory Saal, Cologne
2 May Harlequin, Brussels
3 May Weissbaden, Wartburg
4 May To Act, Weisenhoe
5 May Schwarbingerbraun, Munich
6 May Volkshaus, Zürich
8 May Palasport, Udine
9 May Palasport, Brescia
10 May Palasport, Pesaro
11 May Stadio, Florence
12 May Palalido, Milan
14 May Grand Odeon, Montpellier
15 May Blau-Grana, Barcelona
18 May Plaza del Torros, Murcia
20 May Real Madrid, Madrid
21 May Salle Belgrave, Bordeaux
22 May Salle de Peuple, Clermont
23 May Palais d'Hiver, Lyon
24 May Maison des Sports, Reims
26 May Studio 44, Rouen
27 May Jacques Brel, Lille
28 May Palais des Sports, Paris
30 May Music Machine, London
31 May Music Machine, London

**_Nightclubbing_ tour 1980**

15 Sep Club 688, Atlanta
16 Sep Club 688, Atlanta
17 Sep Club 688, Atlanta
18 Sep Club 688, Atlanta
19 Sep Club 688, Atlanta
20 Sep Club 688, Atlanta
22 Sep Bookie's, Detroit
23 Sep Bookie's, Detroit
24 Sep Bookie's, Detroit
25 Sep Bookie's, Detroit
26 Sep Bookie's, Detroit
27 Sep Bookie's, Detroit
29 Sep Waves, Chicago
30 Sep Waves, Chicago
1 Oct Waves, Chicago
2 Oct Waves, Chicago
3 Oct Beginnings, Schaumberg
4 Oct Madison
5 Oct Madison
6 Oct Madison

**North American tour 1980**

31 Oct Auditorium, Oakland
1 Nov Catalyst Ballroom, Santa Cruz
2 Nov Catalyst Ballroom, Santa Cruz
5 Nov Commodore Ballroom, Vancouver
6 Nov Commodore Ballroom, Vancouver
7 Nov Showbox, Seattle
8 Nov Showbox, Seattle
11 Nov Civic Auditorium, Santa Monica
12 Nov Bacchanal, San Diego
13 Nov Bacchanal, San Diego
15 Nov Rainbow Music Hall, Denver
18 Nov Opry House, Austin
19 Nov Agora, Dallas
20 Nov Agora, Houston
22 Nov Old Man Rivers, New Orleans
23 Nov Tallahasse
25 Nov Agora Ballroom, Fort Lauderdale
26 Nov Park Avenue, Orlando
29 Nov St. Louis
1 Dec Bogart's, Cincinnati
2 Dec Bogart's, Cincinnati
4 Dec Ontario Theatre, Washington D.C.
5 Dec Emerald City, Philadelphia
6 Dec Malibu Beach Club, Long Island
7 Dec Ritz, New York
8 Dec Paradise Theatre, Boston
9 Dec Nassawa
10 Dec Providence
11 Dec Shaboo Inn, Willimantic

**_Party_ UK/European tour 1981**

11 Jun Odd Fellow Palatset, Copenhagen
12 Jun Markthalle, Hamburg
14 Jun Metropol, Berlin
15 Jun Rotation, Hannover
17 Jun Milan
18 Jun Palasport, Bologna
19 Jun Stadio Communale, Turin
20 Jun Salle des Fetes, Marseille
22 Jun Blau-Grana, Barcelona
23 Jun Rock-Ola, Madrid (2 sets)
25 Jun Pabilliao Infante de Sagres, Porto
26 Jun Cascais
28 Jun Velodromo de Anoetz, San Sebastian
29 Jun Salle du Grand Parc, Bordeaux
30 Jun Baltard, Paris
2 Jul University, Leeds
3 Jul Odeon, Birmingham
4 Jul Apollo Theatre, Manchester
5 Jul City Hall, Newcastle
6 Jul Playhouse, Edinburgh
7 Jul Royal Court, Liverpool
8 Jul Polytechnic, Sheffield
9 Jul Rock City, Nottingham
11 Jul Rainbow Theatre, London

POP
THE ADVERT
INBOW THEAT
ay 30th Septem
PSYCHEDE
HAMMERSM
TUESDAY 12th FE
RAINBOW THEATRE 29
FINSBURY PARK
M.A.M. presents
IGGY POP
at 7. p.m.
Sat. MARCH 5
STALLS £2.00
Including VAT
JADE PRESENTS...
IGGY POP
NOV.14th 8:00pm MASONIC AUD.
FISH & COLDCOCK-TICKETS $7.50 AT B.O.
WED. SEPT 2
THURS. SEPT 3, 9P
$12.50 ADVAN
$15.00 DA
CHOCOLATE
CLUB DE VANGUARDIA
presentan:
IGGY POP
+ HUMAN LEAGUE
JUEVES 31 DE MAYO A LAS 21.30 H. EN EL
PABELLON DEL CLUB JUVENTUD DE BADALONA
№ 00139
CLUB 1018
19TH ST. N.Y.C.
IGGY POP
MUST BE 16
IGGY POP
Special Guest:
BALAAM AND THE ANGEL
THIS FRIDAY, JULY 15 - 8 P.M.
PHANTASY THEATRE
12 Advance, $13 Day of Show
Daddy's Dance Hall
International Concert Organisation A/S
presents:
IGGY POP
Mandag den 19. september 1977 kl. 22.00
Sacs presenterar
IGGY POP
Tillbaka efter förra årets succé!
"Träningshallen" Johanneshov
onsdag 24 maj
THE GLASS SPIDER TOUR
SPECIAL GUEST
IGGY POP
ERIKSBERG – Goteborg
Lordag 27 juni kl. 16.00
7. 7. MÜNCHEN · DEUTSCHE
8. 7. HANNOVER · EILENRIE
10. 7. BERLIN · WALDBÜHNE
11. 7. LORELEY (FESTI
12. 7. HAMBURG · STAD
ARMADILLO WORLD HEADQUARTERS
PRESENTS
IGGY POP
MAR 29 1980
AUSTIN TEXAS
SATURDAY
9:00 P.M.
GEN. ADM.
MAR. 29, 1980
IGGY POP
TWISTED ROOTS DIRTY LOOKS
NOVEMBER 20 9:00 PM
TICKETS $8.50
$9.50 DAY OF SHOW
HOLLYWOOD PALLADIUM
466-4311
THE PALLADIUM
THIS THURSDAY
Iggy
OCT. 6—8
TICKETS $7.50
IGGY POP
GRÖNA LUND
Premier Harbour
PRESENTATION
iGGY POP
IN CONCERT
WITH SPECIAL GUESTS
NEW CHRISTS
(ROB YOUNGER & FRIENDS)
ASTOR THEATRE
FRI JULY 1ST
POP
with special guests: COLDCOCK
At the Motor City Roller Rink
(9 Mile & Van Dyke)
THURSDAY, MARCH 20
Club de Vanguardia y
Disco Expres
presentan a
IGGY POP
MARTES 16 DE MAYO A LAS 22 HORAS
NUEVO PABELLON DEL JUVENTUD DE BADALONA
W THEATRE 505
INTERNATIONAL present
IGGY POP
at 7.30 p.m.
rday JULY 11
STALLS
£4.00
LE PALACE
IGG
POP
LUNDI 13 DÉCEMBRE
20 H. 30
AU

***Party*** **North American tour 1981**
31 Jul Ritz, New York
1 Aug Ritz, New York
2 Aug Ritz, New York
5 Aug Lupo's, Providence
6 Aug Metro, Boston
7 Aug Paramount Theatre, Staten Island
8 Aug Left Bank, Mt. Vernon
9 Aug Toad's Place, New Haven
12 Aug Bogart's, Cincinnati
13 Aug Theatre, Royal Oak
14 Aug Holiday Ballroom, Chicago
15 Aug Park West Theatre, Chicago
16 Aug Duffy's, Minneapolis
17 Aug Duffy's, Minneapolis
19 Aug Opry House, Lawrence
22 Aug Theatre, Royal Oak
23 Aug The Grove, Oakville
24 Aug Second Chance, Ann Arbor
25 Aug Agora Ballroom, Cleveland
26 Aug Penny Arcade, Rochester
28 Aug Ripley Music Hall, Philadelphia
29 Aug Meadowbrook, Cedar Grove
30 Aug Bayou, Washington D.C.
1 Sep Spit, Long Island
2 Sep Savoy, New York
3 Sep Savoy, New York

***Follow The Sun*** **tour 1981**
26 Oct Bus Stop, Lansing
27 Oct Theatre, Royal Oak
29 Oct Pittsburgh
30 Oct Marble Bar, Owingsmills
31 Oct Mosque Ballroom, Richmond
1 Nov Viceroy Park, Charlotte
2 Nov Pier, Raleigh
5 Nov Music Hall, Memphis
6 Nov Agora, Atlanta
7 Nov Main Street, Gainesville
8 Nov Agora, Fort Lauderdale
10 Nov Riverboat President, New Orleans
11 Nov Cardi's, Houston
12 Nov Cardi's, Dallas
13 Nov Club Foot, Austin
14 Nov Club Foot, Austin
17 Nov Dooley's, Tempe
19 Nov Bacchanal, San Diego
20 Nov Palladium, Hollywood
24 Nov Old Waldorf, San Francisco
25 Nov Old Waldorf, San Francisco
27 Nov Sacramento
28 Nov Market Street Theatre, San Francisco
30 Nov Silverdome, Pontiac
1 Dec Silverdome, Pontiac
2 Dec Music Hall, Toronto
3 Dec Music Hall, Toronto
4 Dec Kitchner
5 Dec Ottawa
6 Dec Montreal

***Zombie Birdhouse*** **tour 1982**
13 Oct City Gardens, Trenton
14 Oct Peppermint Lounge, New York
15 Oct Peppermint Lounge, New York
16 Oct Peppermint Lounge, New York
18 Oct Toad's Place, New Haven
19 Oct Chance, Poughkeepsie
20 Oct Channel, Boston
23 Oct Spectrum, Montreal
2 Nov Agora Ballroom, Cleveland
7 Nov Duffy's, Minneapolis
14 Nov Club Foot, Austin
15 Nov Club Foot, Austin
24 Nov Adam's Avenue, San Diego
26 Nov Rissmiller's, Los Angeles
27 Nov Rissmiller's, Los Angeles
9 Dec Ritz, New York
13 Dec Palace, Paris
15 Dec The Venue, London
16 Dec The Venue, London (2 sets)
*Dates missing.*

***The Breaking Point*** **tour 1983**
11 Feb Keystone, Berkeley
12 Feb Keystone, Berkeley
13 Feb Stone, Palo Alto
15 Feb WWU Viking Union Lounge, Bellingham
16 Feb Commodore Ballroom, Vancouver
17 Feb Commodore Ballroom, Vancouver
18 Feb Eagles Hippodrome, Seattle
19 Feb Starry Night, Portland
20 Feb EMU, Eugene
23 Feb Sooner Theatre, Norman
24 Feb Hot Klub, Dallas
25 Feb Club Foot, Austin
26 Feb Bonham Ballroom, San Antonio
27 Feb Mars, Corpus Christi
28 Feb Numbers 2, Houston
2 Mar Trinity's, Baton Rouge
3 Mar Tupelo's, New Orleans
6 Mar Theatre, Tampa
7 Mar Agora, Hallandale
9 Mar I&I, Athens
11 Mar Club 688, Atlanta
12 Mar Alabama
13 Mar Bogart's, Cincinnati
14 Mar Stanley Theatre, Pittsburgh
17 Mar Peppermint Lounge, New York
18 Mar Peppermint Lounge, New York
20 Mar Living Room, Providence
21 Mar Agora Ballroom, New Haven
24 Mar Paradise Club, Boston
25 Mar Uncle Sam's, Hull
26 Mar Zoo, Brooklyn

**Australasian tour 1983**
9 Jun Honolulu
10 Jun Honolulu
11 Jun Honolulu
12 Jun Honolulu
17 Jun Koseinenkin Hall, Osaka
19 Jun Nakano Sun Plaza, Tokyo
20 Jun Nakano Sun Plaza, Tokyo
21 Jun Nihon Seinenkan, Tokyo
28 Jun Capitol Theatre, Sydney
29 Jun Capitol Theatre, Sydney
1 Jul Astor Theatre, Melbourne
2 Jul Seaview Ballroom, Melbourne
3 Jul Seaview Ballroom, Melbourne
5 Jul Cardiff
6 Jul Greenfield Taverna, Newcastle
8 Jul Bombay Rock, Surfers' Paradise
10 Jul Whispers, Brisbane
14 Jul Seals Club, Maroubra
*Possibly further Australian dates.*

***Blah Blah Blah*** **tour 1986**
29 Oct Oscar's, Santa Barbara
30 Oct One Step Beyond, Santa Clara
31 Oct Wolfgang's, San Francisco
2 Nov Palace, Los Angeles
3 Nov Palace, Los Angeles
6 Nov Metro, Chicago
7 Nov Phantasy Theatre, Cleveland
8 Nov St. Andrew's Hall, Detroit
9 Nov Concert Hall, Toronto
11 Nov Metro, Boston
12 Nov Trocadero, Philadelphia
13 Nov Ritz, New York
14 Nov Ritz, New York
23 Nov Zaal Brielpoort, Deinze
24 Nov Muziekcentrum Vredenburg, Utrecht
26 Nov Draken, Stockholm
27 Nov Draken, Stockholm
29 Nov Rockefeller Music Hall, Oslo
30 Nov Falkonerteatret, Copenhagen
2 Dec Metropol, Berlin
3 Dec Knops Musikhalle, Hamburg
4 Dec Philipshalle, Düsseldorf
5 Dec Pfalzbau, Ludwigshafen
7 Dec Musikhalle, Frankfurt
8 Dec Theater, Munich
9 Dec Kurhalle Oberlaa, Vienna
11 Dec Palalido, Milan
12 Dec Volkshaus, Zürich
13 Dec Bourse du Travail, Lyon
15 Dec Grande Halle de la Vilette, Paris
17 Dec Brixton Academy, London
18 Dec Brixton Academy, London

**North American tour with the Pretenders 1987**
14 Jan Plattsburgh
15 Jan Williamsport
16 Jan Williamsburg
18 Jan State College
19 Jan Charlottesville
20 Jan Philadelphia
22 Jan Lexington
23 Jan Atlanta
24 Jan Memphis
25 Jan Nashville

28 Jan Fort Myers
29 Jan Lakeland
30 Jan Miami
5 Feb College Station
6 Feb Houston
7 Feb Lakefront Arena, New Orleans
9 Feb Austin
11 Feb Dallas
12 Feb Norman
15 Feb Denver
17 Feb Tempe
18 Feb Tucson
19 Feb San Diego
21 Feb Sport Arena, Los Angeles
22 Feb Sport Arena, Los Angeles
28 Feb Coliseum, Oakland
2 Mar Wolfgang's, San Francisco (solo)
3 Mar Coliseum, Seattle
5 Mar PNE Coliseum, Vancouver
7 Mar Corral, Calgary
8 Mar Coliseum, Edmonton
10 Mar Arena, Winnipeg
13 Mar Cumberland Civic, Portland
15 Mar Centrum, Worcester
17 Mar Forum, Montreal
18 Mar Civic Center, Ottawa
19 Mar Maple Leaf Gardens, Toronto
21 Mar Ohio Center, Columbus
22 Mar Hara Arena, Dayton
24 Mar Pavilion, Chicago
26 Mar Richfield Coliseum, Cleveland
27 Mar Cobo Hall, Detroit
28 Mar Sports Arena, Toledo
30 Mar Capitol Centre, Washington D.C.
31 Mar Nassau Coliseum, Uniondale
1 Apr Bay Street, Long Island (solo)
2 Apr Park Arena, Hershey
4 Apr Stone Pony, Asbury Park (solo)
5 Apr 1018, New York (solo)

*All dates as opening act for the Pretenders except where noted.*

**Japanese tour 1987**

Apr Osaka
Apr Tokyo
Apr Tokyo

**UK/European tour 1987**

6 Jun Törnävä Festivalpark, Seinäjoki, Provinssirock
8 Jun De Berckt Sportpark, Baarlo, Pinkpop
9 Jun Zenith, Paris
11 Jun Colston Hall, Bristol
12 Jun Royal Concert Hall, Nottingham
14 Jun City Hall, Sheffield
15 Jun City Hall, Newcastle
16 Jun Playhouse, Edinburgh
18 Jun Royal Court, Liverpool
19 Jun Apollo Theatre, Manchester
20 Jun Odeon, Birmingham
23 Jun Hammersmith Odeon, London
24 Jun Hammersmith Odeon, London
27 Jun Eriksbergsvarvet, Gothenburg
28 Jun Oslo, Kalvöyafestivalen
30 Jun Brunnsparken, Örebro
1 Jul Gröna Lund, Stockholm
3 Jul Roskilde, Roskildefestivalen
4 Jul Torhout, Rock Torhout/Werchter
5 Jul Festival Terrein, Werchter, Rock Torhout/Werchter
7 Jul Deutsches Museum, Munich
8 Jul Eilenriedehalle, Hannover
10 Jul Waldbühne, Berlin, Bizarre Festival
11 Jul Freilichtbühne, Loreley, Bizarre Festival
12 Jul Stadtpark, Hamburg

***Instinct* tour 1988**

8 Jul Whisky A Go-Go, Hollywood
9 Jul Scream, Hollywood
10 Jul Fillmore West, San Francisco
12 Jul Metro, Chicago
14 Jul St. Andrew's Hall, Detroit
15 Jul Phantasy Theatre, Cleveland
17 Jul 930 Club, Washington D.C.
18 Jul Chestnut Cabaret, Philadelphia
19 Jul Channel, Boston
20 Jul Ritz, New York
22 Jul City Gardens, Trenton
23 Jul Lobster A Go-Go, Hamptons
24 Jul Toad's Place, New Haven
Aug five dates in South America, including Rio de Janeiro, Sao Paulo, and Buenos Aires
26 Aug Reading Festival
27 Aug Winterthur, Musik Festwoche
30 Aug Tel Aviv

## Line-ups of Iggy's groups

**The Iguanas 1962-65**

Jim McLoughlin (guitar)
Nick Kolokithas
Don Swickerath
Sam Swisher
Iggy (drums)

**The Prime Movers 1965-66**

Daniel Erlewine
Michael Erlewine
Jack Dawson
Robert Sheff
Iggy (drums)

**The Stooges 1967**

Iggy (hawaiian guitar, various instruments)
Ron Asheton (bass)
Scott Asheton (drums)

**The Stooges 1968-April 1970**

Iggy (vocals *from here on* )
Ron Asheton (guitar)
Dave Alexander (bass)
Scott Asheton (drums)

**The Stooges April-August 1970**

Ron Asheton (guitar)
Steven Mackay (sax)
Dave Alexander (bass)
Scott Asheton (drums)

**The Stooges August 1970-late 1970**

Ron Asheton (guitar)
Billy Cheatham (guitar)
Steven Mackay (sax)
Zeke Zettner (bass)
Scott Asheton (drums)

**The Stooges late 1970-early 1971**

Ron Asheton (guitar)
James Williamson (guitar)
Zeke Zettner (bass)
Scott Asheton (drums)

**The Stooges early 1971-July 1971**

Ron Asheton (guitar)
James Williamson (guitar)
Jimmy Recca (bass)
Scott Asheton (drums)

**The Stooges June 1972-spring 1973**

James Williamson (guitar)
Ron Asheton (bass)
Scott Asheton (drums)

**The Stooges spring 1973-February 1974**

James Williamson (guitar)
Scott Thurston (piano, harmonica)
Ron Asheton (bass)
Scott Asheton (drums)

***The Idiot* tour 1977**

Ricky Gardiner (guitar)
David Bowie (keyboards)
Tony Sales (bass)
Hunt Sales (drums)

***Lust For Life* tour 1977**

Stacey Heydon (guitar)
Scott Thurston (keyboards, guitar)
Tony Sales (bass)
Hunt Sales (drums)

***TV Eye* tour 1978**
Fred "Sonic" Smith (guitar)
Scott Thurston (keyboards, guitar)
Gary Rasmusen (bass)
Scott Asheton (drums)

***New Values* UK/European tour 1979**
Jackie Clark (guitar)
Scott Thurston (guitar, keyboards)
Glen Matlock (bass)
Klaus Kruger (drums)

***New Values* North American tour 1979**
Brian James (guitar)
Ivan Kral (keyboards, guitar)
Glen Matlock (bass)
Klaus Kruger (drums)

***Soldier* UK tour 1980**
Rob Duprey (guitar)
Ivan Kral (keyboards, guitar)
Billy Rath (bass)
Klaus Kruger (drums)

***Soldier* North American tour 1980, European tour 1980, *Nightclubbing* tour 1980, North American tour 1980**
Rob Duprey (guitar)
Ivan Kral (keyboards, guitar)
Michael Page (bass)
Douglas Bowne (drums)

***Party* UK/European tour 1981**
Rob Duprey (guitar)
Ivan Kral (guitar)
Richard Sohl (keyboards)
Michael Page (bass)
Douglas Bowne (drums)

***Party* North American tour 1981**
Rob Duprey (guitar)
Gary Valentine (guitar)
Richard Sohl (keyboards)
Michael Page (bass)
Douglas Bowne (drums)

***Follow The Sun* tour 1981**
Rob Duprey (guitar)
Carlos Alomar (guitar)
Gary Valentine (guitar)
Michael Page (bass)
Clem Burke (drums)

***Zombie Birdhouse* tour 1982, *The Breaking Point* tour 1983, Australasian tour 1983**
Frank Infante (guitar)
Rob Duprey (guitar, keyboards)
Michael Page (bass)
Larry Mysliewicz (drums)

***Blah Blah Blah* tour 1986**
Kevin Armstrong (guitar)
Shamus Beghan (keyboards, guitar)
Phil Butcher (bass)
Gavin Harrison (drums)

**North American tour with the Pretenders 1987, Japanese tour 1987**
Kevin Armstrong (guitar)
Shamus Beghan (keyboards, guitar)
Phil Butcher (bass)
Andy Anderson (drums)

**UK/European tour 1987**
Kevin Armstrong (guitar)
Shamus Beghan (keyboards, guitar)
Barry Adamson (bass)
Andy Anderson (drums)

***Instinct* tour 1988**
Andy McCoy (guitar)
Shamus Beghan (keyboards, guitar)
Alvin Gibbs (bass)
Paul Garisto (drums)

# DISCOGRAPHY

## Albums

*UK/US discography. Only foreign releases of interest included.*

**The Stooges: *The Stooges***
1969 ; I Wanna Be Your Dog ; We Will Fall ; No Fun ; Real Cool Time ; Ann ; Not Right ; Little Doll.
Producer: John Cale.
Released: Elektra EKS 74051 August 1969 (US), September 1969 (UK). Reissued as Elektra K 42032 in March 1977 (UK).

**The Stooges: *Fun House***
Down On The Street ; Loose ; TV Eye ; Dirt ; 1970 ; Fun House ; LA Blues.
Producer: Don Gallucci.
Released: Elektra EKS 74071 August 1970 (US), December 1970 (UK). Reissued as Elektra K 42055 in March 1977 (UK).

**Iggy and the Stooges: *Raw Power***
Search And Destroy ; Gimme Danger ; Your Pretty Face Is Going To Hell ; Penetration ; Raw Power ; I Need Somebody ; Shake Appeal ; Death Trip.
Producer: Iggy Pop.
Released: Columbia KC 32111 May 1973 (US), CBS 65586 June 1973 (UK). Reissued as CBS Embassy 31464 in May 1977 (UK) and as CBS 32083 in November 1981 (UK).

**Iggy and the Stooges: *Metallic KO***
Raw Power ; Head On ; Gimme Danger ; Rich Bitch* ; Cock In My Pocket* ; Louie Louie*.
Recorded: Michigan Palace, Detroit, October 6, 1973. *Michigan Palace, Detroit, February 9, 1974 (last performance).
Released: Skydog SGIS 008 1976 (France). Reissued by Import Records as Import IMP 1015 in 1977 (US).

**Iggy Pop: *The Idiot***
Sister Midnight ; Nightclubbing ; Funtime ; Baby ; China Girl ; Dum Dum Boys ; Tiny Girls ; Mass Production.
Producer: David Bowie.
Released: RCA PL 12275 March 1977

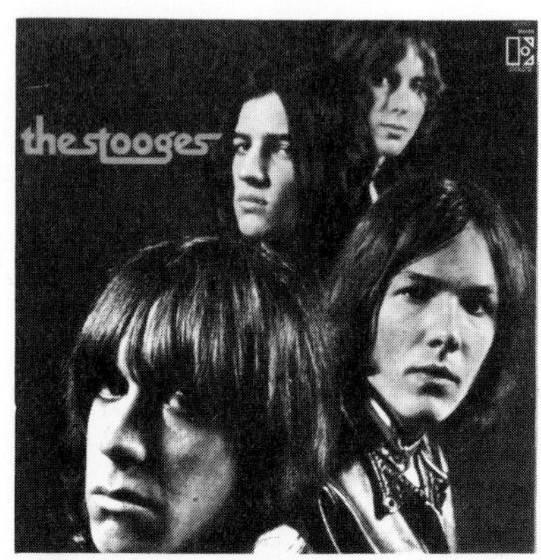
the stooges

IGGY POP
The Idiot

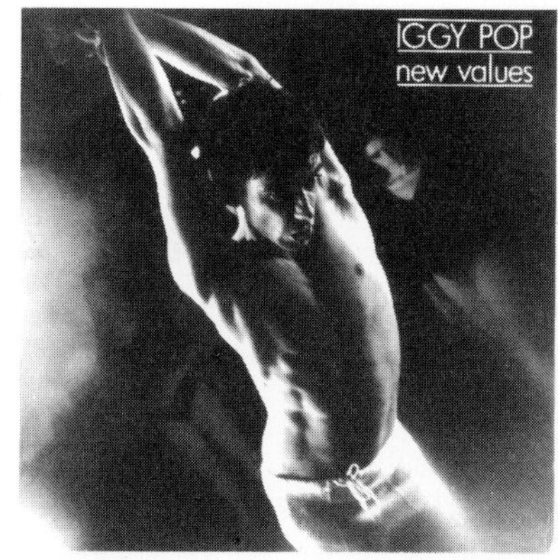
IGGY POP
new values

the stooges
fun house

Iggy Pop
Lust For Life

IGGY POP
SOLDIER

IGGY POP & JAMES WILLIAMSON
KILL
CITY

iGGY POP

METALLIC 'KO
IGGY AND THE STOOGES

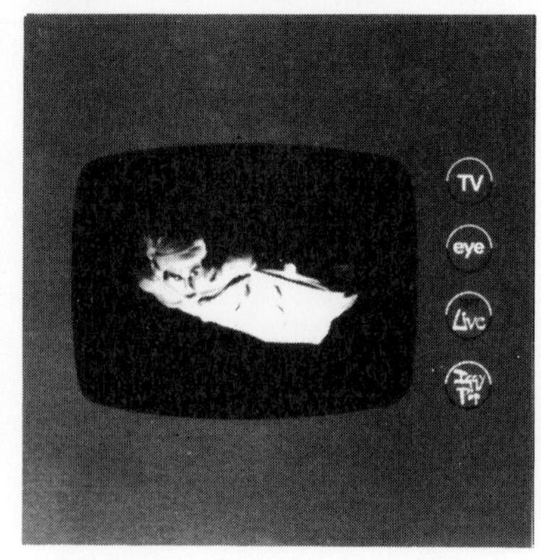
TV
eye
Live

gy Pop "Zombie Birdhouse"

(UK), RCA APL1-2275 March 1977 (US). Reissued as RCA International INTS 5172 in October 1981 and as RCA NL 82275 in October 1984.

**Iggy Pop: *Lust For Life***
Lust For Life ; Sixteen ; Some Weird Sin ; The Passenger ; Tonight ; Success ; Turn Blue ; Neighbourhood Threat ; Fall In Love With Me.
Producer: David Bowie.
Released: RCA PL 12488 September 1977 (UK), RCA APL1-2488 September 1977 (US). Reissued as RCA International INTS 5114 in October 1981 and as RCA NL 82488 in October 1984.

**Iggy Pop and James Williamson: *Kill City***
Kill City ; Sell Your Love ; Beyond The Law ; I Got Nothin' ; Johanna ; Night Theme ; Night Theme (reprise) ; Consolation Prizes ; No Sense Of Crime ; Lucky Monkeys ; Master Charge.
Producer: James Williamson.
Released: Bomp BLP 4001 November 1977 (US), also available on green vinyl. Issued by Radar Records as Radar RAD 2 in February 1978 (UK). Reissued as Visa IMR 1018 in 1978 (US), Line LLP 5157 in 1982 (Germany), and Line LILP 4.00131 (white vinyl) in 1986 (Germany).

**Iggy Pop: *TV Eye Live 1977***
TV Eye* ; Funtime* ; Sixteen ; I Got A Right ; Lust For Life ; Dirt* ; Nightclubbing ; I Wanna Be Your Dog**.
Producers: Iggy Pop and David Bowie.
Recorded: Uptown Theatre, Kansas City, October 26, 1977. *Agora Ballroom, Cleveland, March 21/22, 1977. **Aragon, Chicago, March 28, 1977.
Released: RCA PL 12796 May 1978 (UK), RCA APL1-2796 May 1978 (US).

**Iggy Pop: *New Values***
Tell Me A Story ; New Values ; Girls ; I'm Bored ; Don't Look Down ; The Endless Sea ; Five Foot One ; How Do Ya Fix A Broken Part ; Angel ; Curiosity ; African Man ; Billy Is A Runaway.
Producer: James Williamson.
Released: Arista SPART 1092 April 1979 (UK), Arista 4237 October 1979 (US).

**Iggy Pop: *Soldier***
Loco Mosquito ; Ambition ; Take Care Of Me ; Get Up And Get Out ; Play It Safe ; I'm A Conservative ; Dog Food ; I Need More ; Knocking 'Em Down ; Mr. Dynamite ; I Snub You.
Producer: Pat Moran.
Released: Arista SPART 1117 February 1980 (UK), Arista 4259 February 1980 (US).

**Iggy Pop: *Party***
Pleasure ; Rock And Roll Party ; Eggs On Plate ; Sincerity ; Houston Is Hot Tonight ; Pumpin' For Jill ; Happy Man ; Bang Bang* ; Sea Of Love* ; Time Won't Let Me*.
Producer: Thom Panunzio, *Tommy Boyce.
Released: Arista SPART 1158 June 1981 (UK), Arista 4278 September 1981 (US).

**Iggy Pop: *Zombie Birdhouse***
Run Like A Villain ; The Villagers ; Angry Hills ; Life Of Work ; The Ballad Of Cookie McBride ; Ordinary Bummer ; Eat Or Be Eaten ; Bulldozer ; Platonic ; The Horse Song ; Watching The News ; Street Crazies.
Producer: Chris Stein.
Released: Animal CHR 1399 September 1982 (UK), Animal APE 6000 September 1982 (US).

**Iggy Pop: *Blah Blah Blah***
Real Wild Child ; Baby, It Can't Fall ; Shades ; Fire Girl ; Isolation ; Cry For Love ; Blah Blah Blah ; Hideaway ; Winners And Losers.
Producers: David Bowie and David Richards.
Released: A&M AMA 5145 October 1986 (UK), A&M SP 5145 October 1986 (US).

**The Stooges: *Rubber Legs***
Rubber Legs ; Open Up And Bleed ; Johanna ; Cock In My Pocket ; Head On ; Cry For Me.
Recorded: Studio rehearsal, early 1973.
Released: Fan Club FC 037 November 1987 (France).

**Iggy and the Stooges: *Death Trip***
Death Trip* ; Head On ; Rubber Legs ; radio ad ; Raw Power ; I'm A Man** ; The Ballad Of Hollis Brown**.
Recorded: Studio rehearsal 1973. *Different mix of the *Raw Power* track. **Iggy Pop/James Williamson jams, 1972/73. Radio ad from St. Louis, August 17, 1973.
Released: Revenge MIG6 March 1988 (France). Also available as picture disc, Revenge MIG6P.

**Iggy and the Stooges: *Metallic 2xKO***
Raw Power ; Head On ; Gimme Danger ; Search And Destroy ; Heavy Liquid ; Open Up And Bleed ; I Got Nothin'* ; Rich Bitch* ; Cock In My Pocket* ; Louie Louie*.
Recorded: Michigan Palace, Detroit, October 6, 1973. *Michigan Palace, Detroit, February 9, 1974 (last Stooges performance).
Released: Skydog SKI 622321 March 1988 (France). Double LP.

**Iggy Pop: *Instinct***
Cold Metal ; High On You ; Strong Girl ; Tom Tom ; Easy Rider ; Power & Freedom ; Lowdown ; Instinct ; Tuff Baby ; Squarehead.
Producer: Bill Laswell.
Released: A&M AMA 5198 June 1988 (UK), A&M SP 5198 June 1988 (US).

## Compilation albums

**The Stooges featuring Iggy Pop: *No Fun***
1969 ; Real Cool Time ; No Fun ; Dirt ; Down On The Street ; Loose ; TV Eye ; I Wanna Be Your Dog ; 1970.
Released: Elektra K 52234 August 1980 (UK), Elektra EF 7095 August 1980 (US). The US version is credited to Iggy and the Stooges.

**Iggy and the Stooges: *I'm Sick Of You***
I'm Sick Of You ; Tight Pants ; I Got A Right ; Johanna ; Consolation Prizes ; Scene Of The Crime ; Gimme Some Skin ; Jesus Loves The Stooges.
Released: Line LLP 5126 1981 (Germany). Reissued as Line LILP 4.00093 in 1986 (white vinyl). Also issued as Disc AZ 2414 in 1981 (France).

**Iggy Pop: *I Got A Right***
I'm Sick Of You ; Tight Pants ; I Got A Right ; Scene Of The Crime ; Gimme Some Skin ; Kill City ; I Got Nothin' ; Johanna ; Consolation Prizes ; No Sense Of Crime ; Lucky Monkeys.
Released: Invasion/Enigma E 1019 1983 (US).

**Iggy Pop: *Iggy Pop***
Tell Me A Story ; New Values ; Girls ; The Endless Sea ; Five Foot One ; Don't Look Down ; I'm Bored ; How Do Ya Fix A Broken Part ; Angel ; Curiosity ;

BLAH . BLAH . BLAH

IGGY POP

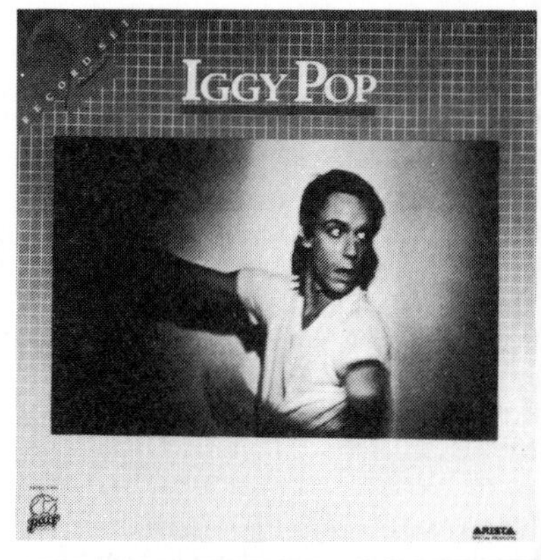
IGGY POP
ARISTA

the Stooges
Rubber legs

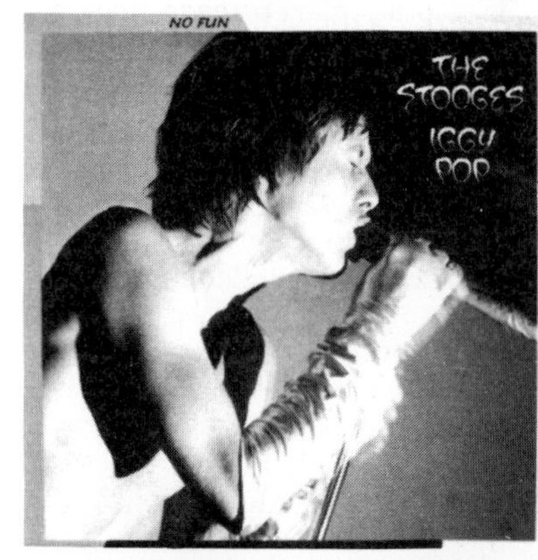
NO FUN
THE STOOGES
IGGY POP

IGGY
POP
CHOICE CUTS

IGGY
AND THE
STOOGES

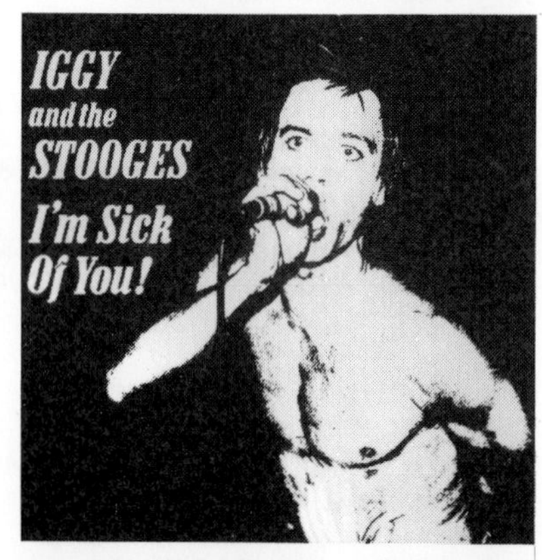
IGGY
and the
STOOGES
I'm Sick
Of You!

IGGY POP
I GOT A RIGHT

METALLIC 2x KO
IGGY AND THE STOOGES

IGGY
POP
I Got a Right

THE BEST OF
BOMP
IGGY and The STOOGES
The WEIRDOS
The FLAMIN' GROOVIES
The POPPEES
SHOES

African Man ; Billy Is A Runaway ; Get Up And Get Out ; I Snub You ; Eggs On Plate ; Sincerity.
Released: Arista ARPDL 2-1051 1984 (US). Double LP.

**Iggy Pop: *Choice Cuts***
China Girl ; Nightclubbing ; Sister Midnight ; Funtime ; Baby ; Lust For Life ; Sixteen ; Some Weird Sin ; The Passenger ; Neighbourhood Threat.
Released: RCA PL 84957 September 1984 (Germany).

**Iggy Pop: *I Got A Right***
I Got A Right ; I'm Sick Of You ; I Got Nothin' ; Beyond The Law ; Johanna ; Gimme Some Skin ; Scene Of The Crime ; Consolation Prizes ; Kill City.
Released: Revenge Mig 2 1987 (France).

## Albums with Iggy tracks

***Garden Of Delights***
Down On The Street.
Released: Elektra S3-10 1971 (US).

***The Guitars That Destroyed The World***
Search And Destroy.
Released: CBS S 65654 1973 (Holland).

***Michigan Rocks***
1969.
Released: Seeds and Stems 77001 1977 (US).

***Punk Collection***
Funtime.
Released: RCA PL 42339 1977 (Italy).

***The Best Of Bomp***
Gimme Some Skin ; I Got A Right.
Released: Bomp LP 4002 1978 (US). Reissued as Line LLP 5006 in 1979 (Germany) and Disc AZ 2428 in 1982 (France).

***La Creme De Skydog***
Open Up And Bleed (Michigan Palace, February 9, 1974).
Released: Skydog SGC 0017 1978 (France).

***Animal Sampler***
The Horse Song ; The Villagers.
Released: Animal CAGE 1 1982 (UK).

***Repo Man***
Repo Man.
Released: MCA MCF 3223 1984 (UK). MCA 250683-1 1984 (Germany).

***Elektrock***
1969 ; I Wanna Be Your Dog ; No Fun ; TV Eye ; 1970.
Released: Elektra 960403-1 1985 (US).

***Dogs In Space***
Dog Food ; Endless Sea.
Released: MMA Music MX 218329 1986 (Australia).

***High In The Mid-60's (Pebbles Vol. 19)***
Again And Again.
Released: Pacific IAP 10028 1986 (US). The track is an outtake from the Iguanas' "Mona" session, but this one supposedly has Iggy singing lead vocals.

## Guest appearances by Iggy

**David Bowie: *Low***
What In The World.
Released: RCA PL 12030 January 1977 (UK), RCA APL1-2030 January 1977 (US).

**David Bowie: *Tonight***
Dancing With The Big Boys.
Released: EMI America DB1 September 1984 (UK/US).

**Ryuichi Sakamoto: *Neo Geo***
Risky.
Released: CBS 460095 October 1987 (UK).

## Singles and EPs

*UK/US discography. Only foreign releases of interest included.*

**1965**
The Iguanas: Mona / I Don't Know Why.
Forte 201 (US).

**1969**
The Stooges: I Wanna Be Your Dog / 1969.
Elektra 45664 (US).

**1970**
The Stooges: Down On The Street / I Feel Alright (1970).
Elektra 45695 (US).

**1973**
Iggy and the Stooges: Search And Destroy / Penetration.
Columbia 45877 (US).

**1977**
Iggy Pop: China Girl / Baby.
RCA PB 9093 (UK).

Iggy Pop: Sister Midnight / Baby.
RCA 10989 (US).

Iggy Pop: Success / The Passenger.
RCA PB 9160 (UK).

Iggy and the Stooges: I Got A Right / Gimme Some Skin.
Siamese PM 001 (US) and (France).

Iggy and the Stooges: *I'm Sick Of You* EP: I'm Sick Of You / Tight Pants ; Scene Of The Crime.
Bomp EP 113 (US). Reissued as 12" EP as Line LMS 3009 in 1979 (Germany).

Iggy Pop and James Williamson: *Jesus Loves The Stooges* EP: Consolation Prizes ; Johanna / Jesus Loves The Stooges.
Bomp EP 114 (US). Reissued as 12" EP as Line LMS 3006 in 1979 (Germany).

**1978**
Iggy and the Stooges: *(I Got) Nothing* EP: Gimme Danger / Heavy Liquid ; I Got Nothing.
Skydog SGIS 12 (France). 12" record. Recorded live at Michigan Palace, Detroit, February 9, 1974.

Iggy Pop and James Williamson: Kill City / I Got Nothin'.
Radar ADA 4 (UK).

Iggy Pop: I Got A Right / Sixteen.
RCA PB 9213 (UK).

**1979**
Iggy Pop: I'm Bored / African Man.
Arista ARIST 255 (UK).

Iggy Pop: Five Foot One / Pretty Flamingo.
Arista ARIST 274 (UK). Also available as picture disc: ARIPD 274.

Iggy Pop: I'm Bored / African Man.
Arista ARIST 0438 (US).

**1980**
Iggy Pop: Loco Mosquito / Take Care Of Me.
Arista ARIST 327 (UK).

**1981**
Iggy Pop: Bang Bang / Sea Of Love.
Arista ARIST 407 (UK).

Iggy Pop: Pumpin' For Jill / Time Won't Let Me.
Arista ARI 8112 (US).

**1982**
Iggy Pop: The Passenger / Nightclubbing.
RCA GOLD 549 (UK).

Iggy Pop: Run Like A Villain / Platonic.
Chrysalis CH FLY 2634 (UK).

**1986**
Iggy Pop: Cry For Love / Winners And Losers.
A&M AM 358 (UK).

Iggy Pop: Cry For Love (dance mix) / Cry For Love (edited) ; Winners And Losers.
A&M AMY 358 (UK). 12" record.

Iggy Pop: Cry For Love / Winners And Losers.
A&M AM 2874 (US).

Iggy Pop: Cry For Love (dance mix) / Cry For Love (edited) ; Little Miss Emperor.
A&M AM SP-12203 (US). 12" record.

Iggy Pop: Real Wild Child / Little Miss Emperor.
A&M AM 368 (UK).

Iggy Pop: Real Wild Child (extended) / Real Wild Child ; Little Miss Emperor.
A&M AMY 368 (UK). 12" record.

**1987**
Iggy Pop: Real Wild Child / Fire Girl.
A&M AM 2909 (US).

Iggy Pop: Shades / Baby, It Can't Fall.
A&M AM 374 (UK).

Iggy Pop: Shades ; Cry For Love (extended) / Baby, It Can't Fall (extended).
A&M AMY 374 (UK). 12" record.

Iggy Pop: Fire Girl / Blah Blah Blah (live Zürich, December 12, 1986).
A&M AM 392 (UK).

Iggy Pop: Fire Girl (remix) / Fire Girl ; Blah Blah Blah (live Zürich).
A&M AMY 392 (UK). 12" record.

Iggy Pop: Isolation / Hideaway.
A&M AM 397 (UK). Available with poster cover.

Ryuichi Sakamoto: Risky / Sakamoto track.
CBS 6510177 (UK). Iggy sings on A-side.

Ryuichi Sakamoto: Risky / Sakamoto tracks.
CBS 6510176 (UK). 12" record.

Iggy Pop: I Got A Right / No Sense Of Crime.
Revenge SS1 (France). Coloured vinyl.

The Stooges: Gimme Danger / I Need Somebody.
Fan Club Stooges 1 (not sold separately from *Rubber Legs* LP).

**1988**
Iggy and the Stooges: *Pure Lust* EP: I Got A Right ; Johanna / Gimme Some Skin ; I Got Nothin'.
Revenge CAX1 (France). 12" record. Coloured vinyl.

Iggy and the Stooges: Johanna / Purple Haze.
Revenge SS6 (France). Coloured vinyl.

Iggy and the Stooges: *Raw Power* EP: Raw Power ; Head On / Purple Haze ; Waiting For The Man ; radio ad.
Revenge CAX2 (France). 12" record. Coloured vinyl.

Iggy and the Stooges: *Gimme Danger* EP: Gimme Danger ; Open Up And Bleed / Heavy Liquid ; I Got Nothin' ; Dynamite Boogie.
Revenge CAX3 (France). 12" record. Coloured vinyl.

## Bootlegs

**Iggy Pop: *A Real Wild Child***
I Got A Right ; Gimme Danger ; Some Weird Sin ; Real Wild Child ; Sister Midnight ; Blah Blah Blah ; Nightclubbing ; Fire Girl ; Five Foot One ; Shades ; Loose ; TV Eye ; Down On The Street ; China Girl ; The Passenger ; Winners And Losers ; Lust For Life ; Raw Power ; Cry For Love ; Search And Destroy.
Recorded: Musikhalle, Frankfurt, December 7, 1986. Double LP.

**Iggy Pop, David Bowie: *Alarm***
China Girl* ; Sister Midnight ; China Girl ; Bowie tracks.
Recorded: Mantra Studios, Chicago, March 28, 1977. *Agora Ballroom, Cleveland, March 22, 1977. LP.

**Iggy Pop: *Beat My Brain***
The Passenger* / Lust For Life ; Funtime ; No Fun.
Recorded: Agora Ballroom, Cleveland, March 22, 1977. *Daddy's Dance Hall, Copenhagen, September 19, 1977. 7" EP. Reissued with a different cover.

**Iggy Pop, David Bowie: *Black Sheep Boys Remixed***
Nightclubbing* ; The Passenger** ; I'm Crying*** ; Hang On Sloopy ; Hassles ; Ordinary Bummer ; Street Crazies ; Gloria ; Bowie tracks.
Recorded: Keystone, Berkeley, February 12, 1983.
*L'Hippodrome, Paris, September 23, 1977. **Markthalle, Hamburg, September 17, 1977. ***The Grove, Oakville, August 23, 1981. LP.

**Iggy Pop: *Cry For Love***
Some Weird Sin ; Real Wild Child ; Sister Midnight ; Blah Blah Blah ; Baby, It Can't Fall ; Nightclubbing ; Fire Girl ; Five Foot One ; Loose ; TV Eye ; The Passenger ; Lust For Life ; Nightclubbing ; Fire Girl ; I Got A Right ; TV Eye ; Down On The Street ; China Girl ; Cry For Love.
Recorded: Muziekcentrum Vredenburg, Utrecht, November 24, 1986. Double LP.

**Iggy Pop: *Duet At The Mantra***
I Need Somebody* ; Dirt* ; Funtime* ; Mass Production** ; Shake Appeal ; Search And Destroy ; Raw Power ; Hard To Beat ; Loose**.
Recorded: Original mix of *Raw Power*. *Mantra Studios, Chicago, March 28, 1977. ** Live 1983. LP.

**Various artists: *Echoes In Time, Volume 2***
Mona ; other artists.
Recorded: Iguanas' single. LP.

**Iggy Pop: *Fire Engine***
Fire Engine / Warrior Tribe.
Recorded: Synchro Sound Studios, Boston, 1983. Produced by Ric Ocasek. 7" single.

**Iggy Pop: *Garden Of Evil***
Repo Man(1) ; Warrior Tribe(2) ; 96 Tears(3) ; Flesh And Blood(4) ; One For

My Baby(5) ; Fire Engine(2) ; Fortune Teller(6) ; Search And Destroy(7) ; Driftin' From Town To Town(8) ; Old Mule Skinner(2) ; Pretty Flamingo(9) ; Speak To Me(10) ; Puppet World(11).
Recorded: (1)From the soundtrack album. (2)Synchro Sound Studios, Boston, 1983. (3)Seaview Ballroom, Melbourne, July 2, 1983. (4)Metropol, Berlin, June 14, 1981. (5)Stardust Ballroom, Los Angeles, November 30, 1979. (6)"The Old Grey Whistle Test" BBC TV, April 24, 1979. (7)Mantra Studios, Chicago, March 28, 1977. (8)KROQ, Los Angeles, April 1974. (9)Single b-side. (10)Outtake from *Party*. (11)Bookie's, Detroit, September 26, 1980. LP.

**Iggy Pop: *Heroin Hates You***
Real Cool Time ; Knocking 'Em Down ; Take Care Of Me ; Dog Food ; You Really Got Me ; New Values ; TV Eye ; Play It Safe ; Funtime ; I Wanna Be Your Dog ; One For My Baby ; China Girl ; Five Foot One ; No Fun ; Jenny Take A Ride* ; Neighbourhood Threat* ; That's How Strong My Love Is* ; Gloria**.
Recorded: Stardust Ballroom, Los Angeles, November 30, 1979. *L'Hippodrome, Paris, September 23, 1977. **State University, San Diego, November 16, 1977. Double LP.

**Iggy Pop: *His Hausmeister's Voice***
Eggs On Plate ; Bang Bang ; Funtime ; Rock And Roll Party ; Lust For Life ; Dog Food ; New Values ; Sincerity ; Five Foot One ; Louie Louie ; Flesh And Blood ; Search And Destroy.
Recorded: Metropol, Berlin, June 14, 1981. LP.

**Sonic Youth: *I Wanna Be Your Dog***
I Wanna Be Your Dog / Sister.
Recorded: A-side live with Iggy, Town & Country Club, London, June 4, 1987. 7" single.

**Iggy Pop: *Iggy & Ziggy***
Raw Power ; 1969 - No Fun - 96 Tears ; Gimme Danger ; Sister Midnight ; Search And Destroy ; I Wanna Be Your Dog ; China Girl.
Recorded: Paramount Theatre, Seattle, April 9, 1977. LP.

**Iggy Pop: *I'm The Original One***
I'm The Original One / Speak To Me.
Recorded: *Party* outtakes. 7" single.

**Iggy Pop: *Interview Picture Disc***
Interview.
Recorded: England 1986. LP.

**Iggy Pop: *Kinky Busyness***
I Got A Right ; Gimme Danger ; Shades ; TV Eye ; Down On The Street ; China Girl ; Loose ; Winners And Losers ; Lust For Life ; Raw Power ; Cry For Love ; Search And Destroy.
Recorded: Volkshaus, Zürich, December 12, 1986. LP.

**Iggy Pop, David Bowie: *Kiss Away The Darkest Day***
Raw Power ; TV Eye ; Gimme Danger ; No Fun ; Search And Destroy ; I Wanna Be Your Dog ; Turn Blue ; Bowie tracks.
Recorded: Mantra Studios, Chicago, March 28, 1977. LP.

**Iggy Pop, David Bowie: *The Laecherling***
Dirt* ; I Need Somebody* ; Funtime* ; Shake Appeal ; Search And Destroy ; Raw Power ; Hard To Beat ; Bowie tracks.
Recorded: Original mix of *Raw Power*. *Mantra Studios, Chicago, March 28, 1977. LP.

**Iggy Pop, David Bowie: *Liquor & Drugs***
Re-release of *Kiss Away The Darkest Day*.

**Iggy Pop: *Liquor And Drugs***
Brakes On ; One For My Baby ; I'm The Original One ; Speak To Me ; There Is A Place* ; Crawling King Snake* ; Fire Engine** ; Warrior Tribe** ; Old Mule Skinner**.
Recorded: *Party* outtakes. *Brunnsparken, Örebro, May 27, 1978 (jam before concert). **Synchro Sound Studios, Boston, 1983, sessions with Ric Ocasek. LP.

**Iggy Pop: *Live At San Diego Sport Center***
Hassles / Louie Louie - Hang On Sloopy.
Recorded: Keystone, Berkeley, February 12, 1983 (not San Diego). 7" single.

**Iggy Pop, David Bowie: *Missing Link***
Bowie tracks ; Gloria ; Louie Louie ; Ordinary Bummer.
Recorded: Live 1983. LP

**The Iguanas: *Mona***
Mona / I Don't Know Why.
Recorded: A pirate of the original recording. 7" single.

**Iggy Pop and the Stooges: *Night Of The Iguana***
Raw Power ; Rich Bitch ; Wet My Bed ; I Got Nothin' ; Cock In My Pocket ; Search And Destroy ; Gimme Danger ; Heavy Liquid.
Recorded: Academy of Music, New York, December 31, 1973. LP.

**Iggy Pop: *Nightclubbing***
One Two Brown Eyes ; I Wanna Be Your Dog ; Modern Guy ; Lust For Life ; Rock Action ; Fall In Love With Me ; Shake Appeal ; Gloria ; TV Eye ; Nightclubbing ; I Got A Right ; Raw Power ; One For My Baby* ; The Passenger** ; Real Cool Time*** ; Knocking 'Em Down*** ; Dog Food*** ; You Really Got Me*** ; New Values*** ; TV Eye*** ; Play It Safe*** ; Funtime*** ; No Fun***.
Recorded: State University, San Diego, November 16, 1977. *Palais d'Hiver, Lyon, May 23, 1980. **Berlin, September 18, 1977. ***Old Waldorf, San Francisco, November 27, 1979. Double LP.

**Various artists: *Ohne Titel***
Mona ; I Don't Know Why ; The Passenger* ; live jam* ; That's How Strong My Love Is - Fame** ; other artists.
Recorded: The Iguanas 1965 single. *Brunnsparken, Örebro, May 27, 1978 (pre-concert jam). ***Lust For Life* tour 1977. LP.

**Iggy and the Stooges: *Open Up And Bleed***
Open Up And Bleed / Open Up And Bleed.
Recorded: Whisky A Go-Go, Hollywood, September 16, 1973. 7" single.

**Iggy Pop: *Out On The Edge***
Fall In Love With Me* / Girls ; Kill City.
Recorded: *TV Eye* tour 1978. *Markthalle, Hamburg, September 17, 1977. 7" EP.

**Iggy Pop: *Paris Palace***
Cock In My Pocket ; Kill City ; Fortune Teller ; New Values ; Billy Is A Runaway ; I Wanna Be Your Dog ; Five Foot One ; Dirt ; Batman Theme ; Louie Louie ; Shake Appeal ; I'm Bored.
Recorded: Palace, Paris, May 16, 1979. LP.

IGGY
POP
CRY
FOR
LOVE

THE LAECHERLING
& BRIAN ENO

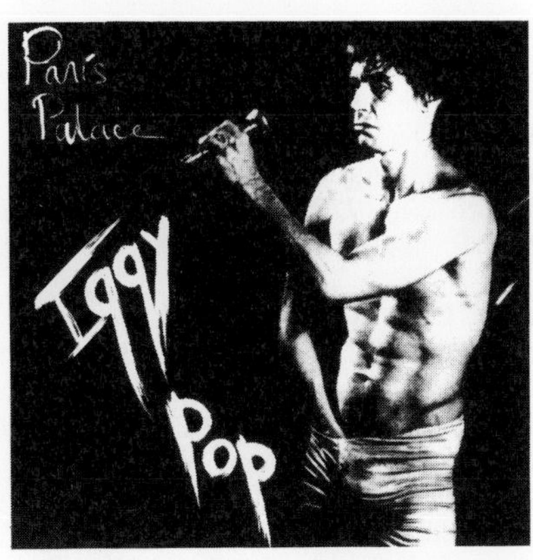
Paris Palace
Iggy Pop

IGGY POP
STOWAWAY D.O.A.
FEATURING DAVID BOWIE

Liquor And Drugs
Iggy Pop

STEREO
IGGY POP
PRIMEVIL
Vol. 2

Iggy Pop
Suck
On This

IGGY POP & STOOGES
night of the iguana
1: Raw Power
Head On
Wet My Bed
I Got Nothing
2: I Got A Cock -
In My Pocket
Search & Destroy
Gimme Danger
New Orleans
Rich Bitch
LIVE IN NEW YORK 1973
BANG

STEREO
IGGY POP
Vol. 3
PRIMEVIL

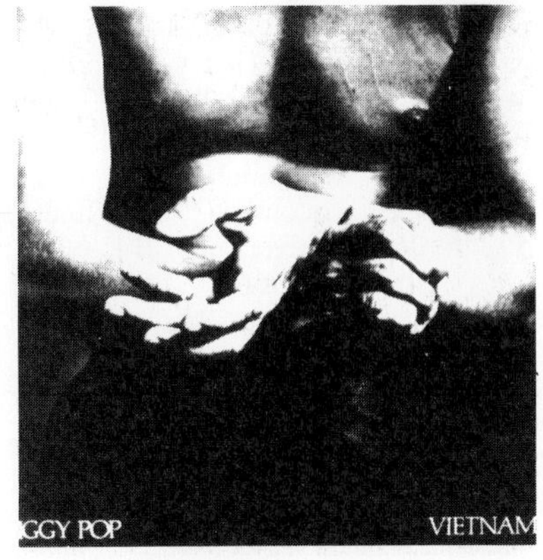
GGY POP
VIETNAM

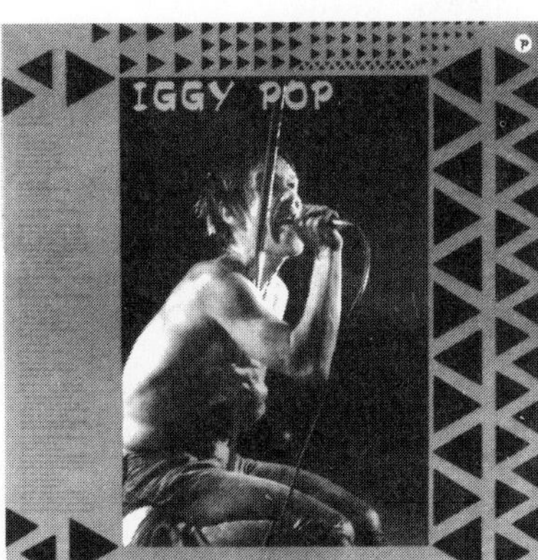
IGGY POP

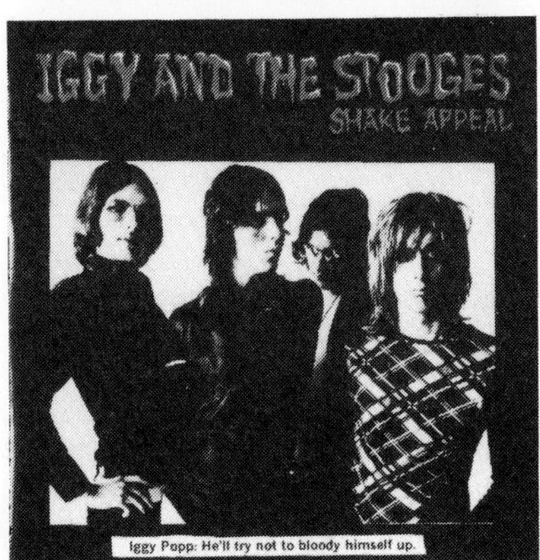
IGGY AND THE STOOGES
SHAKE APPEAL
Iggy Popp: He'll try not to bloody himself up.

IGGY POP
The Wild One

**Iggy Pop: *Primevil Live 1983***
Fire Engine ; Loose ; Penetration ; Fortune Teller ; Five Foot One ; No Fun - Waiting For The Man ; I'm Bored ; One For My Baby ; Run Like A Villain ; Louie Louie ; I'm A Conservative ; Mass Production ; Dum Dum Boys.
Recorded: Seaview Ballroom, Melbourne, July 3, 1983. LP.

**Iggy Pop: *Primevil Vol. 2***
Mona(1) ; TV Eye(2) ; 1970(2) ; Open Up And Bleed(3) ; Wet My Bed(4) ; I Got Nothin'(5) ; Raw Power(6) ; Fame(7) ; Shake Appeal(8) ; The Passenger(9) ; On Every Other Street(9) ; Flesh And Blood(10) ; 96 Tears(11).
Recorded: (1)The Iguanas' single. (2)Crosley Field, Cincinnati, Cincinnati Pop Festival, June 13, 1970. (3)American Theatre, St. Louis, August 18, 1973. (4)Bimbo's, San Francisco, January 1974. (5)Michigan Palace, Detroit, February 9, 1974. (6)Mantra Studios, Chicago, March 28, 1977. (7)*Lust For Life* tour 1977. (8)Markthalle, Hamburg, September 17, 1977. (9)Brunnsparken, Örebro, May 27, 1978. (10)Metropol, Berlin, June 14, 1981. (11)Seaview Ballroom, Melbourne, July 2, 1983. LP.

**Iggy Pop: *Primevil Vol. 3***
Gimme Danger(1) ; Heavy Liquid(1) ; Cock In My Pocket(2) ; I Need Somebody(2) ; That's How Strong My Love Is(3) ; Nightclubbing(4) ; The Winter Of My Discontent(5) ; The End(5) ; I'm A Conservative(5) ; Kill City(6) ; Dirt(6) ; Batman Theme(6).
Recorded: (1)Michigan Palace, Detroit, February 9, 1974. (2)American Theatre, St. Louis, August 18, 1973. (3)*Lust For Life* tour 1977. (4)Markthalle, Hamburg, September 17, 1977. (5)Stage West, Hartford, March 8, 1980. (6)Top Rank, Brighton, June 6, 1979. LP.

**Iggy and the Stooges: *Shake Appeal***
Shake Appeal ; Search And Destroy / Raw Power ; Hard To Beat.
Recorded: Original mix of *Raw Power.* 10" EP.

**Iggy and the Stooges: *Studio Rehearsals 73-74***
Rubber Legs ; Open Up And Bleed ; Johanna ; Cock In My Pocket ; Cock In My Pocket ; Rubber Legs ; Head On ; Cry For Me.
Recorded: Studio rehearsal, early 1973. LP.

**Iggy Pop: *Stowaway D.O.A.***
I Wanna Be Your Dog ; TV Eye ; Dirt ; Gimme Some Skin* ; Funtime ; Raw Power ; Turn Blue ; I Got A Right*.
Recorded: Agora Ballroom, Cleveland, March 22, 1977 (not Santa Monica as stated). **Raw Power* sessions, 1972. LP.

**Iggy Pop: *Suck On This***
Raw Power ; TV Eye ; Dirt ; 1969 ; Turn Blue ; Funtime ; Gimme Danger ; No Fun ; Sister Midnight ; I Need Somebody ; Search And Destroy ; I Wanna Be Your Dog ; Lust For Life* ; The Passenger* ; Nightclubbing* ; One Two Brown Eyes*.
Recorded: Ohio, March 1977. *Civic Auditorium, Santa Monica, November 18, 1977. Double LP.

**Patti Smith: *Teenage Perversity And Ships In The Night***
Iggy doesn't perform but he comes up on stage and makes comments.
Recorded: Roxy, Los Angeles, January 30, 1976. LP.

**The Stooges: *TV Eye***
TV Eye / I Feel Alright (1970).
Recorded: Crosley Field, Cincinnati, Cincinnati Pop Festival, June 13, 1970. 7" single.

**Iggy Pop: *Vietnam***
Shake Appeal(1) ; TV Eye(1) ; Nightclubbing(1) ; Brakes On(1) ; Lust For Life(1) ; I'm All Right(1) ; Puppet World(2) ; One For My Baby(2) ; Funtime(2) ; I'm Crying(3) ; Fortune Teller(4) ; Penetration(5) ; One For My Baby(6).
Recorded: (1)Waves, Chicago, October 1, 1980. (2)Bookie's, Detroit, September 26, 1980. (3)Palais d'Hiver, Lyon, May 23, 1980. (4)"The Old Grey Whistle Test" BBC TV, April 24, 1979. (5)Brunnsparken, Örebro, May 27, 1978. (6)Old Waldorf, San Francisco, November 27, 1979. LP.

**Various artists: *Whitman's Punk Sampler***
Neighbourhood Threat ; other artists.
Recorded: Civic Auditorium, Santa Monica, November 18, 1977. LP.

**Iggy Pop: *Whoa Daddy!***
Beside You / When Dreaming Fails / Family Affair / Purple Haze.
Recorded: 1985 *Blah Blah Blah* demos. Double 7" single.

**Iggy Pop, David Bowie: *Why Does David Bowie Like Dressing Up In Ladies' Clothes?***
Re-release of *Alarm.*

**Iggy Pop: *The Wild One***
Real Wild Child ; Nightclubbing ; TV Eye ; China Girl ; Lust For Life ; Cry For Love ; Blah Blah Blah*.
Recorded: Ritz, New York, November 14, 1986. *Volkshaus, Zürich, December 12, 1986. LP.

**Iggy Pop: *The Winter Of My Discontent***
The Winter Of My Discontent ; Lust For Life ; Eggs On Plate ; I Need More ; Dum Dum Boys ; TV Eye* ; The Villagers** ; Life Of Work** ; Run Like A Villain** ; Louie Louie** ; Eat Or Be Eaten*** ; I'm A Conservative*** ; Street Crazies***.
Recorded: Music Hall, Toronto, December 3, 1981. **The Idiot* tour 1977. **Keystone, Berkeley, February 12, 1983. ***Trinity's, Baton Rouge, March 2, 1983. LP.

**Iggy Pop, David Bowie: *Zowie & A Couple Of Kooks***
Re-release of *Alarm.*

## Unreleased Iggy material

*A list of songs by Iggy Pop/the Stooges never officially released on studio LPs, but recorded or performed live.*

**Asthma Attack**
**I'm Sick**
The two earliest known Stooges tunes, from 1968.

**The Dance Of Romance**
**Goodbye Bozos**
Originating from 1968, "Goodbye Bozos" was later developed into "Little Doll," while "The Dance Of Romance" became "Ann" on the Stooges' first LP.

**Big Time Bum**
**Private Parts**
**Searching For Head**
**Way Down In Egypt**
Four songs from the Stooges' post-*Fun House* ("jazz") period, mid-to-late 1970.

**I Need You**
**Who Do You Love**
**You're Looking Fine**

**You Want My Action**
These and several other Pop/Williamson tunes were played live in 1971. Some titles are tentative.

**Fresh Rag**
**Nigger Man**
**Penetration**
Three *Raw Power* outtakes recorded in London, June-August 1972. "Penetration" is different from the LP version. "Fresh Rag" is supposedly a re-working of a Joe Tex number.

**Black Ace**
**Come Hungry Sweet Child**
**Cry For Me***
**Emotional Problems**
**I Gotta Problem**
**Love Light**
**Love Sick**
**Mellow Down Easy**
**My Girl Hates My Heroin**
**My Veins Are Crying**
**Nowhere**
**On The Beach**
**Problems**
**Rubber Legs***
**Sack O Shit**
Unreleased Pop/Williamson songs, written after the *Raw Power* sessions, late 1972/early 1973. *Released on *Rubber Legs* LP.

**Cock In My Pocket***
**Head On***
**Heavy Liquid***
**Open Up And Bleed***
**Rich Bitch***
**Sex Drive****
**She-Creatures Of The Hollywood Hills**
**Wet My Bed**
Performed live by the Stooges in 1973-74. *Released on *Metallic KO* and *Metallic 2xKO*. **Supposedly played live by the Stooges towards the end, in 1974 (no known tape recordings).

**Hats Off**
*Kill City* outtake from 1975.

**Drink To Me**
**Moving On**
Two songs recorded with David Bowie in Los Angeles in 1975. These sessions also included "Turn Blue" (later on *Lust For Life* ) and "Sell Your Love" (*Kill City* ).

**Modern Guy**
**Rock Action**
Played live on a few rare occasions on the *Lust For Life* tour in 1977.

**Hassles**
**Sacred Cow**
**The Winter Of My Discontent**
Written during the *Soldier* sessions in 1979 and performed live in 1980 and on some later tours. There also exists two unreleased songs from the *New Values* sessions earlier in 1979.

**Ass On The Line**
**Bad Actor**
**Brakes On**
**Get Off My Back**
**I Can Be Tough**
**I'm The Original One**
**Low Life**
**Out With The Fellows**
**Prized Possessions**
**Puppet World**
**Speak To Me**
**The Story Of Johnny Moore**
**Texas Girl**
**Wayward Youth**
**Why Are You Bothering Me**
A wealth of songs were written by Ivan Kral and Iggy for the *Party* sessions in 1980.

**Flesh And Blood**
**Joe And Billy**
Played live in 1981.

**Pain And Suffering**
Recorded for the Canadian TV film *Rock 'n' Rule*, 1981.

**Fire Engine**
**Old Mule Skinner**
**Warrior Tribe**
Ric Ocasek demos from 1983.

**Beside You**
**When Dreaming Fails**
Two of the demos from Iggy's collaboration with Steve Jones in Los Angeles, 1985.

## Songs by other artists performed by Iggy

*This is a list of songs by other artists played by Iggy Pop/the Stooges in live performance, but never captured on vinyl. Songs performed at one-off shows or sound-checks/jams are not included.*

**Batman Theme**
(Neal Hefti)
A surprising selection played on the UK/European *New Values* tour in 1979. It was performed as a spoof with Jackie Clarke as Robin and Iggy as Batman. Nelson Riddle recorded the original theme to the *Batman* TV series, and Link Wray made a fine interpretation in 1965.

**Fame**
(Carlos Alomar/David Bowie/John Lennon)
A segment of this song was occasionally played on the *Lust For Life* tour, 1977, as part of a medley with "That's How Strong My Love Is." Carlos Alomar's riff to "Fame" is a direct lift from an old rhythm and blues song called "Footstomping," originally done by the Flares. "Fame" is the only Bowie song (apart from the Bowie/Iggy collaborations) that Iggy has been known to perform.

**Fortune Teller**
(Naomi Neville)
This song was played on Iggy's UK/European *New Values* tour in 1979 and the 1983 Australasian tour. The original recording was made by black New Orleans singer Benny Spellman, in 1962 (as the B-side to his minor hit "Lipstick Traces"). The song was written by pianist Allen Toussaint using his mother's maiden name.

**Gloria**
(Van Morrison)
Iggy has played Them's classic song on several tours from 1977 and onwards. It was originally the B-side of Them's first hit, "Baby Please Don't Go," released in 1964.

**Hang On Sloopy**
(Wes Farrell/Bert Russell)
This 1965 international smash hit for the McCoys was played by Iggy on the *Breaking Point* tour in 1983. Co-writer Bert Russell is a pseudonym for famed rhythm and blues (and Them) producer Bert Berns. The song was first released in 1964 by Vibrations (as "My Girl Sloopy").

**House Of The Rising Sun**
(Traditional)
This rock standard was played on a few rare occasions on the 1983 *Breaking Point* tour. Animals' famous version was released in 1964 and made number one on both sides of the Atlantic.

**I'm All Right**
(Nanker/Phelge)
Iggy played this Rolling Stones (Nanker/Phelge is a pseudonym for

Jagger/Richard) tune on the American tours in 1980. The Rolling Stones' original version first appeared on the EP *Got Live If You Want It*, and on the US version of the LP *Out Of Our Heads*, both from 1965.

**I'm Crying**
(Eric Burdon/Alan Price)
Iggy performed this Animals song in 1980. "I'm Crying" was the follow-up single to "House Of The Rising Sun," in 1964.

**Jenny Take A Ride**
(Bob Crewe/Enotris Johnson/Richard Penniman/Ma Rainey)
Iggy performed this song on the 1977 *Lust For Life* tour. The song was the breakthrough for Mitch Ryder and the Detroit Wheels (previously Billy Lee and the Rivieras) in 1965. The song is actually a medley (pieced together by Mitch's producer Bob Crewe) of the old Chuck Willis blues "C.C. Rider" (Rainey) and Little Richard's (real name Penniman) 50's hit "Jenny Jenny."

**Louie Louie**
(Richard Berry)
This three-chord classic was performed by the Stooges in January/February 1974 with partly new lyrics by Iggy, "A fine little bitch, she waits for me, just a whore from across the way, every night I take her, we fuck all alone, she ain't the kind I'd lay at home/Ah, Louie Louie, oh baby, we gotta go/I feel a rose down in her hair, her ass is black and her tits are bare/Ah, Louie Louie, oh baby....." Iggy has also performed the song live in 1979, 1981, and 1983. Written by Richard Berry in the 50's, "Louie Louie" was made famous by the Kingsmen who scored a huge US hit with the song in 1963. "Louie Louie" is hailed by many as the "greatest rock tune ever." Certainly, many songs have been based on it (including Iggy's own "I'm A Conservative"), and it must be one of the most covered songs of all time.

**New Orleans**
(F. Guida/J. Royster)
Gary U.S. Bond's big US hit from 1960 was developed into "Heavy Liquid" and was a regular in the Stooges' set in 1973/74.

**96 Tears**
(Rudy Martinez)
Question Mark and the Mysterians' "punk" classic from 1966 was played as part of a medley (with "1969" and "No Fun") on some of the shows on *The Idiot* tour in 1977. In more ways than one, this Flint (Michigan) group of Mexican guys were forerunners to the Stooges; their singer (Rudy Martinez a.k.a. Question Mark) was insulting audiences and being way too far out on stage as far back as 1966. Their repertoire also featured such Stooges-like titles as "If I Can't Have You Bitch — I'm Gonna Make You Like Me," "You Captivate Me," and "I Need Somebody."

**One For My Baby**
(Harold Arlen/Johnny Mercer)
Iggy has performed this ballad, the story of the end of an affair, with Iggy bending the ear of Joe the barman (the song is often mis-titled "Set 'Em Up Joe" on bootlegs, etc), on several tours from 1978 and onwards. Originally featured in the American film, *Young At Heart* (directed by Gordon Douglas), 1955, this Frank Sinatra number was included on his widely acclaimed *Frank Sinatra Sings For Only The Lonely*, 1958.

**One Two Brown Eyes**
(Van Morrison)
Iggy played this Them song on a few occasions on the *Lust For Life* tour in 1977. The song was the B-side of Them's first single release, "Don't Start Crying Now," in 1964.

**The Shadow Of Your Smile**
(Johnny Mandel/Paul Francis Webster)
This is another Frank Sinatra number. It was occasionally sung acapella by Iggy when there was some equipment breakdown in the Stooges' set. The song was written for the American film, *The Sandpiper* (directed by Vincente Minnelli), 1965, and it won an Academy Award.

**That's How Strong My Love Is**
(Jamison)
Otis Redding's number from 1964 was regularly played on the *Lust For Life* tour in 1977. The original recording was made by O.W. Wright, also in 1964.

**Waiting For The Man**
(Lou Reed)
Velvet Underground's sordid tale of scoring heroin in New York, from their first LP, *The Velvet Underground & Nico* (released 1967), was performed on Iggy's Australasian tour in 1983 in a medley with "No Fun."

**You Really Got Me**
(Ray Davies)
The Kinks' crude classic was played on Iggy's 1979 American *New Values* tour. "You Really Got Me," a UK number one in 1964, was the Kinks' third single.

## Cover versions of Iggy songs

*This is a list of officially released cover versions of songs recorded and released by Iggy Pop/the Stooges. Single (7"/12") releases unless LP title is given.*

**Ann**
(The Stooges)
Broken Jug
Feedtime (*Cooper S* and *Hard To Beat* compilation album)
Redd Kross (*Teen Babes From Monsanto*)

**Bang Bang**
(Ivan Kral/Iggy Pop)
David Bowie (*Never Let Me Down*)

**Cock In My Pocket**
(Iggy Pop/James Williamson)
Nuns

**China Girl**
(David Bowie/Iggy Pop)
David Bowie (*Let's Dance*)

**Dirt**
(The Stooges)
DT and the Stoodes (*Metallic OK*)
Folamour
Henry Paul French Group
Magnolia Strip (*Hard To Beat*)
Naked Prey (*Under The Blue Marlin*)
1984 (*La Creme De Skydog* comp.)
Occasional Dead Flies (*A Real Cool Time* comp.)

**Don't Look Down**
(Iggy Pop/James Williamson)
David Bowie (*Tonight*)

**Down On The Street**
(The Stooges)
Exploding White Mice (*Hard To Beat*)
Olympic Sideburns

**Funtime**
(David Bowie/Iggy Pop)
Peter Murphy (*Love Hysteria*)

**Gimme Danger**
(Iggy Pop/James Williamson)
Celibate Rifles (*Hard To Beat*)

**I Got A Right**
(Iggy Pop/James Williamson)
The Henchmen
Miracle Workers (*Dimension Of Sound* comp.)
Murphy's Law
Prevaricators (*Detente*)

**I Got Nothin'**
(Iggy Pop/James Williamson)
ME 262 (*Hard To Beat*)

**I Need Somebody**
(Iggy Pop/James Williamson)
Seminal Rats (*Hard To Beat*)

**I Wanna Be Your Dog**
(The Stooges)
Anti-Pasti
Fantomes (*La Creme De Skydog*)
Henry Paul French Group
Joan Jett and the Blackhearts (*Up Your Alley*)
Las Vulpess
NRG (*Hard To Beat*)
Gary Oldman (*Sid & Nancy - Love Kills*)
Paralisis Permanente (*El Acto*)
The Primitives (CD single)
Sonic Youth (*Confusion Is Sex*)
Sid Vicious (*Sid Sings* and *Love Kills NYC*)

**Kill City**
(Iggy Pop/James Williamson)
Johnny Kannis (*Hard To Beat*)

**Little Doll**
(The Stooges)
Miracle Workers
Spaceman 3

**Loose**
(The Stooges)
Birthday Party (*Drunk On The Pope's Blood*)
Bollock Brothers (*Punk - A World History*, comp.)
Fuzztones (*Live In Europe*)
Vocal Lizard (*Hard To Beat*)
D.I. (*Clockwork Orange County* comp.)

**Lust For Life**
(David Bowie/Iggy Pop)
The Smithereens

**Neighbourhood Threat**
(David Bowie/Ricky Gardiner/Iggy Pop)
David Bowie (*Tonight*)

**Nightclubbing**
(David Bowie/Iggy Pop)
Human League (*Holiday 80* double EP)
Grace Jones (*Nightclubbing*)

**1970/I Feel Alright**
(The Stooges)
Damned (*Damned Damned Damned*, *Live At The Roundhouse*, and *Mindless Directionless Energy*)
Flesh For Lulu
GBH (*Baby's Revenge*)
Hanoi Rocks (*All Those Wasted Years*, *Rock 'n' Roll Divorce*, and *Dead By Christmas*)
Hard Ons (*Hard To Beat*)
Mission Of Burma (*The Horrible Truth About Burma*)

**1969**
(The Stooges)
The Mission
Njurmännen (cassette LP)
The Outcasts
Psychotic Turnbuckles (*Hard To Beat*)
Sisters Of Mercy

**No Fun**
(The Stooges)
Dr. Mix and the Remix (*Wall Of Noise*)
Plunderers (*Hard To Beat*)
Sex Pistols (*The Original Sex Pistols - Live* and *Flogging A Dead Horse*)

**Not Right**
(The Stooges)
Stress of Terror (*Hard To Beat*)

**Open Up And Bleed**
(Iggy Pop/James Williamson)
Harem Scarem (*Hard To Beat* and *Pilgrim's Progress*)
These Immortal Souls

**The Passenger**
(Ricky Gardiner/Iggy Pop)
Fiendens Musik
Siouxsie and the Banshees (*Cities In Dust*)

**Penetration**
(Iggy Pop/James Williamson)
No Mans Land (*Hard To Beat*)

**Raw Power**
(Iggy Pop/James Williamson)
DMZ (*DMZ Live*)

**Real Cool Time**
(The Stooges)
God (*Hard To Beat*)
Nomads (*A Real Cool Time*)

**Rich Bitch**
(Iggy Pop/James Williamson)
D.O.A.

**Search And Destroy**
(Iggy Pop/James Williamson)
Dead Boys (*Return Of The Living Dead* and *We've Come For Your Children*)
Dictators (*Manifest Destiny*)
Hellmenn (*Hard To Beat*)
Heretics
Smack (*Live Desire*)
The Strand
Sid Vicious (*Sid Sings* and *Love Kills NYC*)

**Sister Midnight**
(Carlos Alomar/David Bowie/Iggy Pop)
David Bowie (re-titled "Red Money," but it is basically "Sister Midnight" with new lyrics) (*Lodger*)

**Tight Pants**
(Iggy Pop/James Williamson)
The Girlies (*Hard To Beat*)

**Tonight**
(David Bowie/Iggy Pop)
David Bowie (*Tonight*)

**TV Eye**
(The Stooges)
Asylum (*Hard To Beat*)
Radio Birdman (*Radios Appear*, Australian release)
Destructors

**Your Pretty Face Is Going To Hell**
(Iggy Pop/James Williamson)
Thrust (*Hard To Beat*)

A few *unreleased* Iggy songs have also been covered. Matt Gimmick's *Detroit Renaissance 78* EP features covers of unreleased Stooges material from 1971 (supposedly). The group Raw Power has made a version of "She-Creatures Of The Hollywood Hills" (Iggy Pop/James Williamson), included on the Australian Stooges cover double LP, *Hard To Beat*.

# AUDIO TAPES

## Concerts

*Information in brackets: approximate length (minutes) and sound quality (EX = excellent, VG = very good, G = good, F = fair, P = poor). The asterisked concert recordings are from soundboard or TV/radio broadcasts. Only known tapes (circulating on the open market) are included.*

**1970**
13 Jun Crosley Field, Cincinnati, Cincinnati Pop Festival (10/VG)*

**1971**
May Kiel Auditorium, St. Louis (35/P)

**1973**
30 Jul Max's Kansas City, New York (40/G)
6 Aug Max's Kansas City, New York (50/G)
18 Aug American Theatre, St. Louis, lst set (55/G)
18 Aug American Theatre, St. Louis, 2nd set (50/G)
15 Sep Whisky A Go-Go, Hollywood (30/G)
16 Sep Whisky A Go-Go, Hollywood (55/VG)
17 Sep Whisky A Go-Go, Hollywood (20/F)
Sep Whisky A Go-Go, Hollywood (25/G)
Nov Latin Casino, Baltimore (75/G)
31 Dec Academy of Music, New York (45/G)

**1974**
Jan Bimbo's, San Francisco (35/VG)
Jan Sports Center, Toledo (5/F)

***The Idiot* tour 1977**
2 Mar City Hall, Newcastle (65/F)
3 Mar Apollo Theatre, Manchester (60/G)
4 Mar Hippodrome, Birmingham (25/VG)
7 Mar Rainbow Theatre, London (70/VG)
13 Mar Le Plateau Theatre, Montreal (70/VG)
14 Mar Seneca College, Toronto (70/G)
18 Mar Palladium, New York (60/VG)
22 Mar Agora Ballroom, Cleveland (60/EX)*
25 Mar Masonic Auditorium, Detroit (65/VG)
28 Mar Mantra Studios, Chicago (60/EX)*
9 Apr Paramount Theatre, Seattle (70/VG)
15 Apr Civic Auditorium, Santa Monica (70/F)
16 Apr Civic Auditorium, San Diego (70/G)

***Lust For Life* tour 1977**
17 Sep Markthalle, Hamburg (70/VG)
18 Sep Berlin (40/VG)*
19 Sep Daddy's Dance Hall, Copenhagen (60/VG)
20 Sep Konserthuset, Stockholm (60/VG)
23 Sep L'Hippodrome, Paris (75/VG)
25 Sep Apollo Theatre, Manchester (60/G)
6 Oct Palladium, New York (60/VG)
8 Oct Le Plateau Theatre, Montreal (65/VG)
15 Oct Civic Center, Baltimore (40/G)
22 Oct Aragon Ballroom, Chicago (65/VG)
16 Nov State University, San Diego (65/EX)*
18 Nov Civic Auditorium, Santa Monica (70/VG)

***TV Eye* tour 1978**
16 May Pabellon del Juventud, Badalona (50/G)
24 May Domino, Stockholm (60/VG)
25 May Chateau Neuf, Oslo (60/VG)
27 May Brunnsparken, Örebro (30/VG)
29 May Det Ny Teater, Copenhagen (55/G)
13 Jun Music Machine, London (60/VG)

***New Values* UK/European tour 1979**
20 Apr Russell's, Manchester (60/VG)
21 Apr Eric's, Liverpool (60/G)
22 Apr Top Rank, Sheffield (65/VG)
25 Apr Music Machine, London (60/VG)
29 Apr Coatham Bowl, Redcar (65/VG)
4 May Barbarella's, Birmingham (60/G)
12 May University, Leeds (65/G)
13 May Lyceum, London (65/VG)
16 May Palace, Paris (45/VG)
28 May Palasport, Parma (70/VG)
31 May Pabellon del Juventud, Badalona (75/VG)
6 Jun Top Rank, Brighton (80/VG)
8 Jun Hammersmith Odeon, London (75/G)

***New Values* North American tour 1979**
29 Oct Hot Club, Philadelphia (75/G)
31 Oct Palladium, New York (70/G)
4 Nov My Father's Place, New York (65/EX)*
14 Nov Masonic Auditorium, Detroit (75/VG)
19 Nov Oriental Theatre, Milwaukee (75/VG)
27 Nov Old Waldorf, San Francisco (60/EX)*
30 Nov Stardust Ballroom, Los Angeles (60/EX)*
4 Dec Tempe (65/G)
9 Dec Hurrah's, New York (70/VG)

***Soldier* UK tour 1980**
2 Feb Friars, Aylesbury (75/VG)
4 Feb City Hall, Newcastle (80/P)
7 Feb Apollo Theatre, Manchester (70/VG)
8 Feb Odeon, Birmingham (75/VG)
12 Feb Hammersmith Palais, London (60/VG)

***Soldier* North American tour 1980**
17 Feb Old Man Rivers, New Orleans (80/VG)
18 Feb Old Man Rivers, New Orleans (55/VG)
1 Mar Emerald City, Cherry Hill (65/VG)
4 Mar My Father's Place, New York (70/VG)
5 Mar Irving Plaza, New York (70/VG)
8 Mar Stage West, Hartford (75/VG)
12 Mar William Paterson College, Wayne (80/VG)
18 Mar Agora Ballroom, Cleveland (70/VG)
31 Mar Dooley's, Tempe (70/VG)
4 Apr Palladium, Hollywood (75/G)

**European tour 1980**
24 Apr Markthalle, Hamburg (45/VG)
4 May To Act, Weissenhoe (70/G)
6 May Volkshaus, Zürich (75/G)
11 May Stadio, Florence (75/VG)
12 May Palalido, Milan (80/VG)
14 May Grand Odeon, Montpellier (75/VG)
15 May Picadero, Barcelona (70/VG)
23 May Palais d'Hiver, Lyon (35/EX)*
31 May Music Machine, London (55/VG)

***Nightclubbing* tour 1980**
20 Sep Club 688, Atlanta (80/VG)
26 Sep Bookie's, Detroit (75/EX)*
1 Oct Waves, Chicago (60/EX)*

**North American tour 1980**
13 Nov Bacchanal, San Diego (40/VG)
18 Nov Opry House, Austin (70/VG)
22 Nov Old Man Rivers, New Orleans (70/VG)
3 Dec Paradise Theatre, Boston (70/G)
11 Dec Shaboo Inn, Willimatic (70/VG)

***Party* UK/European tour 1981**
11 Jun Odd Fellow Palatset, Copenhagen (75/VG)
14 Jun Metropol, Berlin (70/VG)
17 Jun Milan (75/VG)
18 Jun Palasport, Bologna (70/VG)
22 Jun Blau-Grana, Barcelona (70/VG)
28 Jun Velodromo de Anoetz, San Sebastian (75/G)
3 Jul Odeon, Birmingham (80/F)
4 Jul Apollo Theatre, Manchester (90/F)
7 Jul Royal Court, Liverpool (80/VG)
8 Jul Polytechnic, Sheffield (80/VG)
9 Jul Rock City, Nottingham (80/VG)
11 Jul Rainbow Theatre, London (70/F)

***Party* North American tour 1981**
2 Aug Ritz, New York (65/VG)
7 Aug Paramount Theatre, Staten Island (65/VG)
8 Aug Left Bank, Mt. Vernon (60/VG)
9 Aug Toad's Place, New Haven (65/VG)
16 Aug Duffy's, Minneapolis (70/VG)
23 Aug The Grove, Oakville (40/VG)
26 Aug Penny Arcade, Rochester (55/VG)
29 Aug Meadowbrook, Cedar Grove (75/VG)

***Follow The Sun* tour 1981**
11 Nov Cardi's, Houston (75/VG)
13 Nov Club Foot, Austin (50/G)
14 Nov Club Foot, Austin (50/G)
19 Nov Bacchanal, San Diego (45/VG)
25 Nov Old Waldorf, San Francisco (50/EX)*
30 Nov Silverdome, Pontiac (25/F)
1 Dec Silverdome, Pontiac (40/VG)
3 Dec Music Hall, Toronto (45/EX)*

***Zombie Birdhouse* tour 1982**
13 Oct City Gardens, Trenton (75/VG)
14 Oct Peppermint Lounge, New York (75/VG)
23 Oct Spectrum, Montreal (70/VG)
7 Nov Duffy's, Minneapolis (80/EX)*
24 Nov Adam's Avenue, San Diego (65/VG)
9 Dec Ritz, New York (75/VG)
13 Dec Palace, Paris (85/VG)
15 Dec The Venue, London (75/VG)
16 Dec The Venue, London, 1st set (70/VG)
16 Dec The Venue, London, 2nd set (70/VG)

***The Breaking Point* tour 1983**
12 Feb Keystone, Berkeley (85/EX)*
15 Feb WWU Viking Union Lounge, Bellingham (75/VG)
16 Feb Commodore Ballroom, Vancouver (75/VG)
17 Feb Commodore Ballroom, Vancouver (75/VG)
18 Feb Eagles Hippodrome, Seattle (45/VG)
25 Feb Club Foot, Austin (75/VG)
26 Feb Bonham Ballroom, San Antonio (75/VG)
27 Feb Mars, Corpus Christi (65/VG)
2 Mar Trinity's, Baton Rouge (70/VG)
3 Mar Tupelo's, New Orleans (75/VG)
6 Mar Theatre, Tampa (75/VG)
9 Mar I&I, Athens (70/G)
11 Mar Club 688, Atlanta (70/VG)
13 Mar Bogart's, Cincinnati (70/VG)
14 Mar Stanely Theatre, Pittsburgh (65/VG)
17 Mar Peppermint Lounge, New York (60/G)
18 Mar Peppermint Lounge, New York (35/VG)
20 Mar Living Room, Providence (75/VG)
21 Mar Agora Ballroom, New Haven (60/VG)
26 Mar Zoo, Brooklyn (70/VG)

**Australasian tour 1983**
17 Jun Koseinenkin Hall, Osaka (75/VG)
19 Jun Nakano Sun Plaza, Tokyo (85/VG)
1 Jul Astor Theatre, Melbourne (60/VG)
2 Jul Seaview Ballroom, Melbourne (60/EX)*
3 Jul Seaview Ballroom, Melbourne (60/EX)*
5 Jul Cardiff (80/VG)
6 Jul Greenfield Taverna, Newcastle (70/VG)
8 Jul Bombay Rock, Surfers' Paradise (70/VG)
10 Jul Whispers, Brisbane (50/VG)
14 Jul Seals Club, Maroubra (70/G)

***Blah Blah Blah* tour 1986**
30 Oct One Step Beyond, Santa Clara (90/VG)
31 Oct Wolfgang's, San Francisco (90/VG)
7 Nov Phantasy Theatre, Cleveland (90/VG)
8 Nov Detroit, St. Andrew's Hall (85/EX)*
11 Nov Metro, Boston (90/VG)
12 Nov Trocadero, Philadelphia (85/VG)
13 Nov Ritz, New York (80/VG)
14 Nov Ritz, New York (70/EX)*
23 Nov Zaal Brielpoort, Deinze (90/VG)
24 Nov Muziekcentrum Vredenburg, Utrecht (65/EX)*
26 Nov Draken, Stockholm (85/VG)
27 Nov Draken, Stockholm (85/VG)
30 Nov Falkonerteatret, Copenhagen (80/VG)
2 Dec Metropol, Berlin (75/VG)
3 Dec Knops Musikhalle, Hamburg (85/VG)
4 Dec Philipshalle, Düsseldorf (90/VG)
5 Dec Pfalzbau, Ludwigshafen (90/VG)
7 Dec Musikhalle, Frankfurt (90/VG)
8 Dec Theater, Munich (90/VG)
9 Dec Kurhalle Oberlaa, Vienna (85/VG)
12 Dec Volkshaus, Zürich (90/EX)*
15 Dec Grande Halle de la Vilette, Paris (90/VG)
17 Dec Brixton Academy, London (90/VG)
18 Dec Brixton Academy, London (90/VG)

**North American tour with the Pretenders 1987**
7 Feb Lakefront Arena, New Orleans (45/VG)
28 Feb Coliseum, Oakland (40/VG)
2 Mar Wolfgang's, San Francisco (80/VG)
19 Mar Maple Leaf Gardens, Toronto (45/VG)
21 Mar Ohio Center, Columbus (45/VG)
26 Mar Richfield Coliseum, Cleveland (45/VG)
27 Mar Cobo Hall, Detroit (45/VG)
1 Apr Bay Street, Long Island (60/EX)*
4 Apr Stone Pony, Asbury Park (70/VG)
5 Apr 1018, New York (80/EX)*

**Japanese tour 1987**
Apr Tokyo (30/EX)*

**UK/European tour 1987**
6 Jun Törnävä Festivalpark, Seinäjoki, Provinssirock (90/EX)*
8 Jun De Berckt Sportpark, Baarlo,

Pinkpop (60/G)
9 Jun Zenith, Paris (90/VG)
12 Jun Royal Concert Hall, Nottingham (90/VG)
15 Jun City Hall, Newcastle (90/VG)
16 Jun Playhouse, Edinburgh (90/VG)
19 Jun Apollo Theatre, Manchester (90/VG)
20 Jun Odeon, Birmingham (90/VG)
23 Jun Hammersmith Odeon, London (90/EX)*
24 Jun Hammersmith Odeon, London (90/EX)*
27 Jun Eriksbergsvarvet, Gothenburg (65/VG)
28 Jun Oslo, Kalvöyafestivalen (90/F)
30 Jun Brunnsparken, Örebro (90/VG)
1 Jul Gröna Lund, Stockholm (90/VG)
3 Jul Roskilde, Roskildefestivalen (55/VG)
4 Jul Torhout, Rock Torhout/ Werchter (80/VG)
5 Jul Festival Terrein, Werchter, Rock Torhout/Werchter (30/EX)*
11 Jul Freilichtbühne, Loreley, Bizarre Festival (85/VG)
12 Jul Stadtpark, Hamburg (90/VG)

***Instinct* tour 1988**
10 Jul Fillmore West, San Francisco (75/VG)
15 Jul Phantasy Theatre, Cleveland (75/VG)
19 Jul Channel, Boston (75/EX)*
20 Jul Ritz, New York (80/EX)*
22 Jul City Gardens, Trenton (75/VG)
24 Jul Toad's Place, New Haven (75/VG)

*Many additional tapes from 1988 will probably emerge.*

## Interviews

*Quality is EX unless otherwise is noted.*

**1973**
17 Aug St. Louis radio (5/G)

**1974**
Apr KROQ, Los Angeles (15/F)

**1975**
- Los Angeles radio (5/VG)

**1977**
13 Mar Capital Radio, London (15)
24 Mar WABX, Detroit (25)
7 May "Rock Around The World" Suffolk Cablevision, USA (50)
18 May Radio 2SM, Sydney (5/VG)
14 Oct Boston radio (25)
Nov KSAN, San Francisco (10)

**1979**
26 Apr Capital Radio, London (20)
28 May "Sounds" DRS, Switzerland (10)
9 Jun "Rock On" BBC, England (10)
Jun Radio 2JJ, Sydney (50)
11 Jul Radio 2SM, Sydney (10)
28 Oct "Radio Radio" WPIX, New York (60)

**1981**
11 Jul Capital Radio, London (10)

**1982**
18 Dec "Rock On" BBC, England (20)

**1985**
- US radio (30)

**1986**
26 Sep WNEW, New York (30)
Oct "Rockdepartementet" SR, Sweden (15)
Oct "Rrox" SR, Sweden (15)
8 Nov WLLZ, Detroit (10)
14 Dec "Rock Is Dead" DRS, Switzerland (10)
15 Dec "Sounds" DRS, Switzerland (30)
Dec "Saturday Live" BBC, England (10)

**1987**
16 Jan "Rockline" WNEW, New York (40)
23 Jan "Paul Anthony Show" Radio Signal, London (10)
22 Apr Japanese radio (45)
Jun Piccadilly Radio, Manchester (30)

*In addition to these radio interviews, a number of private interview tapes (interviews made by fans and press conference recordings) are circulating.*

## Studio sessions, outtakes and demos

**1972**
Original mix of *Raw Power* tracks (30/EX)
I Need Somebody ; Hard To Beat (Your Pretty Face Is Going To Hell) ; Death Trip ; Raw Power ; Search And Destroy ; Shake Appeal.
Broadcast by WABX, Detroit, early 1973. The Stooges' own mix of the album has much more drums and bass than th finished mix. There are also some voc differences and more prominent backin vocals on some tunes.

**1972/73**
Iggy Pop/James Williamson jam (180/VG)
The Ballad Of Hollis Brown ; Waiting Fo The Man ; I'm A Man ; I'm So Glad Purple Haze ; various rock and blues jam. The exact date and source of these tapes ar unknown. Several tracks have bee released by Revenge Records from France Some of the jams are quite tedious an stoned-out (à la the *Jesus Loves Th Stooges* EP).

**1973**
Studio session
Search And Destroy ; Cock In My Pocke ; Come Hungry Sweet Child part 2 Come Hungry Sweet Child ; Cock In M Pocket ; Raw Power ; Come Hungr Sweet Child ; Come Hungry Sweet Chil part 2 ; Your Pretty Face Is Going T Hell.

**1973**
Studio rehearsal (35/EX)
Rubber Legs ; Open Up And Bleed Johanna ; Cock In My Pocket ; Rubbe Legs ; Head On ; Cry For Me.
Probably recorded in Detroit February/March 1973. The session show that even a Stooges rehearsal wa performed as though to an audience; a much energy and urgency are put into th songs as if it had been in front of a packe auditorium. This session has been release on the *Rubber Legs* LP.

**1973**
Detroit rehearsal, February 3
Rubber Legs ; My Veins Are Crying Rubber Legs ; I Need Somebody ; Black Ace ; Johanna ; Head On ; Emotiona Problems.
The Detroit rehearsal tapes were sold by James Williamson to Greg Shaw of Bomp Records in 1977.

**1973**
Detroit rehearsal, February 20
Johanna ; Rubber Legs ; Rubber Legs ; I Gotta Problem ; Open Up And Bleed ; Open Up And Bleed ; jam ; Jesus Loves The Stooges ; Gimme Danger (slow) ; Gimme Danger (fast) ; Gimme Danger.

**1973**
Detroit rehearsal, February 25
Johanna ; On The Beach ; Problems ;

Nowhere ; Johanna ; Mellow Down Easy ; Love Light ; Sack O Shit ; Problems ; Head On.

**1973**
Detroit rehearsals, March 11 and 19
Cock In My Pocket ; Head On ; Search And Destroy ; Search And Destroy ; Search And Destroy ; Search And Destroy Raw Power ; Raw Power ; Raw Power ; Death Trip ; various jams.

**1973**
Detroit rehearsals, March 17 and 18
Emotional Problems ; Emotional Problems ; I Gotta Problem ; jam ; Head On ; Head On ; I Need Somebody.

**1973**
Detroit rehearsal, March
I Gotta Problem ; Raw Power ; Rubber Legs ; My Girl Hates My Heroin ; Open Up And Bleed ; jam ; Jesus Loves The Stooges ; Gimme Danger.

**1979**
*Soldier* session (60/VG)
Live session recorded at Rockfield Studios, Wales, August 27, 1979. Includes early versions of many *Soldier* tunes.

**1980**
*Party* outtakes (15/VG)
I'm The Original One ; Speak To Me ; Brakes On ; One For My Baby.

**1983**
Demos with Ric Ocasek (15/EX)
Fire Engine ; Warrior Tribe ; Old Mule Skinner.
Recorded at Synchro Sound Studios, Boston, 1983, prior to Iggy's Australasian tour.

**1985**
*Blah Blah Blah* demos (25/EX)
Purple Haze ; Family Affair ; Cry For Love ; Fire Girl ; Beside You ; When Dreaming Fails.

# VIDEO TAPES

## Promos

| | |
|---|---|
| 1977 | Lust For Life |
| 1979 | I'm Bored |
| 1979 | Five Foot One |
| 1980 | Loco Mosquito |
| 1980 | Knocking 'Em Down |
| 1980 | Dog Food |
| 1986 | Cry For Love |
| 1986 | Real Wild Child |
| 1987 | Shades |
| 1987 | Isolation |
| 1987 | Risky *(no appearance)* |
| 1988 | Cold Metal |

## Live appearances and concerts on TV

*Length of programme in brackets (minutes).*

**1970**
Aug "Midsummer Rock" USA (8)

**1977**
Sep Danish TV (5)
Sep "TopPop" Holland (5)
Oct "So It Goes" England (13)

**1978**
May "TopPop" Holland (5)
May "Szene 78" Germany (5)

**1979**
24 Apr "The Old Grey Whistle Test" England (8)
Jul "Countdown" Australia (5)

**1981**
23 Aug "The New Music" Canada (5)
8 Sep "Bananas" Germany (5)

**1982**
28 Oct Canadian TV: live with the Untouchables (60)
17 Dec "The Tube" England (12)

**1986**
21 Nov "The Tube" England (8)
15 Dec "Zenith" France (5)
16 Dec "Zenith" France (2)
20 Dec "No. 73" England (5)
27 Dec "MTV Saturday Night Concert" USA (67)

**1987**
15 Jan "Top Of The Pops" England (5)
6 Jun "Provinssirock 87" Finland (88)
Aug "Hold Tight" England (5)

## Interviews and documentaries

**1977**
3 Mar "Granada Reports" Manchester (5)
11 Mar "90 Minutes Live" Canada (30)
6 May "Dinah!" USA (25)
Sep "TF1 Actualites" France (5)

**1978**
13 Feb "Öronaböj" Sweden (25)

**1979**
8 Jul "Ten 10 Sun" Sydney (20)
Dec "Wyld Ryce" Minneapolis (15)

**1981**
13 Jan "Tomorrow Show" USA (15)
12 Mar "Videowest Show" New York (5)

**1982**
8 Dec "Late Night With David Letterman" USA (16)

**1983**
Jun "Sounds" Australia (15)
Aug "After Dark" Australia (15)

**1985**
\- "MTV Music News" USA (1)

**1986**
Oct "MTV Music News" USA (1)
9 Oct "Aktuellt" Sweden (3)
18 Oct "Les Enfants du Rock" France (5)
23 Oct "Södra Station" Sweden (5)
7 Nov "The Tube" England (9)
24 Nov "Musik Szene" Germany (8)
Nov "Cutting Edge" USA (5)
Dec "UK Despatch" England (13)
Dec "Videospeilet" Norway (5)
Dec "MTV Music News" USA (1)
13 Dec "Mini-Mag" France (11)
14 Dec "Lust For Life" Holland (45)
Dec "Kluzz" Norway (8)
Dec "MTV Music News" USA (1)
30 Dec "Today Show" USA (7)

**1987**
\- "Pinky" Italy (6)

18 Jan "Music Box" England (18)
4 Feb "Cargo de Nuit" Belgium (10)
14 Feb "Les Enfants du Rock" France (2)
16 Feb "Late Night With David Letterman" USA (10)
17 Feb "Beatbox" Denmark (10)
Feb "MTV Music News" USA (2)
16 May "Les Enfants du Rock" France (6)
23 May "Les Enfants du Rock" France (3)
29 Jul "The New Music" Canada (15)
18 Aug "Les Enfants du Rock" France (5)

**1988**
2 Jul "The MTV Week In Rock" USA (5)
21 Jul "Late Night With David Letterman" USA (10)
1 Aug "Rockfile" England (5)

## Private concert films

*The quality grading takes into consideration the sound quality, distance from stage, camera work, etc.*

**1968**
- The Stooges (1/G)

**1969/70**
- The Stooges (2/VG)
- The Stooges (2/VG)

**1977**
13 Mar Le Plateau Theatre, Montreal (3/P)
19 Mar Tower Theatre, Philadelphia (10/VG)
Mar/Apr US concert (3/G)

**1978**
24 May Domino, Stockholm (2/G)

**1979**
9 Dec Hurrah's, New York (20/F)

**1981**
24 Aug Second Chance, Ann Arbor (20/VG)
25 Nov Old Waldorf, San Francisco (52/EX)
3 Dec Music Hall, Toronto (32/VG)

**1986**
26 Nov Draken, Stockholm (35/G)
17 Dec Brixton Academy, London (90/EX)

**1987**
24 Jun Hammersmith Odeon, London (84/G)
30 Jun Brunnsparken, Örebro (76/VG)
30 Jun Brunnsparken, Örebro (84/EX)
1 Jul Gröna Lund, Stockholm (82/VG)
1 Jul Gröna Lund, Stockholm (55/VG)
1 Jul Gröna Lund, Stockholm (50/G)
4 Jul Torhout, Rock Torhout/Werchter (58/G)
11 Jul Freilichtbühne, Loreley, Bizarre Festival (83/G)

## Miscellaneous

**1982**
- Pain And Suffering video (from *Rock 'n' Rule*, Canadian TV film) (5)

**1984**
14 Sep "MTV Video Music Awards 1984" USA (Iggy collects Bowie's award for the "China Girl" promo) (2)

**1986**
23 Dec "MTV Guest VJ" USA (Iggy plays his favourite videos) (50)

**1987**
20 Mar Private video of Iggy at A&A record store, Toronto (20)

# FILMOGRAPHY

***The Color Of Money*** **(1986)**
Director: Martin Scorsese.
Starring: Paul Newman, Tom Cruise, Mary Elizabeth Mastrantonio, Iggy Pop.

***Sid And Nancy*** **(1986)**
Director: Alex Cox.
Starring: Gary Oldman, Chloe Webb, David Hayman, Iggy Pop.

# BIBLIOGRAPHY


***Blah Blah Blah Tour***
By Per Nilsen (Rosebud, 1987).

***I Need More – The Stooges An[d] Other Stories***
By Iggy Pop with Anne Wehrer (Karz Cohl, 1982).

***The Lives & Crimes Of Iggy Pop***
By Mike West (Babylon Books, 1982 Second edition 1987).

***The Wild One — The True Stor[y] Of Iggy Pop***
By Per Nilsen with Dorothy Sherma[n] (Omnibus Press and Rosbud. First editio[n] 1988).


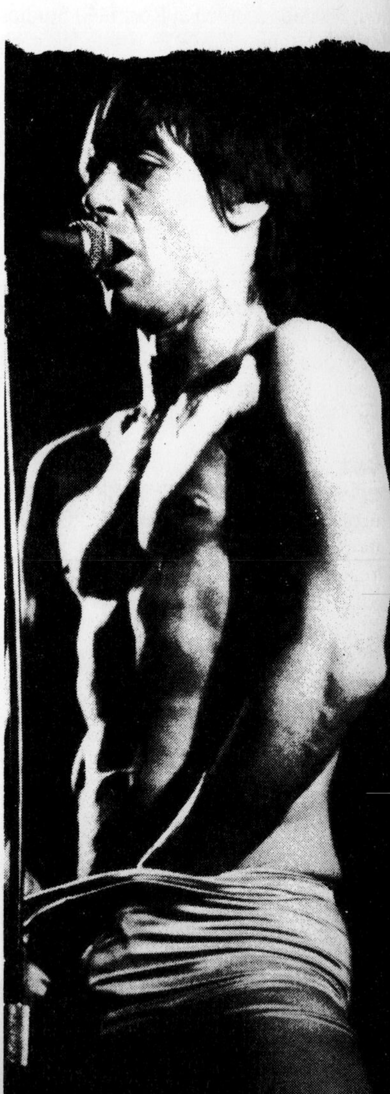